Praise for a Foot in Both Worlds

Over the years, I have met dozens of shamans from all six inhabited continents and have seen many of them at work, so I am well aware of the healing power of their interventions. It comes as a welcome surprise to see their work integrated into 21st-century psychotherapy. This remarkable book spells out how a dedicated shamanic practitioner has helped his clients recover from their dysfunctional behaviors, attitudes, and beliefs. He not only restores their well-being but also leaves them in a better mental and physical state than they were before treatment. Many terms and procedures will seem strange to readers, but the case studies demonstrate the efficacy of how Brockman incorporates these ancient time-tested practices into a contemporary psychotherapeutic setting. If you are open to consider new ways to wholeness, you must read this book.

Dr. Stanley Krippner, Ph.D, co-author of *Healing States: A Journey Into the World of Spiritual Healing and Shamanism* With Alberto Villoldo, Ph.D.

How fortunate you are to have this extraordinary book. Howard Brockman, an expert psychotherapist, uses the tools of shamanic healing and energy psychology to guide you through nonordinary reality (NOR). When you come back to ordinary reality, you have become transformed to better cope with life's challenges. You may or may not intentionally spend time in NOR or the imaginal realm. Immersion in NOR allows you to go beyond time and space to experience precognitive dreams that come true. Or, with a lucid dream or shamanic journey, you can meet a helper to guide you through a health challenge or puzzling personal issue. Fasten your seat belt to step into the nonordinary realms for an exciting and rewarding adventure. I highly recommend *A Foot in Both Worlds: How Shamanic Healing and Energy Psychology Are Transforming Therapeutic Practice.*

Marcia Emery, Ph.D. author of *Intuition Workbook, The Intuitive Healer, and Power Hunch.*

A FOOT IN BOTH WORLDS

Howard Brockman's related books

Dynamic Energetic Healing™: Integrating Core Shamanic Practices With Energy Psychology Applications and Processwork Principles

Essential Self-Care for Caregivers and Helpers: Preserve Your Health, Maintain Your Well-Being And Create Effective Boundaries

A FOOT IN BOTH WORLDS

How Shamanic Healing
and Energy Psychology are
Transforming Psychotherapy

HOWARD BROCKMAN, LCSW

Columbia Press, LLC
1620 Commercial St. SE
Salem, Oregon 97302

Copyright © 2025 by Howard Brockman

All rights reserved. No part of this book may be reproduced, utilized, or transmitted in any form or by any means, electronic or mechanical, including photocopying, recording, or by any information storage and retrieval system, without permission in writing from the publisher.

Dynamic Energetic Healing™ is a unique energy-based psychotherapy model under the ownership of Howard Brockman.

Editor: Linda Jenkins
Cover illustration: Tara Thelen
Cover and book design: Deborah Perdue, Illumination Graphics
Proofreader: Sara J. Fowler

Image Credits
Images in this book were generated using artificial intelligence (AI) tools provided by OpenAI's ChatGPT with DALL·E. © Howard Brockman, 2025. Original illustration page 128 by Andrea Carlson.

ISBN: 978-0-9766469-9-0 (paperback)
ISBN: 978-0-9766469-6-9 (ebook)

Library of Congress Control Number: 9780976646990

Acknowledgments

I want to thank my creative team that helped shape my manuscript as it came together from start to finish. My editor, Linda Jenkins, spent many months scrutinizing each sentence of each chapter as she and I went back and forth over email to ensure that what I intended to express to the reader was being conveyed. Linda edited my first two books, each of which won publishing awards for excellence. I owe her an enormous amount of gratitude for her excellent work.

My proofreader, Sara Fowler, worked with exactitude to identify any inconsistencies in spelling, punctuation and formatting and to ensure that the manuscript adhered to specific style guidelines. Her attention to detail will ensure that the reader can enjoy the clarity, accuracy and continuity that naturally flows from one paragraph to the next. Her polish adds a bright shine to the finished product.

My designer, Deborah Perdue of Illumination Graphics, patiently supported me as text and images were added to, and footnotes were modified in, the manuscript. She worked diligently and without protest as changes were continually requested by Linda, Sara and myself. She was constantly having to revise the manuscript as modifications continued to be required, especially during the proofreading process. Deborah works with artist Tara Thelen who created the wonderful cover illustration that captures the essence of the title and theme of the book. She too was patient as we went back and forth to refine the final cover. To all of you I say Thank You.

A special acknowledgment goes to Dr. Stanley Krippner, an extraordinary individual. When I sent him a rough draft of the manuscript hoping he would provide an endorsement, Dr. Krippner read through the entire draft, providing me with commentary and corrections in the margin that were extremely helpful. I felt that my manuscript was reviewed and critiqued by a college professor with substantial expertise in the realm of parapsychology and consciousness. In fact, Dr. Krippner was the Alan Watts Professor of Psychology at Saybrook University in southern California. Occasionally, we are gifted by our meetings with special individuals, and Dr. Krippner is one of these special people.

DISCLAIMER

Shamanic healing methods, energy psychology techniques, and other described methods presented in this book should not be considered an exclusive approach for confronting psychological and/or medical problems.

This book is intended as an informational guide only. The remedies, approaches, and techniques described herein are meant to supplement, and not to be a substitute for, professional medical care or treatment. Proper use of the methods described in this book requires a thorough understanding, proper analysis, and supervised training. They should not be used to treat a serious ailment without prior consultation with a qualified healthcare professional. All matters regarding your health require medical supervision.

Neither the author nor anyone else who was involved in the creation, production, or support of the book shall be liable for any direct, incidental, economic, non-economic, punitive, or consequential damages.

DEDICATION

To Anita, Noah and Elias, whose love and constancy supports me
to stay grounded amidst my otherworld incursions

CONTENTS

Preface		xiii
PART 1:	**A Brief Historical Overview of Psychotherapy**	**1**
Chapter 1	Freudian Psychoanalysis	3
Chapter 2	Carl Gustav Jung's Analytic Psychology	11
Chapter 3	John Bowlby's Object Relations	19
Chapter 4	Behaviorism	23
Chapter 5	Cognitive Behavioral Therapy	31
Chapter 6	Humanistic Person-Centered Therapy	35
Chapter 7	The Therapeutic Alliance	39
Chapter 8	"Lobotomy Gets Them Home"	53
Chapter 9	The Psychopharmacological Revolution	63
Chapter 10	Psychotherapy Outside the United States	91
Chapter 11	Cross-Cultural Psychotherapy Considerations	97
PART 2:	**Integrating Shamanic Strategies in Dynamic Energetic Healing™**	**103**
Chapter 12	Sacred Imagination, Psychotherapy and the Living Earth	105
Chapter 13	Frontal Occipital Holding as the Vehicle for Shamanic Healing	127
Chapter 14	Power Animals and Shamanic Journeying	137
Chapter 15	How Shamanic Practices Provide Replenishment	145
Chapter 16	Merging and Shapeshifting— Three Personal Examples	155
Chapter 17	Dissociation, Soul Loss and Soul Retrieval	167
Chapter 18	Traumatic Residue as Energetic Imprints	175
Chapter 19	Energetic Boundaries, Intrusions and Extraction of Psychotoxic Energies	181
Chapter 20	Earthbound Spirits	189

| PART 3: | Clinical Case Studies in Dynamic Energetic Healing™ | 197 |

Introduction to Case Studies		199
Case Study 1	Animal Earthbound Spirit Attachments	208
Case Study 2	Intrusions, Psoriatic Arthritis and a Parasitic Attachment	216
Case Study 3	Bowel Dysfunction Relieved from Releasing an Energetic Intrusion	226
Case Study 4	How Releasing an Energetic Intrusion Changed a Student's Life	229
Case Study 5	Releasing Multiple Layers of an Energetic Intrusion	239
Case Study 6	Healing PTSD in Two Sessions	243
Case Study 7	Energetic Intrusion and Soul Stealing	249
Case Study 8	Covid Collective Field Discharged via Dismemberment	257
Case Study 9	Collective Energetic Intrusions	261
Case Study 10	Author's Personal Examples of Collective Intrusions	265
Case Study 11	Confronting Ancestral Spirits That Contribute to Physical Illness	271
Case Study 12	An Ancestral Spirit Comes in Love	275
Case Study 13	Spontaneous Healing through Shamanic Merging	279
Case Study 14	Soul Stealing and Soul Retrieval	285
Case Study 15	Clearing a House of Residual Psychotoxic Energy	288
Case Study 16	Spirit Attachment and Releasement	292
Conclusion	Shamanic Practices and the Living Earth	296
Notes		303
Suggestions for Further Reading		310
Index		318

Preface

This book is written for psychologists, psychotherapists, social workers, professional counselors, and professional and spiritual coaches. Additionally, people who are working in the healing arts, including acupuncturists, body workers and Reiki practitioners, will find this book very helpful. It is also written for anyone who is currently involved in or considering using psychotherapy to feel better and find a safe way to get out of mental and emotional anguish.

In the many psychology graduate programs offered throughout the United States, students are introduced to and taught the basics of a wide variety of psychotherapy models as they learn about the history of Western psychotherapy. While there is usually a practicum requirement providing opportunities to receive clinical supervision while learning how to work with a certain population, these clinical contexts are typically limited to one or two therapeutic orientations, often determined by where the clinician is placed. Once psychotherapists are licensed to practice, they begin their clinical practice based on their graduate training. As each licensing board requires a specified number of continuing education credits for renewing their license either annually or every two years, clinicians are drawn to particular therapy models that pique their interest to integrate into their practice when meeting with clients. In this way, most psychotherapists end up specializing in how they approach their work with clients. While this tends to develop competence in their specialized approach it also limits them, since they must exclude hundreds of other possible therapy models.

Since Sigmund Freud developed psychoanalysis at the turn of the last century, literally hundreds of different psychotherapy models have been advanced. In psychology, a model refers to a particular theoretical framework or approach that involves certain assumptions about human behavior. There may be several theories within a particular approach, but they all tend to share these assumptions. Each model has its relative strengths, weaknesses and biases, and brings something different to the way we attempt to understand human behavior.

In **Part 1**, I review and comment on how Western psychotherapy has evolved, focusing on eight significant psychotherapy models. As psychotherapists continue to practice their preferred approach and participate in learning new therapy models through their continuing education, it is often the case that the historical antecedents they learned about in graduate school fade into the background. In my review and commentary about these eight important psychotherapy models (leading up to cross-cultural influences), I discuss how this Western approach to help people feel better mentally and emotionally is both diverse and, at the same time, becoming more narrow. As you read through Part 1, you will discover that this is not actually paradoxical. It is an outgrowth of an attempt to be more scientific.

While Western psychology tries to validate itself as scientific with evidence-based research, the therapeutic relationship continues to emphasize and support subjectivity. There are actually many contradictions within this attempt to help individuals come into mental and emotional balance, largely because of the many different therapy models that are available to use. This is not necessarily a bad thing providing a new client knows what he or she is looking for and that a good connection is made with their therapist. More than anything, it is my intent to help you decide for yourself to what degree you are available to consider new ideas and possibilities both personally and within your professional practice.

This book has two primary themes: a Western Eurocentric secular approach to help people be happier and self-satisfied through the agency of psychology, and the incorporation of the ancient indigenous practices of core shamanic healing and energy psychology into the psychotherapy session. Each individual's personal journey for balance and for healing previously acquired trauma includes the myriad mental and emotional factors that most people don't spend much time discussing, unless of course they are participating in psychotherapy. Many people are prone to share with friends and family that they may be feeling depressed or anxious about a variety of things, be it their primary relationship or their family or the state of the world. This is not to say that people from historically earlier times ignored these issues, for much is written about these topics in literature as well as in philosophy, going all the way back to Plato. What has shifted since the early twentieth century is the emphasis on the scientific study of the human mind that includes the evolving brain-based medical model of neuropsychology, as well as what has come to be known as evidence-based, reproducible positive outcomes from a variety of psychological models.

I begin by discussing and reviewing Western psychotherapy. In the abbreviated historical overview, I have highlighted many of the most influential Western psychotherapy models and theories since Sigmund Freud. My analysis and commentary are in no way intended to present a comprehensive history of Western psychotherapy. I have judiciously selected eight of the many significant psychotherapy models in order to provide the reader with insights into how this field has developed and changed since the early 1900s. My intent is to illustrate and comment on how Western psychology has evolved in its effort to address various expressions of mental and emotional distress.

As a practicing psychotherapist with over forty years of experience, I believe it is essential to acknowledge the role of Western psychology in our efforts to navigate the complexities of the human experience and the world we inhabit. Psychology has evolved over time in an effort to deepen our understanding of the underlying mental and emotional factors that influence human behavior. Its emphasis has largely been about why some individuals are happy and successful while others find themselves continually failing in their personal and professional pursuits.

The publication of the first edition of the *Diagnostic and Statistical Manual of Mental Disorders* (DSM-1) in 1952 marked a turning point for the psychiatric community.[1] It began the systematic cataloging of mental disorders, a practice that has continued through subsequent editions, culminating in the updated DSM-5 released in 2022. While the DSM provides a conceptual framework for diagnosing and treating mental health conditions, criticism has emerged regarding the potential arbitrariness of these classifications. There are critics who assert that this labeling may inadvertently do a disservice to individuals by reducing complex human experiences into medically determined categories. In essence, the DSM has succeeded in medicalizing the complexity and diversity of the way human beings variously and uniquely experience being in the world.

More to the point, labeling individuals in order to fit them into neat diagnostic categories can influence how we perceive them and how they perceive themselves. Once assigned a diagnostic label, individuals may be subject to preconceptions and stereotypes, potentially shaping both their own self-image and the stigma that comes from the perceptions of others. This is the reason many clients of mine over the years have chosen not to use their medical insurance for reimbursement, since a DSM diagnosis is required for reimbursement. They fear that should this confidential information become available (especially more recently as institutional healthcare records are now being regularly hacked by cybercriminals), the potential social and employment consequences could be devastating, especially with the pervasiveness of social media. A recently recognized form of cyberbullying and blackmail called *doxing* has unfortunately become increasingly common. This occurs when sensitive or confidential medical and personal information is revealed online for harassment and exposure. All of this underscores the importance of approaching each person holistically, recognizing the multifaceted nature of human experience beyond diagnostic categories.

For psychotherapists, it is essential to tread lightly between diagnostic frameworks and the individual complexity of our clients. While diagnostic labels can provide a useful framework for understanding and communicating about mental health conditions, applying them must be approached with thoughtfulness and caution, recognizing the inherent limitations and potential biases they engender. Ultimately, one's aim as a psychotherapist must be to cultivate a therapeutic environment that honors the uniqueness and dignity of each individual, fostering healing and growth beyond the constraints of diagnostic labels as the therapeutic relationship supports the client's growth and healing.

Some of the chapters in Part 1 are relatively brief, simply highlighting the primary principles and practices that are intended to help people be more present to themselves through the lens of Western psychology. However, my purpose in providing this abbreviated historical overview is to stimulate thinking about how people can change, supported by the methods that these psychological models provide. The chapters on behaviorism, lobotomy and the psychopharmacological revolution are more lengthy because these approaches have been shown to do greater harm in their attempts to reengineer the human mind. I believe you will find them interesting and thought provoking.

As I reviewed the treatment strategies used in the 1940s and early 1950s for mental health disorders, it became evident to me that the treatments were characterized by extreme and often harmful interventions. Many individuals with mental illness were confined to asylums, where psychotherapy was essentially nonexistent. At that time, there was a pervasive stigma surrounding untreated mental health issues. Practices such as lobotomy and electroconvulsive therapy (ECT) were commonly employed in attempts to manage intractable symptoms.

All of this began to change with the introduction of antipsychotic and antidepressant medications, alongside the growing acceptance of benzodiazepines. This marked a significant shift toward a psychopharmacological approach to mental health treatment. This shift has reflected a growing acceptance of the medical model within the field of mental health, with psychiatrists assuming prominent roles as the authoritative clinicians.

As medications continued to gain prominence in the latter part of the 1950s, there was a decisive move away from the use of extreme interventions like lobotomy and ECT. The reliance on psychopharmacotherapy as the primary method for treating mental illness became increasingly utilized. This shift represented a pivotal moment in the history of mental health care, with medication-based approaches becoming the cornerstone of psychiatric treatment. Psychiatrists now called the shots. Even behaviorism, with its evidence-based classical conditioning, began to lose its prominence.

As the profession of psychology matured and became more widely accessible, psychotherapists began moving away from psychoanalysis to more diverse and available psychodynamic therapies to help clients understand how their early family dynamics impacted their behaviors and thought patterns. New approaches began to unfold, including humanistic, transpersonal, behavioral and cognitive behavioral therapy (CBT). Eventually, holistic or integrative orientations emerged that focus on helping people feel better about themselves with an emphasis on self-esteem, interpersonal boundaries and fostering positive connections with others. Today, prospective psychotherapy clients have a multitude of options for addressing their unhappiness and perseverating mental and emotional disturbances.

Why do people seek out psychotherapy and counseling? The most common issues that compel people to look for a therapist include marital and relationship conflicts, anxiety, depression, coping with loss, poor self-esteem with persistent negative inner self-talk, loneliness, emotional dysregulation such as intense anger or fear, lack of self-confidence, chronic physical dysfunction resulting from ongoing stress and post-traumatic stress disorder (PTSD), purposelessness or lack of a "soul mission," compulsive behaviors, and the long list of psychiatric disorders such as schizophrenia and bi-polar, narcissistic, sociopathic and borderline personality disorders.

For example, some prospective clients are unhappy with their primary or marital relationship and seek better understanding of the interpersonal psychodynamics, particularly with respect to difficult and acrimonious communication issues. Within this category of couple counseling, many different approaches have emerged. These may include CBT to reveal repetitive negative or erroneous thinking patterns, Imago Relationship Therapy to help identify childhood wounds and projections onto one's partner, and Internal Family Systems that identify various inner parts that need to be expressed and often acted out.

Other clients seek out individual psychotherapy for help with eliminating their depressed mood or chronically anxious feeling state. When either of these disorders become persistent, uncovering old interpersonal patterns from one's family of origin is often the focus within the psychodynamic approach to therapy. Helping clients recognize current life triggers through talk therapy can be helpful if the therapist is sufficiently skilled.

With hundreds of psychotherapy models, each containing their own therapeutic bias, knowledgeably selecting a therapist who has been trained within a specific orientation can be daunting. Let me provide you with some examples of the hundreds of psychotherapy models currently available to prospective clients:

Adlerian therapy
Art therapy
Attachment-based psychotherapy
Behavior modification
Biofeedback
Body psychotherapy
Contemplative psychotherapy
Dance movement therapy
Depth psychotherapy
Dialectical behavior therapy
Dreamwork
Dynamic Energetic Healing™ (DEH)
Emotional freedom techniques (EFT)
Encounter groups
Eye movement desensitization and reprocessing (EMDR)
Family constellations
Gestalt therapy
Grief counseling
Hakomi
Holotropic breathwork
Hypnosis assisted therapy
Interpersonal psychotherapy
Jungian psychotherapy
Mindfulness-based cognitive therapy
Music therapy
Object relations psychotherapy
Play therapy
Process-oriented therapy
Psychodrama
Reichian therapy

Sandplay therapy
Sex therapy
Somatic therapy
Systematic desensitization
Transactional analysis
Transpersonal therapy
Wilderness therapy[2]

This is just a sampling of the myriad psychotherapy models that prospective clients must evaluate, providing they are sufficiently interested in educating themselves about psychotherapy.

Quite honestly, how is one to know if Jungian or Gestalt psychotherapy is a better fit than object relations or process-oriented psychology approaches? The choices can be overwhelming. Many if not most prospective clients end up with a particular psychotherapist either through a personal recommendation from a friend, or from searching websites on the internet, hoping that some therapist has room for them in their caseload. As we are recovering from the pandemic, a majority of psychotherapists report that their caseloads have become so full that they are simply unable to accept any new clients. Because this has become so prevalent, a prospective client might throw caution to the wind and simply hope that the therapist who has an opening and the psychotherapy model he or she is trained in will be a good match for them. For example, a prospective client may have researched Jungian psychotherapy with an emphasis on dream analysis and intuitively resonates with this, yet due to their need to establish some kind of therapeutic relationship as their problems continue to negatively impact their life, they eventually find a therapist who emphasizes CBT but who has no training in dream analysis. Circumstances dictate that a therapist using CBT is better than no therapist at all.

This became particularly problematic during the height of the pandemic. Even after Covid-19 infections peaked, most psychotherapists had to close off their practice to new clients due to overwhelming demand. Millions of people who were regularly interacting with colleagues in their offices were now isolated at home in front of their computer, working remotely and feeling quite lonely. Even now in 2025, children and teens throughout the country are experiencing an epidemic of loneliness due to the isolation that computer-driven distance learning classes have created. The newly emergent phenomenon of remote telehealth has grown, largely replacing in-person psychotherapy sessions with telehealth remote interactions. I feel grateful that for the majority of my forty-three years as a psychotherapist, I was able to meet with my clients in that most special and emotionally intimate context in my physical office space. I always enjoy that up-close connection with people and I have heard similar feedback from many of my colleagues.

However, the shift to remote telehealth meetings for the majority of my clients has extended my reach far beyond my local clientele and is likely here to stay. In a typical week, I meet with clients living in London, Slovenia, Colorado and southern California. All this has required that psychotherapists adapt themselves to interacting with their clients in front of a screen. While I am meeting with some clients in my office in-person once again, many of my clients find it more convenient to stay in their home office and meet with me over Zoom. This has revolutionized the way psychotherapists conduct the business of interacting with clients. It has also redefined the therapeutic relationship. In my experience, when clients forge a stable and secure therapeutic alliance with their therapist where there is a strong interpersonal connection, successful outcomes are greatly enhanced.

Part 1 of this book is a commentary and brief historical overview of Western psychotherapy. **Chapter 1** starts with Freud and his theoretical overview, including the id, ego and superego. I trace how psychotherapists began to move away from Freud's "talking cure" to consider other approaches and theories for helping clients overcome their neuroses. Freud believed that events in our early childhood significantly impact our behavior and shape our personality as adults. He asserted that people have little free will to make choices in life as our behavior is determined by the influence of the unconscious mind and significant childhood experiences. He emphasized the importance of dreams as a product of our unconscious mind and encouraged his patients to describe them so they could be analyzed for their symbolism to help increase self-awareness. His creative insights continue to serve as the cornerstone of many psychodynamic therapy models.

Chapter 2 highlights Carl Gustav Jung following his departure from Freud (who was his mentor), only to go through his dark night of the soul over several years that ultimately enabled him to develop his theory of archetypes and the collective unconscious. Jung did not agree with Freud's atheism; Jung had a strong spiritual nature that informed much of his emerging theory for how to help his patients. He too realized the importance of dreams and developed techniques to help his patients understand what their dreams and their symbols were communicating to them. Through his sojourn, he developed the therapeutic technique that he named active imagination, an innovative approach that provides opportunities to interact with the repetitive and often tyrannizing inner voices and intrusive images that continually assault many people.

In **Chapter 3** I reflect on the insightful perceptions of John Bowlby and his object relations therapy, which offers profound insights into the dynamics of secure emotional attachment from infancy onward. Bowlby's discerning work emphasized the critical importance of early childhood experiences, particularly the quality of attachment relationships formed with primary caregivers. Drawing on his observations of infant–parent interactions, Bowlby developed his theory of early attachment, positing that secure emotional bonds formed in infancy lay the foundation for healthy social and emotional development as we mature.

By reviewing the client's attachment history and relational patterns, object relations therapy aims to uncover unconscious conflicts, fears, and defenses that may impede the formation of secure attachments and healthy relationships. Through exploration and insight, clients develop greater self-awareness and cultivate more fulfilling and authentic connections to others.

Object relations therapy offers a deep and compassionate approach to healing relational wounds and fostering emotional growth. By discovering the root causes of attachment-related issues, clients can work toward resolving internal conflicts and developing more secure and satisfying relationships in their lives.

As psychotherapy continued to evolve, the more scientific and research-oriented behaviorism model began to gain influence. This is the focus of **Chapter 4**. A core tenet of this model is that with controlled experiments, observable behaviors can be studied because they can be objectively measured. A key underlying assumption in behaviorism is that people do not have free will, and thus it is the environment that determines all behavior. Notable among these theorists are Ivan Pavlov, John Watson and B. F. Skinner. Their arguments initially were about developing ways to measure therapeutic outcomes through controlled experiments that considered how outer stimuli create predictable responses. It wasn't too long before a majority of psychotherapists began to realize that the inner world of clients and their subjective perceptions were being completely marginalized. The pendulum thus began to swing back to emphasizing the collaborative nature of more open and relational psychotherapy that gave rise to cognitive behavioral therapy, as well as person-centered therapy approaches.

Cognitive behavioral therapy (CBT) follows in **Chapter 5**; it now appears to be the go-to talk therapy approach—the dominant psychotherapy model practiced by the vast majority of therapists. Psychotherapists who use this model are mostly concerned with their clients' mental functions such as their memories and perceptions. CBT's emphasis is focused on the client's underlying thinking and mental processing. For example, if a client reveals that he is always coming back to the thought that he is simply a loser, the therapist would orient the client to discuss how this belief came into being and then recommend strategies to stop this repetitive self-devaluing thinking.

Chapter 6 delves into the groundbreaking contributions of Carl Rogers and Abraham Maslow during the late 1950s, which revolutionized the field of psychotherapy and gave rise to humanistic psychology. Rogers challenged the traditional therapist–client dynamic by introducing client-centered therapy, also known as person-centered therapy. He came to believe that the therapist needn't be distant and largely unrelatable. He emphasized the importance of empathy, unconditional positive regard, and genuineness in the therapeutic relationship. Rogers believed that individuals possess an innate drive toward realizing their inherent talents and potentialities, and that the therapist's role is to provide a supportive and nonjudgmental environment for clients to explore their experiences, thought processes and emotions.

Abraham Maslow further expanded on Rogers' ideas with his concept of the hierarchy of needs. Maslow proposed that individuals' needs have a hierarchical ranking, ranging from basic physiological needs to higher-level needs such as self-esteem and self-actualization. According to Maslow, self-actualization represents the fulfillment of one's highest potential and aspirations, leading to a sense of purpose, creativity, and fulfillment in life.

Together, Rogers and Maslow laid the foundation for humanistic psychology, which emphasizes the inherent goodness and potential for growth within each individual. Humanistic therapists focus on facilitating self-discovery, empowerment and personal development rather than diagnosing and treating mental illness.

Their pioneering work paved the way for a more compassionate and client-centered approach to psychotherapy, shifting the focus from pathology to personal growth and self-actualization. The principles of humanistic psychology continue to influence therapeutic practice today, emphasizing the importance of empathy, authenticity, and the therapeutic alliance in promoting overall well-being and psychological flourishing.

The therapist–client relationship is the topic of **Chapter 7** and for good reason. A healthy therapeutic alliance is profoundly healing. Every one of us craves deep connection to others. Spending time with a therapist who is attuned, mindful and listens attentively without judgment provides a context wherein clients can feel safe to venture inward. The more complete the therapist's personal development, the more strongly his or her therapeutic presence conveys this self-assurance and compassionate acceptance. This is modeled through the interactions with clients so it becomes easier for clients to try on new ways of interacting with others. Even so, the therapeutic approach of the psychotherapist must also be a good fit for the client. For example, an individual who is withdrawn and introverted will likely not easily warm up to a therapist who is expecting clients to act out their inner parts through psychodrama. Problem resolution and, ultimately, healing will more readily result when clients feel emotionally safe and supported to reveal to another person what they are most ashamed and fearful of. A magical interpersonal dance ensues.

Chapter 8 describes how the evolving field of psychology addressed societal mental illness before the development of psychiatric medications. During this time, our society was grappling with the severely mentally ill who were increasingly being housed in asylums, many of them having returned shell shocked from World War II; today we call this post-traumatic stress disorder (PTSD). The treatments that had been developed at that time were not able to consistently address the suffering of these unfortunate individuals. A neurologist named Walter Freeman found an article about a procedure being tried in Europe by Portuguese neurologist Egas Moniz that directly affected the human brain. Though Freeman wasn't trained as a surgeon, he nonetheless began to experiment with what became known as the transorbital lobotomy procedure. This involved surgical intervention to compromise the prefrontal cortex by detaching it from the thalamus. It became widely utilized and heralded by Freeman. He was allowed to perform this as an outpatient procedure. Thousands of patients suffered irreparable harm from this psychosurgery that was used for many years. This medical procedure was intended to quiet down the ravings of patients locked up in mental institutions. It is a fascinating and unsettling chapter in the evolution of Western psychology.

Chapter 9 discusses the sweeping shift in mental health treatment that began in the 1950s when the psychopharmacological revolution began in earnest. Lobotomies fell out of favor as powerful new psychotropic medications became available to medicalize and sedate the severely mentally ill. The steady increase in the prescribing and use of psychotropic medications throughout the general population continues to this day. This evolving psychopharmacological model theorizes that chemical imbalances in the brain are responsible for mental illness. I discuss this recasting and the reverberating consequences of this medical/biological model, including long-term consequences, particularly biochemical dependence resulting from continued use of these powerful medications. Ongoing research in this biological model posits that our thoughts, feelings and even our behaviors come forth from our neurochemistry and our genome. One of its underlying assumptions is that our behaviors are inherited. Of course, this model brings the perennial debate about nature versus nurture strikingly to our attention.

Chapter 10 discusses psychotherapy outside of the United States along with the many unique adaptations that are being introduced in various countries. The central question to be considered is how Eurocentric Western psychotherapy models can or cannot adapt to multicultural ways of maintaining psychosocial balance in the world. I discuss cross-cultural issues that must be considered when attempting to apply Western psychotherapy models to cultures that embrace their unique epistemology that is significantly different from our own. This also brings into question what is considered normal versus abnormal within the larger context of cultural relativism. One must remember that Western psychotherapy has only been practiced for approximately 125 years. This begs the question regarding how preliterate and indigenous societies were able to maintain homeostasis communally, as well as individually.

Chapter 11 completes this part of the book as I conclude the discussion of cross-cultural psychotherapy and how non-Western societies implement Western psychotherapy approaches (or don't). Consider that Western Europe and North America account for one billion people while the rest of the world accounts for seven billion. The Western orientation to address mental illness and psychotherapy is approached through a diagnostic lens via the DSM-5 evidence-based framework. The power of community and its unique cultural support is not considered through this framework. This requires an appraisal of each society's belief system about mental illness and how it is different from Eurocentric models. Additionally, many cultures don't even have a place for individual psychotherapy in their worldview, as it is often the community that determines the best treatment approach for individuals who may be acting out in disruptive ways. As a Western reader, it is important to take into account that non-Western countries and societies view the world quite differently than we do, and this must be acknowledged when considering exporting Western psychotherapy approaches to many of these other countries.

In **Part 2** I begin the discussion of an integrative approach to psychotherapy, starting with **Chapter 12**. Poets, novelists, mystics, quantum physicists and shamans experience life as multidimensional. Perhaps you enjoy reading fiction, or maybe you find poetry elusive and difficult to understand and appreciate. Writers have learned to orient in different ways to relate to and describe their experience of reality. They are able to access their imagination to create engaging fictional environments that completely capture our attention as if we were right there in the story. This is true in many of the arts as new realities never before introduced become realized. The plays of Shakespeare, novels that take you into the trenches of World War I, and roaming through star systems as Captain Jean-Luc Picard engages the *Enterprise* to chase down the Borg Queen—these are invented and created realities generated by writers who have accessed and involved us in these new fictional worlds. It is from these creative/created realities that the phrase "life imitates art" has emerged. Through their deep empathy and facility with words, poets and writers are able to capture the essence of the human experience and craft something totally unique through the power of language and imagination. It is their intent to reveal and share their unique experience of reality as they imaginatively perceive and feel into it. Just because you may not relate to what a poet is expressing does not diminish its unique value to reveal aspects of what is otherwise hidden from the rest of us.

Chapter 12 is about intentional dreaming and the power of *sacred imagination*. I begin with the discussion of energy-based approaches to healing and how ancient models such as traditional Chinese medicine and core shamanic practices are successful because of their understanding and application of subtle energy. I discuss the meaning of *epistemology* and how we come to know what is actually true and valid. What follows is how the rational-scientific paradigm contrasts with how we know things subjectively and intuitively. It is here that I introduce what for many readers will be as unfamiliar as quantum physics is to most of us, namely, the animistic orientation to life known as core shamanic practices.

Core shamanic practices are often regarded as the planet's oldest healing methodology—they have been practiced for many thousands of years. This approach's major assertion is that direct revelation is available to anyone willing to consider that there are, indeed, ways to access information other than the rational-scientific approach. Sometimes referred to as a transpersonal model for experiencing the world, shamanic visionary experiences can be easily learned and applied within the Western psychotherapy context. This ancient healing model directly addresses the feelings of isolation and disconnectedness that so many people are experiencing today. The reason for this is that in core shamanic practices, everything is filled with and vibrating with Spirit. When the shamanic practitioner journeys to various spiritual realms, he or she is willing to depart from what we tend to all agree upon as our everyday consensus reality. The shamanic practitioner learns how to be open to and gain access to the realm of the soul. In this domain, there is great spiritual *power* that can be acquired for balance, healing and optimal well-being. In my many Association for Comprehensive Energy Psychology (ACEP)[3] conference seminars and the small-group workshops given in my office, I teach participants how to negotiate *nonordinary reality* (NOR) through learning the shamanic journey. Everyone who I have taught generates shockingly successful and emotionally profound outcomes, and many of these participants achieve this during their very first foray into this rarified spiritual realm.

As you will discover when reading **Chapter 13** on frontal occipital holding, this technique has dramatically impacted clients more than any other strategy used in my Dynamic Energetic Healing™ (DEH) model. Bringing this into play in my psychotherapy sessions has transformed the effectiveness of therapeutic outcomes. Within the essential framework of energy psychology (EP), including behavioral applied kinesiology muscle testing/energy testing, frontal occipital holding creates a bridge that brings in compassionate spirits for transformative healing outcomes. It is difficult to describe in words how powerfully this bridge enables me to have a foot in both worlds: that of our everyday ordinary reality and the nonordinary realms. This ability collapses the barriers between these two dimensions so that the *power* of the helping spirits is accessed and infused into my clients' lives.

Frontal occipital holding was introduced to me as I began to learn how to use energy psychology strategies as therapeutic interventions. As I explain below, the genesis of my transition from more conventional psychotherapy to an energy-based approach required a profound shift and acceptance of an entirely new psychotherapeutic paradigm. While it took several years of EP trainings, incremental practice, and the gradual inclusion of this approach into my psychotherapy practice, the rewards continue to pay large dividends to clients. This is especially highlighted whenever frontal occipital holding is called on.

Over two decades ago, when energy psychology was just beginning to emerge as a new and innovative treatment approach, I began taking as many trainings as I could from the few therapists who were teaching the fundamentals of this new psychotherapeutic model. The first training was over two weekends, one month apart. It was on thought field therapy (TFT)—an approach originated by Dr. Roger Callahan and still used and taught in the growing EP community. It incorporates behavioral kinesiology muscle testing to identify specific combinations of acupressure points that run along the acupuncture meridians. There are combinations of these end points that Callahan had catalogued for treating depression, anxiety, phobias, panic, sadness and loss, and many other common psychotherapeutic issues that clients bring to their therapist. The first weekend training was so different from anything I had previously used with clients that I was confused. Because it was such a new and innovative paradigm, I was skeptical while at the same time trying to be open and available to this new and unfamiliar approach.

At the time, I was deeply engaged in process-oriented therapy, providing adult mixed-gender therapy groups every Tuesday evening for two hours. This was an extroverted, interactive approach that encouraged the acting out of every inner part, expressing as many aspects of whatever feeling states emerged moment to moment. It was psychodrama par excellence that was wild, loud and exuberant. When a colleague strongly encouraged me to take the TFT training, I was initially reluctant; I was thoroughly enjoying the engaging nature of processwork. But she was persuasive so I signed up for the training. I resisted being open to this new approach until one particular demonstration with a woman who hadn't traveled on an airplane for over two decades due to her phobia of flying. Our therapist-trainer worked with her in front of the group, demonstrating the mechanics of muscle testing and then directing the client to tap on specific combinations of acupressure points as each aspect of her long-held fear emerged. It was fascinating to observe but mysterious. By the time thirty minutes had elapsed, the client was completely congruent about considering taking a vacation with her husband on an airplane. She was laughing in delight just considering flying to faraway destinations.

It took me several weeks to process and integrate this new approach after the second weekend. I began to appreciate the precision that the muscle testing provided. It was the guiding process for therapeutic outcomes that emerged relatively quickly, as long-standing issues dissolved not over weeks or months but within the time frame of the weekend training. It blew my mind and disassembled my previous therapeutic biases about how psychotherapy is supposed to be conducted.

I then made the commitment to take any subsequent EP trainings that were within driving distance and enroll in the annual ACEP international conferences held in various locations in the United States. During one of these early three-day trainings in Seattle, I was introduced to an intervention called frontal occipital holding. We were instructed to get a partner sitting close to us; one of us would be the therapist and the other the client. In each pair, the therapist stood on one side of the client, who was seated. The therapist was instructed to place one hand over the occipital ridge on the back of the client's head while placing the other hand on the client's forehead. We were told that frontal occipital holding was a stress management strategy. The client might be inclined to move their head around in order to unwind emotional stress; the therapist was instructed to just stay with the client and allow them to move as they wished. We were told that any impressions or insights that might emerge from either one of us should be debriefed afterward when the therapist felt ready to stop.

At that time I had been practicing shamanic journeying for just over twenty years. I was journeying only occasionally for clients using drumming or rattling in the traditional manner. As I placed my hands in position on my client's head, I waited, not knowing what to expect. After perhaps thirty seconds I began to perceive through my intuitive perception a large tribe of native Americans on their horses flying down from the upper world until they were right next to me. A wizened old woman warrior immediately told me that they had been observing me and liked me because of my sincerity and deep identification with my compassionate helpers. They told me that they would now be working with me to assist in helping and healing my clients. They told me their *power* would be made available for my clients and me, and to just call on them for help.

I was shocked to my core—I never could have anticipated anything like this happening. When I told my partner about my experience, he was just as surprised. He told me that he felt very relaxed afterward and had a feeling of overall well-being.

It was an easy decision for me to include frontal occipital holding as one of the many strategies I began implementing with clients as I transitioned from processwork to EP and eventually what became DEH. Over time as I incorporated DEH into my psychotherapy practice, frontal occipital holding has been consistently called on (through the muscle testing inquiries) when deeply embedded subtle negative energy becomes identified. As you will read in many of the clinical case histories in Part 3 of this book, it is frequently via frontal occipital holding that the compassionate spirits come through me in compressed-time shamanic journeys to facilitate the release of deeply embedded subtle negative energy. It is really quite miraculous.

Chapter 14 addresses the role that power animals play in shamanic journeying. When one is initially learning the fundamentals of the shamanic journey, acquiring a power animal is often the first task that is assigned. Meeting and connecting with a new power animal is exciting and affirming. It is extremely reassuring to discover that a power animal in the lower world is interested in partnering with you in order to teach and guide you in the realm of NOR. These beings in the lower world provide guidance and facilitation for discovering new shamanic environments and new learnings.

As journeyers develop this special relationship over time, they discover that their new power animal has particular locations in NOR that contain unusual concentrations of *power* that are healing and replenishing. Power animals provide guidance and teach us new ways to think about how to support and heal ourselves, our clients and our family, as well as ways to keep us *power-filled*. Power animals often become lifelong spiritual companions that are always available to us for guidance, protection and healing. They teach us different ways of being in our everyday ordinary reality world. They become our guardian spirits.

Each power animal represents a species or category of animal with its own unique abilities. Some power animals provide help in removing psychotoxic energies we have absorbed from others. Other power animals help us reclaim vital essence that was lost due to accidents or trauma. They are instrumental during a soul retrieval, and they can help us to move around within NOR (such as traveling to the upper world from the lower world) since they know the territory of NOR. They are benevolent and loyal, and they support us to stay healthy, enabling us to absorb *power* that carries over into our everyday activities. It is remarkable to consider how compassionate and wise power animals are; they are always available to help and guide us through the challenges of our day-to-day life.

Chapter 15 continues to elaborate on the theme of subtle energy by discussing the need for replenishment. In psychotherapy, clients often feel disempowered due to their early experiences growing up in dysfunctional family systems or from having experienced significant traumatic events. Shamanic healing addresses the loss of personal power as one of the most significant issues that needs to be confronted and healed. When an individual has what we generally call a lack of self-esteem, a shamanic practitioner understands this as a loss of personal power.

The psychopharmacological model provides medication to help clients feel less desperate by modifying their neurochemicals, but this typically does not resolve the underlying causes that are responsible for the presenting symptoms. Shamanic healing strategies address the root cause from which the symptoms continue to persist. Like psychotherapy, a client who is open to receive shamanic healing interventions typically requires a commitment to participate in several sessions to enhance their personal power, and remove energetic blocks and trauma-based psychotoxic imprints that have accumulated over time. This is accomplished through the agency of compassionate spirits that exist in this other dimension of reality. The shamanic practitioner is able to partner with his or her helping spirits or ally figures through the shamanic journey technique.

Those spirits then initiate the infusion of healing *power*, as well as the removal of psychotoxic intrusions that over time continue to weaken the individual.

As I write this, I realize that for many readers there are likely no reference points to latch onto as I describe this very different approach to healing old trauma and returning to balance. Helping spirits who can be interacted with are simply not part of our Western epistemological understanding of how we negotiate everyday reality. This is why it takes some time for neophyte shamanic practitioners to become comfortable with negotiating this different reality.

Western psychotherapy has developed many approaches to address persistent PTSD symptomatology with varying degrees of success. In shamanic healing parlance, often a client has suffered soul loss, or the loss of a significant part of their vital essence that has left them feeling empty or dead inside. Shamanic healing provides soul retrievals to find and reincorporate the lost part or parts of their vital essence that have fled as a consequence of an overwhelming experience or trauma. These split-off inner parts can often be tracked along a client's chronological timeline during the shamanic journey.

Because shamanic healing is an approach with origins from indigenous peoples that operates in the realm of the soul and subtle energy, people who have never experienced it find it difficult to appreciate and accept. But then, consider the therapist who says that an old trauma is trapped in your body and that you therefore need to have deep tissue massage in order to exorcise the trapped traumatic residue through a body-oriented psychotherapy approach—many people would find that difficult to accept as well. Or another therapist may say that an old trauma is trapped in your subconscious mind, so you need deep trance hypnotherapy to restore balance. Yet another therapist says that the trauma is trapped in your nervous system and therefore you need to use biofeedback along with guided imagery and meditation. Core shamanism is an ancient healing approach that proposes its own unique strategies to help a client heal and resolve their trauma and that has a centuries-old track record of success. People tend to be skeptical if they aren't familiar with the theory behind the technique suggested to them. I believe having this background knowledge is important with any new psychotherapeutic or psychospiritual healing approach.

Shamanic healing and energy-based models such as energy psychology and acupuncture will likely generate doubt and skepticism when first introduced. This is human nature. I simply tell my clients that this is a skill set I have learned and practiced for over forty years, and if they would like to experience this for themselves, a new world of possibilities will present itself. If not, that too is understandable and we can consider other approaches or a referral to a different therapist. Nevertheless, my use of shamanic healing interventions as part of my Dynamic Energetic Healing™ model continues to be extremely effective.[4]

Different spiritual practices are designed to help practitioners restore the energy they put out every day in order to stay healthy and regularly revitalized. For shamanic practitioners, this is experienced as an ongoing accumulation of vital energy (called *power*) that is balancing, healing and replenishing. This model also addresses subtle negative energy, which we are all prone to unwittingly absorb from others.

In **Chapter 16** I share three personal experiences that exemplify some of my ongoing experiences with my helping spirits. I describe the difference between visualizing during the shamanic journey and becoming somatically identified with one of my ally figures while in the journey process. In the shamanic healing model, this is known as *merging* with my ally figure where there is very little differentiation between us. What is so fascinating about this process is how powerfully this positively influences clients in our everyday consensus reality. These three personal experiences are excellent examples of how I am able to move back and forth between the nonordinary realms where the spirits reside and create a bridge or passageway to positively impact my clients in our everyday ordinary reality. It is a way of straddling both worlds to generate powerful healing outcomes. This is also called *shapeshifting*, a common phenomenon known to core shamanic practitioners. Shapeshifting is renown throughout the shamanic literature as one of the most mysterious and powerful shamanic healing experiences.

Chapter 17 addresses the fascinating phenomena of dissociation and soul loss. Sigmund Freud identified dissociation as one of many defense mechanisms that occur as one way to compensate for having to deal with emotionally overwhelming experiences. While Freud was trained as a neurologist, he is to be given credit for shifting his attention from the biological to the psychological or psychic adaptations to overly intense emotional experiences. These extraordinarily intense experiences that people dissociate from are subjective to each person's unique neuropsychological makeup.

Consider two siblings who are living under the roof of an emotionally abusive and threatening father. While sibling A may act out and express their indignant anger as a response, no matter the consequences, sibling B may dissociate to try to escape the harsh and repeated lambasting and shaming. Should this continue over many years as part of a dysfunctional family system, sibling B is likely to develop a chronic unconscious response to try to appease and end up being unable to occupy relationships in an honest and sincere manner. This becomes problematic as sibling B matures and seeks meaningful personal relationships because B's ability to stand in their own power has been significantly compromised and has become habituated to dissociating when emotions become overly intense. Unfortunately, this is much more common than you might think; healthy interpersonal conflict is thus not possible.

Dissociation is perceived and addressed differently in core shamanic practices. When accidents, stressors and traumatic events occur, part of one's vital essence leaves to a different dimension of reality, namely NOR. Whether the individual is raised in a Western culture or an indigenous environment, the feeling or perception that "something is very wrong" becomes self-evident. Shamans refer to this serious condition as soul loss—the experience of personal wholeness having become compromised. Through the shamanic journey, the shaman or shamanic practitioner, with the help of their helping spirits, is led to where the person's vital essence is residing. Once located in NOR, a soul retrieval can be brought to bear, essentially rescuing this part that fled and reincorporating it into the person to make things right once again. In this chapter I go into greater detail explaining these fascinating phenomena.

Chapter 18 elaborates on how core shamanic approaches along with EP strategies successfully address residual traumatic residue within an energy-based model of psychotherapy. This traumatic residue is spoken about and better understood as *energetic imprints* that stay stuck in one's *energy body* like many layers of invisible shrink-wrapped plastic. Each layer carries information that can be accessed and ultimately peeled away. Unlike psychiatric medication that largely addresses only the presenting symptoms, EP and core shamanic approaches are able to get to the heart of the issue very quickly. When individuals lose their conviction of feeling self-empowered, they become more available to subtle negative energetic phenomena that disrupt one's homeostasis and create ongoing mind–body discomposure. These imprints can become multilayered over time, accumulating within us. This often creates trauma-based chronic conditions such as dissociation, unconscious death wishes and even suicidal ideation. Unhealed trauma can also promulgate unhealthy mental preoccupations that often disrupt sleep and everyday interactions with friends and partners. Through the help of accurate energy checking, often called behavioral muscle testing, one can trace the energetic origins of these subtle negative energy imprints and identify various effective strategies to release them once and for all.[5]

In **Chapter 19** I discuss why energetic boundaries are so important as a way of reframing what psychotherapists have traditionally understood as interpersonal boundaries. In this energy-based model that is Dynamic Energetic Healing™, there is an emphasis placed on the *energy body* that many people are not familiar with. Remember that this model operates in a realm where subtle energy is the prevailing operational undercurrent. This subtle energy is the focus of my interactions with clients. Once a basic appreciation of the *energy body* is assimilated in the therapy session, the concept of energetic boundaries becomes better understood as the essential foundation of preventing energetic intrusions. These intrusions are explained and show up as a consequence of compromised energetic boundaries.

When individuals lack sufficient self-confidence and tend to not stand up for their beliefs and feeling states in the moment, they become vulnerable to absorbing psychotoxic energetic intrusions from the individual(s) they are interacting with. In many of the case studies presented in Part 3, clients suffered various mental, emotional and often physical compromises that all of their outside efforts were unable to remedy. Remarkably, after releasing an energetic intrusion, clients were able to immediately return to balance and homeostasis with all symptoms quickly resolved. The client's next task was to discuss with me why their energetic boundaries with the person who was the source of the intrusion were compromised. Once the client understands how they did not sufficiently represent themselves congruently, it is much easier to help them create energetic boundaries with that individual.

Some of my clients have previously consulted a psychiatrist to acquire medication, while others have met with their regular doctor in their efforts to resolve their distressing symptoms. In the examples I describe, it was only after releasing the psychotoxicity embedded

PREFACE

in the intrusion or other forms of subtle negative energy that clients began to come back into balance, even on the physical level. This chapter goes into great detail describing the interplay of how energetic intrusions become embedded in a client's *energy body* when energetic boundaries are weak and compromised.

Chapter 20 provides an understanding of how clients are affected when an errant or wandering spirit of a deceased person attaches to their energy field, causing a multitude of problems. Remember, the shamanic universe is populated with not only compassionate helping spirits but the spirits of deceased individuals who, for various reasons, are trapped and wandering in our earthly dimension. Sometimes they are drawn to certain individuals, but often their attachment is random. This always impacts the living person—usually in ways that compromise them. Chapter 20 describes in greater detail many of these impacts and how they are remedied.

Shamans throughout the world know about this aspect of spirit attachment in our middle-world realm that most of us consider the only reality we occupy. In fact, one component of the shamanic practitioner's skill set is referred to as psychopomp work. This is when the practitioner specifically assists the souls of the deceased who are trapped in our middle-world earthly dimension and who are typically lost and frightened. They need help to make their transition to wherever they are destined to continue on their soul's journey. The shamanic practitioner, with the support of his helping spirits, enables the release from this earthly bond to guide the spirit of the deceased to their next destination. This allows the healing resolution of both the released spirit and the person who was affected by it. I have included several case studies in Part 3 that highlight how spirits of the deceased—including ancestral spirits—can impact clients' lives.

For most people unfamiliar with shamanic practices, I do realize this may be hard to take in and may even feel scary to contemplate. It may strike you as a spiritually dubious and disputable practice when compared to culturally familiar Western religious approaches and their connected theological explanations and doctrinal beliefs. However, through training in core shamanic healing, practice and discipline, these perceptions and interventions become accessible, practical and highly effective in generating rapid therapeutic resolutions for clients to whom an earthbound spirit has attached. Of course, this begs the question about the veracity and existence of what occurs after one dies. Yet for shamans and shamanic practitioners, their ongoing relationships with compassionate spirits phenomenologically confirm and reinforce their knowledge of this other dimension of reality and all of its inhabitants.

Part 3 of the book includes sixteen clinical case examples that illustrate how specific presenting symptoms are addressed and resolved when subtle negative energy formulations are identified and released. These clinical examples illustrate what can occur when an individual feels disempowered and vulnerable. In my practice, I often see clients who have become codependent in their relationships and thus have lost their energetic boundaries. When this occurs, a person becomes vulnerable and is operating with compromised personal power. In other words, they have failed to occupy their relationships with their full presence. Frequently, the defense mechanism of dissociation is generated as a result.

In an energy-based shamanic approach, the consequences of harboring old traumatic residue can be serious. Often, disempowered individuals absorb psychotoxic energy from others, resulting in what is known as an *energetic intrusion*. As an experienced shamanic practitioner, I can perceive these intrusions (through the eyes of my helping spirits) in a variety of forms and expressions. They may appear, for example, as a serpentine creature wrapped around the client's throat, a deeply embedded vine like English ivy, or a Velcro-like encasement over and around the trunk of the body.

Additionally, in Part 3 I provide examples of how sensitive individuals are impacted by *collective intrusions*. These energetic intrusions can affect us from enormous collective fields of negatively charged information. When news and information become overwhelmingly negative and frightening, which occurred during the first two years of the Covid-19 pandemic, we can be subject to contamination by these circulating global fields of fear and despair. We typically acquire these collective intrusions from various media inputs that we turn to in order to stay informed. I have called this phenomenon the *dreaming media* because of how unconscious parts of us feel under siege and thus split off to become part of this enormous circulating collective field of influence. I myself have been negatively affected by collective intrusions and describe some of these experiences along with those of my clients.

All of the case studies are discussed in ways that completely mask the identities of the clients. While name, age and even gender may be changed, their anonymity is absolute and protected as part of the requirements outlined in my professional code of ethics.

Through the many thousands of years that shamanism has been practiced, the experiential revelations of its shamans continue to reinforce their knowledge that spirits exist as one representation of the subtle energy manifestation in all things, including plants, animals and humans. If you find this intriguing, I recommend that you inquire at the Foundation for Shamanic Studies to sign up for some of their many workshops to discover for yourself the experiential validity of compassionate spirits and their healing abilities.[6] If you are willing to open up your mind to consider different non-Western indigenous approaches for how deep healing occurs, read on to find out what resonates with you when you learn how to acknowledge and use your sacred imagination.

PART 1:

A BRIEF HISTORICAL OVERVIEW OF PSYCHOTHERAPY

Chapter 1
Freudian Psychoanalysis

Western psychotherapy has evolved significantly since it was founded in the early 1900s by Sigmund Freud (1856–1939). Freud is widely considered the father of Western psychotherapy. His background as a neurologist focused on the brain's physical mechanisms and led him to develop theories for aiding those with psychological struggles. Central to his psychoanalytic model of personality were three inner components: the id, the ego and the superego.

The id, according to Freud, represents our primal energy, which compels us to fulfill our most basic needs and desires. Situated in the unconscious mind, the id drives us to seek food, water and comfort instinctively, without regard for social norms. As we mature, the ego mediates between the id's impulses and the demands of external reality, while the superego guides us toward considering others' needs and transcending selfish desires.

Freud also described how his patients protected themselves from emotional overwhelm by using *defense mechanisms*. His theories about these emerged from his observations of how individuals respond to psychologically threatening situations by *unconsciously* developing strategies to protect their self-identity and self-esteem. This perspective underscores the pivotal role of defense mechanisms in maintaining mental and emotional stability and well-being. He implied that this is something that most of us do as part of how we try to mitigate threats to our self and ward off anxiety.

As Freud refined his theory, he increasingly focused on the unconscious nature of these strategies, emphasizing that individuals are often unaware of their use and creation. This was a profound revelation, since nearly all of us create and utilize defense mechanisms. The theory is a description of how our psyche operates outside of our awareness yet impacts many aspects of our lives. Because defense mechanisms are unconscious, they can hijack us in ways that can compromise our most important relationships. Identifying and eliminating the various maladaptive defense mechanisms is an important therapeutic task of a good psychotherapist.

For instance, habitually interrupting and angrily yelling at one's spouse out of fears that one will get criticized could represent the defense mechanism of projection (see below). This is an example of a defense mechanism that shuts down healthy and honest interpersonal communication. Should this unconscious behavior continue unabated, it could lead to ongoing interpersonal conflict that could end the relationship.

Psychotherapists play a crucial role in helping clients identify and understand the role of these defense mechanisms in their lives, and they help clients facilitate healthier coping strategies. With a sensitive psychotherapist, a client will develop sufficient insight into the underlying fears that are driving their defenses through ongoing increasing self-awareness.

Many of these defense mechanisms have permeated our culture at large, illustrating their widespread recognition and relevance. For instance, the term *denial* is commonly used to describe someone's refusal to acknowledge a problem, while *regression* refers to reverting to earlier patterns of behavior or development (for example, "He regressed back to childlike behaviors by denying that he ate the last piece of cake.").

Chapter 1

As a psychotherapist, I have become increasingly aware of how important it is to recognize and address these defense mechanisms. When individuals can gain insight into their unconscious coping mechanisms, they can then work toward more healthily adaptive ways of managing interpersonal challenges.

While there are numerous defense mechanisms, there are several that I notice clients deal with fairly frequently. Let me give you a few examples.

Dissociation

There are times when in the middle of a session, clients become very tired and begin to yawn repeatedly. When I notice that this persists, I ask what the client is thinking about. Often the client will say that they are just tired and didn't have their second cup of coffee. If I have met with them before and know their history, it becomes evident to me that they are having trouble confronting the truth about a traumatic incident from their past. As we continue to dialogue, I soon realize that this client is having difficulty focusing on the issue at hand, and suddenly cannot recall important details of the traumatic incident that we have previously discussed several times. This is a classic example of what often happens to clients when they dissociate. Because they are not fully in their body, they are suddenly unable to recall the previously discussed event. Since emotions are based in the body, the client is defending himself from feeling the terror of the traumatic event, so dissociation occurs.

This is typically because my eliciting information about the traumatic event is threatening to bring up the client's painful memories. Unconsciously, they are attempting to avoid feeling into the experience. For the moment, the memory becomes inaccessible because that part of their consciousness has dissociated. The part that carries the information about the traumatic event is suddenly unavailable, and thus there is a gap in the continuity of their experience.

This inability to remember may be temporary or it may become a chronic unconscious defense against getting too close to the overwhelming feelings connected to the traumatic memory. In either case, the client is compromised and until the negative emotional charge is depotentiated and the traumatized part is reintegrated, the dissociation will persist. When this occurs, the client does not have all of their internal resources available to them, which decreases their ability to problem solve challenging interpersonal difficulties.

Avoidance

Avoidance is a common defense mechanism that occurs when a client who has experienced a traumatic event avoids talking about it or even thinking about it in order to cope. Avoidance is often related to a profoundly negative and threatening past experience. When the experience is overwhelming to one's normal sense of self-confidence, it is likely a result of trauma. When the event has persisted over time, it can generate classic symptoms of post-traumatic stress disorder (PTSD). Rather than confront and process the memory of the event, clients unconsciously avoid getting near any of the memories or feelings associated with the traumatic event.

Avoidance can be conflated with the defense mechanism of denial—they can work synergistically to protect the client from becoming overwhelmed by the memories of what was an emotionally devastating event. The problem with these defense mechanisms is that the underlying trauma continues to fester, compromising the feeling of being in charge of one's life and perpetuating a victim identity.

Projection

It is not uncommon for a client to tell me about how their spouse is angry all the time, creating an atmosphere of tension between them. As I notice this complaint being repeated over several sessions, it becomes evident to me that this client himself carries a great deal of anger that is manifested in his forceful condemnation and judgment of his spouse. As we dialogue further, it becomes clear that this client's anger began years ago, even before marrying his spouse. He is able to feel okay about himself and maintain his self-esteem by blaming and projecting onto his spouse the anger that is seething within himself. He perceives his own anger simply as an occasional undesirable trait. Rather than explore its roots, he unconsciously defends himself by blaming and projecting it onto his spouse. I see this often in my private practice. It is especially cogent when I meet with couples who want to work on better communication.

Displacement

When a person feels that his spouse is unfairly expressing anger toward him, he may unconsciously redirect his own anger to someone else who doesn't deserve that emotional hostility. This happens especially in cases where he believes that it would be unwise to express his anger directly at his wife or even feels intimidated by her. So he unconsciously chooses to displace his own anger onto another person or even his pet dog by expressing strong hostility toward them. This could result, for example, in his screaming at a child playing baseball in his neighborhood whose ball landed on his lawn. In essence, he has irrationally displaced his anger (that he is feeling toward his spouse) onto an innocent child. This does not help resolve the initial hurt from his spouse, but it satisfies his wounded part by convincing him that he too can express his anger. The therapeutic objective here would be to help him to acknowledge his hurt feelings arising from his spouse's disrespectful treatment and to find ways to occupy the relationship with his wife in a more honest way.

Other common defense mechanisms include repression, compensation and isolation. We owe Freud a debt of gratitude for his keen observations when working with his patients. These observations led him to develop increased awareness of how we all tend to adapt to inhospitable situations by using these unconscious mechanisms.

Freud's psychoanalytic model laid the foundation for what became known as the "talking cure" or talk therapies, emphasizing the exploration of unconscious desires and conflicts through dialogue. Freud believed that through ongoing psychoanalysis, patients could gain insight into their unconscious mind, leading to self-acceptance and resolution of their psychological issues. This often required a strong commitment, returning two to three times per week for many years in order to unwind the buried contents of the unconscious mind. The intended result was greater self-understanding and inner peace.

Over the past 120 years, psychotherapy has undergone significant evolution from Freud's original theories. However, understanding this evolution requires considering the historical context of Western society. The transition from agrarian to industrial societies during the eighteenth and nineteenth centuries brought about profound societal changes. The advent of the Industrial Revolution introduced mechanized production, leading to the proliferation of factories and urbanization. Families who were self-reliant on small plots of land were starting to move into cities, creating a new social dynamic.

While industrialization promised economic opportunities, it also brought long hours of monotonous work and harsh working conditions for many laborers. Factories proliferated, creating a strong demand for dependable workers in order to produce the goods for the citizens in growing and increasingly urbanized cities. While this provided many with opportunities for work previously unavailable, along with the hollow promises of a more secure lifestyle and better wages, what emerged were large numbers of factory workers (primarily men) with extremely long hours of boring and repetitive work under the supervision of demanding task masters. This drudgery became a torment for many of them.

This shift contributed to a rise in psychological problems among workers, including anxiety, depression, and irritability.

As the second industrial revolution began to emerge in the late nineteenth century, electric power became increasingly available, leading to even greater mass production. Factory workers were becoming exhausted and disenchanted but the world had inexorably changed. What had heretofore promised greater opportunities began to feel like a betrayal. While there was no diagnostic category of chronic fatigue syndrome at that time, workers were increasingly becoming unhappy about their plight in life. The term *neurasthenia* became popular in medical circles to describe this collection of work-related symptoms that emerged from this societal shift. This reflected the challenges faced by individuals in adapting to these many new demands. *Webster's New World College Dictionary* describes neurasthenia as:

> A former category of mental disorder, including such symptoms as irritability, fatigue, weakness, anxiety, and localized pains without apparent physical causes, thought to result from weakness or exhaustion or the nervous system.[7]

The neurologists and psychiatrists of this era endorsed this term as a catch-all illness that subsequently generated a host of treatments. These included massage, hypnosis, various physical therapies, "rest cures" and psychoanalysis.

> Psychoanalysis offered an altogether more intriguing and dramatic take upon personal troubles, and had the added benefits of absorbing every symptom of neurasthenia into its own landscape—under the heading of "neurosis."[8]

In the early twentieth century, psychoanalysis emerged into greater public awareness, but its accessibility was limited to the affluent. It also shifted focus away from the underlying causative societal ills of the time to a more focused intrapsychic personal journey. While beneficial for those engaged in ongoing psychoanalytic therapy, it overlooked the pervasive social problems like harsh working conditions leading to psychological suffering. As psychoanalysts diverged from Freud and developed their own models, numerous variations of psychodynamic psychotherapy arose, aiming for broader applicability. This approach elaborated on Freud's ideas, fostering growing self-awareness regarding how past experiences shape present behavior. Various innovative psychotherapy models emerged, diversifying and expanding Western psychotherapy's toolkit and expanding its reach.

Chapter 2
Carl Gustav Jung's Analytic Psychology

Carl Gustav Jung (1875–1961), a student and collaborator of Sigmund Freud's, diverged from Freud's psychoanalytic approach to establish his own school of thought known as analytic psychology.[9] Jung's model introduced novel concepts, notably the collective unconscious, which encompasses the accumulated experiences of humanity's ancestors, including mythological symbols and archetypes from various cultures and religions. This collective unconscious, according to Jung, is shared by all individuals and forms the basis of what ancient cultures referred to as our human interconnectedness. "The collective unconscious is common to all; it is the foundation of what the ancients called the 'sympathy of all things.'"[10]

Jung's fascination with the paranormal contributed to the development of his theory of synchronicity, which emerged as a concept reflecting the interconnectedness of all through the collective unconscious. Many psychotherapists are unaware that Jung's early medical dissertation, published in 1903, focused on the psychology and pathology of occult phenomena.[11] The dissertation underscored his deep interest in spirituality, which remained a consistent theme throughout his life's work.

As Jung's theories evolved, he placed increasing emphasis on achieving personal wholeness through a process he termed *individuation.* This was his way of describing the integration of unconscious aspects of the psyche into one's conscious awareness. Through this striving for wholeness and authenticity, internal conflicts become resolved leading to self-realization. This involved incorporating a spiritual dimension into his analytic psychology approach, supported by his conception of integrating one's ego (representing our everyday ongoing awareness), one's personal unconscious (made up of forgotten or repressed memories), and a second component of the unconscious: the collective unconscious. Jung believed in the powerful therapeutic potential of the collective unconscious, where transformative universal and mythical symbols—which he called archetypes—inherited and shared cross-culturally, could be accessed through dreams and visions. It is these archetypes that populate the collective unconscious. Archetypes represent shared thoughts, emotions and behaviors that are present in every culture throughout human history. Examples of archetypes include the hero, the mother, the soldier, the caregiver and the wizard or magician.

Jung also developed the concepts of the persona and shadow. Our persona is the social mask or veneer that each person presents to the world at large. One might say it is the way we socially compensate that tends to obscure what he labeled as our shadow. Our shadow is the part of us that represents the unconscious aspects of our personality that are usually hidden and repressed. Working to integrate our shadow aspect means that we must first uncover and acknowledge parts of ourselves we are ashamed of or that we have marginalized because of certain fears.

For example, a self-contained individual who prefers a more interior life orientation has compromised the shadow aspect of conviviality and social engagement. While this person may spend time imagining what it would be like to share time socializing with friends, being a recluse creates a barrier to integrating this aspect of his shadow. To achieve individuation, this person would consciously work on acknowledging this part of his shadow, in order to integrate it into his personality and thus become more available to other people.

Another avenue to individuation in Jungian analytic psychology involves recognizing and integrating the opposite gender's traits into one's personality. Jung explained that each person has both feminine and masculine qualities—feminine qualities found in men are known as the anima, and masculine qualities found in women are the animus. The anima and animus are often repressed. In order to live in greater personal balance and completeness, Jung proposed recognizing and then integrating the opposite gender's traits as another component to enduring wholeness. Due to the growing prevalence of transgender identification, Jung's ideas about integrating the anima and animus now need to be reformulated.

Jung believed that women who appear to be ultrafeminine have suppressed their animus and men who cultivate an extreme macho orientation to life have suppressed their anima. Thus, their personalities are unbalanced, precluding individuation as Jung defined it. Cultural reinforcement through repetitive marketing representing the ideal woman or man reflects a constricting cultural trance that causes people to create lifelong problems for themselves. I have had many women clients over the years who have struggled with body image problems and lifelong weight loss preoccupation due to the persistent cultural myth that only thin women are truly valued. This also plays out with our culture's emphasis on the male superhero warrior archetype that only values strength and invincibility. I believe that Jung would not see this as just a twenty-first-century phenomenon: it is central to being human.

Have you heard of the Myers-Briggs Type Indicator (MBTI) as a personality assessment tool? Perhaps you have even identified your own MBTI type. It was designed by Katharine Briggs and her daughter Isabel Briggs Myers in the mid-twentieth century. It is based on Jung's ideas regarding psychological types. Jung posited that each individual has innate preferences for how they incorporate information and stimuli in order to make decisions. The four primary psychological functions Jung identified are thinking, feeling, sensation, and intuition. In addition, Jung introduced and incorporated the predispositions of introversion and extraversion as underlying inclinations of personality.

The MBTI assesses personality types and preferences based on the following dichotomies: extraversion versus introversion, sensing versus intuition, thinking versus feeling, and judging versus perceiving. There are sixteen possible combinations that make up these preferences. An example is INFP (introversion, intuition, feeling and perceiving). When I answered the questionnaire many years ago, I found that the personality type that described me was remarkably accurate and did in fact speak to me. I found this helpful and affirming. When administered to my clients, subsequent discussions lead to deepening awareness about their personalities and how their purpose in life is either being affirmed or denied. Clients also find this helpful in discussing how their personality type impacts their most important relationships.

During the first decade of the twentieth century, Carl Gustav Jung and Sigmund Freud established a cordial professional relationship. Jung collaborated with Freud through reading and commenting on Freud's research papers, but eventually Jung conveyed to Freud his disagreements with Freud's overemphasis on the nature of libido and sexual repression. While Jung embraced Freud's ideas about the personal unconscious, he fervently believed in the pervasive influence of the larger collective unconscious and how the archetypes contained within it deeply influence each person's path in life. As Jung continued to become more spiritually sensitive, he found himself unable to abide Freud's atheism. He also sought to explore broader aspects of the unconscious mind beyond sexuality.

In 1912, through Jung's publication of *Psychology of*

CHAPTER 2

the Unconscious, subsequently republished as *Symbols of Transformation*, his repudiation of the centrality of the libido fractured his relationship with Freud.[12] He had foreknowledge that his split with Freud was coming.

> When I was working on my book about the libido and approaching the end of the chapter "The Sacrifice," I knew in advance that its publication would cost me my friendship with Freud. For I planned to set down in it my own conception of incest, the decisive transformation of the concept of libido, and various other ideas in which I differed from Freud.... I knew that he would never be able to accept any of my ideas on this subject.... I had known that everything was at stake, and that I had to take a stand for my convictions. I realized that the chapter, "The Sacrifice," meant my own sacrifice.[13]

Following his split from Freud in 1913, Jung experienced a profound depression and an acknowledgment of being "menaced by psychosis."[14] To navigate this inner turmoil, he embarked on a journey of confronting his inner voices, narratives, and personified inner figures. This process involved engaging with his moods, images, and bodily sensations, and it served as a bridge between his conscious ego and his unconscious. He realized he had to restrain his conscious waking mind from intruding and exerting influence on his out-of-control stream of images and inner narratives.

Throughout this introspective journey, Jung encountered numerous inner figures, including biblical characters, Egyptian deities, and a guide named Philemon, symbolizing the wise old man archetype. These encounters laid the groundwork for his theories of the collective unconscious and archetypes, which he described as "active principles" facilitating interaction between dimensions of consciousness.

> Philemon and other figures of my fantasies brought home to me the crucial insight that there are things in

15

> the psyche that I do not produce, but which produce themselves and have their own life. Philemon represented a force that was not myself. In my fantasies I had conversations with him and he said things which I had not consciously thought. For I observed clearly that it was he who spoke, not I.[15]

While Jung recovered from his deep inner turmoil after a period of three years, he meticulously documented his inner experiences in a series of black books spanning nineteen years. In these journal entries, he was essentially "confronting" his unconscious through colorful illustrations accompanied by commentary as he recapitulated his many inner visions and conversations with numerous inner figures. These personal reflections were later consolidated into a single volume called *The Red Book: Liber Novus*. *The Red Book* was the distillation of Jung's profound encounters with his many inner figures during his period of mental turbulence. These experiences gave rise to what Jung termed "active imagination," a creative, process-oriented approach to psychotherapy.

Building on Jung's insights, contemporary psychotherapists have adopted active imagination as a technique for engaging with clients. This process involves externalizing internal figures and voices and talking with them. It often incorporates elements of psychodrama, integrating bodily sensations and movement to deepen one's interactions with one's inner figures. Through this method, psychotherapists help guide clients in integrating and harmonizing these inner parts, which gradually diminishes the parts' autonomy. The therapeutic goal is to foster greater self-awareness and inner coherence working toward individuation.

In 1987, I began training with Dr. Arnold Mindell, a Jungian training analyst who had been working and teaching at the C. G. Jung Institute in Zurich, Switzerland, for over twenty years. I spent ten years learning the principles and practices of what came to be known as process-oriented psychology or processwork. Much of processwork is geared toward psychodrama, where all inner parts are personified and interacted with. With his long years of experience at the Jung Institute, Mindell's processwork model was an extension and amplification of Jung's original active imagination work (which for Jung was interior work). While processwork was primarily outgoing and extroverted using Jung's original active imagination principles of interacting with inner figures, inner work was also emphasized on occasion, based on what had become the meditative technique used by Jung.

Overall, it is both remarkable and fascinating just how much Jung's ideas have influenced not just psychotherapy but culture at large.

Chapter 3
John Bowlby's Object Relations

British analyst and psychiatrist John Bowlby (1907–1990) developed object relations therapy through his many years as a psychiatrist and analyst. His pioneering theories on early attachment marked a significant departure from Freudian psychoanalysis, particularly in the realm of understanding human motivation and personality development.

Unlike Freud, who emphasized the role of early sexual drives in shaping personality, Bowlby proposed that the primary focus should be on the quality and dynamics of early relationships, especially with caregivers, whom he termed "objects." (Freud labeled these objects as the significant persons in our early life who we are drawn to *by unconscious desires*.) Bowlby argued that a person's first objects—especially the mother—need to be nurturing and in close contact with the vulnerable infant. This connection begins even before birth for the mother, and then includes the child's ongoing emotional connection to the mother and/or surrogate caregiver that ideally continues to strengthen throughout the person's life.[16]

In Bowlby's view, the nurturing and supportive presence of caregivers, particularly the mother during infancy, is absolutely crucial for healthy psychological development. He stressed the importance of *secure emotional attachments*, wherein individuals feel safe and supported in expressing their deepest fears and emotions without fear of judgment. This concept extended beyond infancy and early childhood to encompass the therapeutic relationship, in which clients need to feel similarly safe and supported in their therapy. Thus, therapy is a safe context in which an individual can experience a surrogate reparenting within an ongoing supportive therapeutic relationship.

Bowlby's object relations model shifted the focus of psychotherapy from solely intrapsychic processes to include the impact of external relationships and environments on individuals. It emphasized the significance of early attachment experiences in shaping personality and emotional well-being, highlighting the importance of fostering secure and nurturing connections in both childhood and adulthood. This was a significant departure from what had been an emphasis on the Freudian intrapsychic orientation to psychoanalysis.

Bowlby's object relations therapy focuses on exploring and understanding the internalized mental representations, or "internal objects," that individuals develop based on their early attachment experiences. This is of key importance, since he asserted that we carry these internal representations of our early caregivers throughout our lives. Thus, they continue to influence us at the unconscious level. These internal objects shape our perceptions of ourselves and others, influencing patterns of relating and interpersonal dynamics into adulthood.

One consequence is that we tend to seek out those early caregivers when forming adult relationships. As a result, we project our internal first objects onto others as we pair bond in our adult relationships. Our adult partner thus represents either a nurturing or critical early caregiver, albeit below the level of our conscious awareness. Our unconscious radar is constantly seeking out that person who treated us in certain ways and who became deeply imprinted.

Bowlby believed that different attachment experiences

would produce not just developmental disparities, but noticeably different ways that people related to others behaviorally. These interactional styles might reflect tendencies in people to feel secure, as well as avoidant and anxious. These early attachment influences also reflect how individuals form their responses to conflict, stress and even intimacy as they mature. Bowlby's therapeutic goals aimed to help clients integrate and resolve unresolved attachment-related issues, fostering increasingly greater self-awareness, emotional regulation, and interpersonal fulfillment.

Chapter 4
Behaviorism

Psychodynamic therapies (including the approaches developed by Freud, Jung and Bowlby) focus on exploring the nebulous inner world of feelings, family of origin dynamics and unconscious impulses. In contrast, behavioral therapies emphasize the measurement and treatment of observable behaviors, often through evidence-based scientific research and clinical trials.

People often associate behaviorism with the much-heralded experiments of Ivan Pavlov (1849–1936), the early twentieth century physiologist whose research into conditioned reflexes was popularized by Pavlov's dogs. Pavlov researched the physiology of the digestive system, for which he was awarded the Nobel Prize for Physiology or Medicine in 1904.[17] He is most recognized for his study on classical conditioning that has come to be known as Pavlovian conditioning, as published in *Conditioned Reflexes* in 1926.[18]

Pavlov's experiments demonstrated how dogs could be *conditioned* to associate a neutral stimulus (such as the ringing of a bell) with a reflex response (such as salivation). Over time, the dogs learned to anticipate food whenever they heard the bell, leading to the conditioned response of salivation even in the absence of food. The bell thus became *a conditioned stimulus* that generated *a conditioned reflex*. Pavlov's dog experiments marked the beginning of research into classical conditioning and behavior modification, which laid the foundation for the emerging new field of behaviorism.[19]

The behaviorist orientation continued with the research of John B. Watson (1878–1958), an early twentieth century psychologist who is generally regarded as the originator and developer of the field of behaviorism within the field of psychotherapy. In 1908, Watson was accepted to the faculty at Johns Hopkins University. Five years later he published his influential article "Psychology as the Behaviorist Views It," which is often referred to as "The Behaviorist Manifesto." It was in this article that Watson explained the prominent features of his new ideas he called "behaviorism."[20]

> Watson's behaviorist theory focused not on the internal emotional and psychological conditions of people, but rather on their external and outward behaviors. He believed that a person's physical responses provided the only insight into internal actions. He spent much of his career applying his theories to the study of child development and early learning.[21]

While many or even most contemporary psychotherapists may find behaviorist interventions too narrow and rigid in many ways, one must understand that the goal of the behaviorist approach is to identify what interventions can be used to predict and control behavior and reactions. For example, directing clients to uncover deeply hidden unconscious traumatic memories is sidestepped, as it is the outer manifestations of traumatic sequelae that are targeted via behaviorist methods. This is in stark contrast to Bowlby's object relations theory, which proposes infants need to be unconditionally supported and nurtured by their mother and other significant caregivers in order to achieve a secure emotional attachment as a foundation for a healthy emerging personality. Watson was against providing infants and children with too much affection, fearing they would grow up to be overly dependent and needy adults.

While working at Johns Hopkins University in 1920, Watson and his colleague Rosalie Rayner carried out what has often been regarded as one of the most controversial experiments in Western psychology. It has come to be known as the Little Albert Experiment. The subject of their behaviorist experiment was a child who at the start of the experiment was nine months old. Watson was inspired by Pavlov's work with dogs and classical conditioning. His intention was to create or "condition" a phobia in a child who initially was emotionally stable.

Before the actual experiment was to begin, Albert (a pseudonym) was introduced to a number of objects and animals such as a dog, a white rat, a monkey, wool and cotton. His emotional responses were neutral—he demonstrated no apparent fear. When he was eleven months and three days old, he was placed on a mattress on a table with a white rat that he was provided to play with. Each time Albert touched the rat, Watson and Rayner made a loud noise by striking a steel bar with a hammer next to Albert. Naturally, this shocked Albert and he cried and became fearful. This continued until his initial unconditioned neutral response to the rat became a conditioned emotional response as Albert became fearful and cried, trying to crawl away from the rat. One week later, when exposed only to the rat, he once again became upset and began crying. Further experiments demonstrated a generalized conditioned fear response to what were previously neutral responses. As a result, Albert also became upset by a furry rabbit, a dog and other objects with hair.

Watson's experiment demonstrated how he could elicit a fearful reaction and thus condition a fear response in poor innocent Albert. After the tests were completed at the hospital lab, Albert was taken away by his parents and the conditioned emotional reaction was apparently never reversed.[22] Today we would never consider doing such an experiment as it would be not only unlawful but unethical, given the anticipated emotional risks to the child. What's more, this experiment had only one subject and no control subjects.

The use of classical conditioning and its behaviorist roots is graphically depicted in Anthony Burgess's 1962 book *A Clockwork Orange*, later produced as a movie by director Stanley Kubrick in 1972. I remember reading Burgess's novel in a college literature class as we discussed the issue of moral choice that distinguishes us from lower animals. The lead character is a sociopathic juvenile delinquent named Alex who, with his gang, targets unsuspecting victims as they carry out random acts of rape, other forms of violence and theft. Eventually he gets caught and is sentenced to fourteen years in prison. At some point in prison, Alex is chosen to undergo the so-called Ludovico technique. As he is forced to watch violent images, he is injected with a drug that makes him nauseous and sick. The images are accompanied by classical music.

Alex is released from prison once the authorities are convinced that he is unable to pursue violent actions or even think violent thoughts.[23] While Burgess was illustrating the power of behavior modification, specifically aversion therapy, his main point was how human beings can be manipulated and conditioned to become unable to exercise free choice, even if their choice is to do antisocial behaviors. During Alex's conditioning process, one of the soundtracks used is Beethoven's ninth symphony. Classical music had been one of Alex's pleasures, but he becomes unable to enjoy it after it is incorporated into his conditioning process.

Burgess's novel is yet another critique of behavioral approaches to modify behavior that not everyone will be in agreement with. Advertisers and marketers know the effectiveness of behaviorist tools to persuade and manipulate prospective purchasers to buy their products. In fact, when John Watson left his university teaching job, he entered advertising and within two years came to prominence as a significant influencer in that field. He is known to have led the way in several successful advertising campaigns that included the ads for Ponds cold cream and Maxwell House coffee.[24]

My appraisal of behaviorism would not be complete without including the influence of B. F. Skinner (1904–1990) and operant conditioning. Like previous behaviorists, Skinner believed that in order to help people make their desired changes, studying observable behavior is more productive than analyzing internal thought processes. He focused on studying the environmental causes of an action and the consequences of the action. He wanted to know how a particular action or behavior emerged and how to reinforce it or eliminate it. He called this "operant conditioning." He defined an *operant* as a behavior that impacts a particular environment and leads to specific consequences. He described operant behaviors as those under our control, versus any type of reflexive response or action that is not. Thus, he believed that the major influence on human behavior is learning from our environment.[25] Skinner also elaborated on the concept of reinforcement as a stimulus or event that consistently strengthens the behavior it targets.

While Pavlov and Skinner were both behaviorists, there is an important distinction between them. Pavlov's work centered on the involuntary responses to stimuli, such as dogs' salivation and gastric responses; Skinner focused on learned responses to a particular environment.

Like Watson before him, Skinner believed that psychology should be approached as a science and researched in an objective and scientific manner. He believed that there isn't much of a difference between how humans and animals learn, so his research on operant conditioning could be carried out on animals and be generalized to people. In his research he developed what has come to be known as the Skinner box. The device has a bar that an animal (particularly rats) can press in order to receive food as reinforcement. Using the box, Skinner could quantitatively measure the higher response rates—the number of bar presses—that followed rewards (such as food) and the lower response rates—fewer bar presses—that occurred when there was a lack of any reward. Unlike Pavlov and Watson (who focused on a preceding stimulus to measure behavior), Skinner determined that through operant conditioning, the behaviors (that is, the responses/bar presses) were dependent on what occurred after (the stimulus/food pellet).

Punishment can also be incorporated in the operant conditioning process. Skinner defined punishment as a detrimental or adverse response (such as a mild electric shock) that weakens the behavior it follows.[26]

Two well-known and controversial books Skinner wrote describe how his research in operant conditioning can create a more coherent and unified society. He was firm in his belief, supported by his scientific research, that free will and moral choice get in the way of creating a society that is happy and well ordered. In his 1948 book *Walden Two*, he laid out a fictional representation of his beliefs. The novel describes a behaviorist utopian society in which the citizens are essentially brought up in a system of rewards and punishments—behavior modification. He describes what is essentially the behavioral engineering of children that he believed would lead to more harmonious relationships throughout their lives.

> Now that we know how positive reinforcement works, and why negative doesn't, we can be more deliberate and hence more successful, in our cultural design. We can achieve a sort of control under which the controlled . . . nevertheless feel free. They are doing what they want to do, not what they are forced to do. That's the source of the tremendous power of positive reinforcement—there's no restraint and no revolt. By a careful design, we control not the final behavior, but the inclination to behave—the motives,

the desires, the wishes. The curious thing is that in that case the question of freedom never arises.[27]

Walden Two was controversial with the public and with Skinner's academic colleagues. The majority of psychotherapists were still oriented to the psychodynamic approach, and many were unsure about his scientific orientation, because it excluded unconscious internal conflicts and repressed traumatic residue—the so-called less tangible elements of the human psyche. The following quote from *Walden Two* illustrates Skinner's beliefs.

> Society attacks early, when the individual is helpless. It enslaves him almost before he has tasted freedom. The "ologies" will tell you how its [sic] done. Theology calls it building a conscience or developing a spirit of selflessness. Psychology calls it the growth of the superego. Considering how long society has been at it, you'd expect a better job. But the campaigns have been badly planned and the victory has never been secured.[28]

In Skinner's *Beyond Freedom and Dignity*, he reflects that

> Ethical control may survive in small groups, but the control of the population as a whole must be delegated to specialists—to police, priests, owners, teachers, therapists, and so on, with their specialized reinforcers and their codified contingencies.... It is a mistake to suppose that the whole issue is how to free man. The issue is to improve the way in which he is controlled.[29]

Despite the successes that some researchers were able to accomplish, behaviorism began to fall out of favor in the late 1950s. Its focus was primarily on observable behaviors and stimulus–response associations. Criticism began to emerge, seeing behaviorism as a way to manipulate for specific ends that reduced people to automatons. Many in the therapeutic community believed that behavioral therapies were essentially reductionistic.

The critics asserted that people are more complex than simply responding to external stimuli that elicit a predictable response.

As a therapeutic model, behaviorism largely ignores the complexity of what motivates human beings, including our internal mental processes and our various shifting feeling states. Behaviorism focuses on how our outer environment influences our behavior, choosing to ignore each individual's uniqueness and thus our differences. Put succinctly, it oversimplifies human behavior. It fails to take into account and celebrate each individual's uniqueness that, to a large degree, determines our respective successes in all areas of life, including the creative arts.

Behaviorism also tends to ignore and minimize that people and animals can and do adapt their behavior as they become more aware of new information. People do change and learn new ways to problem solve without the use of reinforcement and negative consequences, such as punishment or aversive therapeutic approaches. Behaviorism marginalizes a person's creativity, personal motivation and emotional responses as avenues to make changes. By focusing solely on how individuals respond to outer stimuli and observable behavior, free agency to make positive changes is discredited in place of environmentally deterministic stimulus–response.

As we will see in Chapter 6, it was in the late 1940s and early 1950s that both Carl Rogers and Abraham Maslow began promoting a more holistic and integrative approach to working with troubled clients. They departed from Skinner's approach by emphasizing how people are learning new information all the time as self-aware, evolving human beings. A humanistic approach emerged, wherein the client is presumed to have the inherent capabilities to solve their dilemmas with sufficient support to work through what had previously been internal confusion.

Overall, while behaviorism made significant contributions to the field of psychology, its limitations became increasingly apparent as the field progressed, leading to its decline in the late 1950s and beyond.

Chapter 5
Cognitive Behavioral Therapy

In the early twentieth century, the prevailing approach among American psychoanalysts was deeply rooted in Freudian theory, focused on investigating clients' inner conflicts and aiding them in adapting to societal norms and expectations. This involved delving into past experiences to shed light on current behaviors, a practice that remains prevalent today.

Therapists often guide clients toward understanding how past influences shape present actions, empowering them with the insight to reframe self-defeating behaviors.

In the 1950s, clinical psychologist Albert Ellis (1913–2007) began to challenge the conventional beliefs embedded in psychoanalysis, a process he himself went through that was expected of most psychotherapists at the time. As he became a practicing psychoanalyst, Ellis couldn't help but notice that the effectiveness of patients under his charge was not dependent upon how frequently he would meet with them. Whether it was daily or once a week, their progress was much the same. He discovered that when he became more confrontational, his patients seemed to let go of their underlying irrational beliefs more quickly. Over time, he developed what became known as rational emotive behavioral therapy or REBT. When being more direct with his patients by challenging their irrational beliefs, patients were able to more readily let go of them. This was a radical change from the tenants of psychoanalysis where the analyst was more patient and passive as patients rambled on about their inner life and neurotic tendencies. Ellis went on to establish his own institute in New York to train psychologists, provide psychotherapy as well as psychological assessments. He insisted that it was the underlying irrational beliefs that were the cause of his patients' emotional distress.

In the 1960s, psychiatrist Aaron Beck (1921–2021) continued to challenge the efficacy of traditional psychoanalysis, particularly in treating depression. Similar to Ellis, Beck was initially trained in psychoanalysis and even underwent analysis. He started to think that for the medical community to continue to endorse psychoanalysis, new research supporting its effectiveness needed to be conducted. His emphasis was on discovering how effective the classic Freudian model was for treating depression. Beck's research revealed that psychoanalysis fell short in effectively addressing depression. He identified "automatic thoughts" as the underlying triggers of depressive moods, labeling these recurring thoughts as "cognitive distortions." Beck developed cognitive behavioral therapy (CBT) to help clients identify and challenge these maladaptive beliefs, which he believed constrained their potential for a positive future.[30]

The cornerstone of CBT is "thought stopping," which entails strengthening one's will to stop unproductive thinking patterns. This is often addressed through identifying and acknowledging one's self-sabotaging perseverating beliefs that continue to create problems. Once these thinking patterns are acknowledged with the help of the therapist, the individual can begin to problem solve persistent difficulties and work on developing self-confidence through role playing and daily practice. While insight regarding one's thinking is an important component of CBT, clients are also tasked with challenging themselves to make behavioral changes in their everyday lives. In a manner of speaking, they are encouraged to "do better."

There have been many studies reporting that CBT's apparent success is evidence based, supporting this practical approach to making changes in one's day-to-day life. In many respects, CBT has become the go-to therapeutic approach as the modern-day version of talk therapy. CBT's widespread adoption is supported by numerous studies validating its effectiveness, positioning it as a leading contemporary therapeutic approach.

However, the approach has many critics. Common criticisms include that just because one can acknowledge that a thought is irrational does not necessarily mean that one can suppress it or suppress the persistent belief that is behind it. The objection is that while CBT tends to address current problems, it frequently does not address the underlying root cause from the past that generated the maladaptive beliefs. Additionally, challenges arise when clients struggle to follow through on homework assignments requiring persistence and discipline, especially in cases of significant emotional trauma.

For instance, coping with profound loss or trauma may prove resistant to cognitive reframing techniques. While CBT offers valuable tools for managing certain difficulties, its applicability to complex psychological issues such as post-traumatic stress disorder (PTSD) remains debated. It is extremely difficult to think away one's thoughts about despair, hopelessness and self-recrimination. Moreover, its reliance on verbal communication and ongoing discussion about the client's underlying operational beliefs may overlook deeper emotional wounds, prompting the therapist to recommend psychiatric medication to augment the ongoing CBT.

In conclusion, while CBT can be helpful for many individuals, its limitations underscore the need for a multifaceted approach to psychotherapy. Recognizing the diverse complexities of the human psyche, therapists must tailor their therapeutic approach and interventions to each client's unique needs, acknowledging that no single therapy model is universally effective. It is challenging for prospective clients to know in advance which therapeutic approach is going to be most effective for them. Nevertheless, clients need to take personal responsibility to research what approach resonates with them before making a commitment to engage a particular therapist.

Chapter 6

Humanistic Person-Centered Therapy

Carl Rogers's (1902–1987) client-centered therapy, also known as person-centered therapy, emerged as a significant departure from traditional psychoanalytic approaches in the late 1940s. Unlike Freudian psychoanalysis, which emphasized the authority of the analyst and delved into unconscious conflicts, Rogers's approach was nondirective and focused on the therapeutic relationship itself as the primary tool or technique for healing. At that time, he proposed a radical reframing of the therapeutic relationship. This client-centered approach redefined the role of the psychotherapist as a person who was genuine and empathic.[31]

In client-centered therapy, the therapist takes on an unconditionally supportive role, prioritizing active listening and complete acceptance of the client's emotions in the present moment. Rogers believed that fostering a collaborative therapeutic alliance with clients and providing unconditional positive regard would create a safe environment for growth and healing.

Rogers's approach was grounded in several key principles, including the belief in individuals' innate capacity for self-direction and healthy choices. Unlike behaviorists, Rogers emphasized the subjective reality of each person and worked to support clients in strengthening their own self-concept within their unique life circumstances. He firmly believed that when clients felt unconditionally supported, they would naturally start orienting to their strengths and begin succeeding in their therapeutic goals. This included coming to realize their emerging purpose in life.

Critics argued that Rogers's focus on subjective experience might tend to overlook unconscious defense mechanisms, but Rogers maintained that providing clients with genuine emotional support could ultimately empower them to overcome past limitations and strive toward their full potential. This view was also echoed by psychologist Abraham Maslow, as discussed below.

Overall, client-centered therapy represented a significant shift in psychotherapeutic practice, emphasizing the importance of empathy, acceptance and collaboration in facilitating personal growth and healing. The impact of this approach continues to this day.

Abraham Maslow's (1908–1970) hierarchy of needs, alongside Carl Rogers's client-centered therapy, forms the foundation of the humanistic approach to psychotherapy. Both theorists championed self-actualization—the realization of an individual's full potential—as the ultimate goal of therapy. Maslow's hierarchy outlines a progression of needs, from basic safety and physiological requirements to more complex needs such as love, self-esteem, partnering and, ultimately, self-actualization.[32] This model suggests that for individuals to achieve their fullest potential, including developing one's special and unique talents, their more fundamental needs must first be satisfied.

Rogers's approach is deeply focused on fostering a nurturing therapeutic relationship characterized by empathy, authenticity, and unconditional positive regard. This relationship is seen as essential for facilitating personal growth and self-discovery, allowing clients to overcome internalized negative beliefs and progress toward self-actualization. The concept of unconditional positive regard is particularly significant, emphasizing the therapist's acceptance of the client without judgment, which supports the client's self-worth and positive self-image.

The humanistic perspective contrasts sharply with both the psychoanalytic and behaviorist approaches, which tended to focus more on pathology and behavioral modification, respectively. Instead, humanistic psychotherapy underscores the inherent value and potential of the individual, promoting a more optimistic and supportive therapeutic process.

The caring and unconditionally supportive alliance created by the therapist becomes the central catalyst for consistent incremental positive change. In this approach, younger, emotionally injured parts are essentially reparented through the experience of ongoing unconditional support. If a person has grown up in a family system of criticism and shame, the psychotherapist can be the stand-in or surrogate parent who, over time, supports the development of an increasingly self-confidant individual.

However, the practical application of person-centered therapy often faces challenges, notably from insurance companies that may limit coverage for mental health services. This financial barrier can restrict access to the prolonged and consistent therapeutic engagement that is typically necessary for the person-centered approach to be most effective. Insurance companies have continued to reduce outpatient mental health benefits, often contracting with managed care companies that scrutinize treatment plans while imposing caps on how much they will pay and how many sessions they will allocate.

Despite these challenges, the humanistic approach has profoundly influenced the field of psychotherapy, promoting a shift toward more empathic, supportive and client-focused practices. This evolution reflects an ongoing dialogue within the field of psychotherapy about the most effective ways to facilitate psychological healing and growth. While a person-centered approach is about what takes place within the therapeutic relationship as an alliance is promulgated and sustained, the behaviorist approach emerged that challenged the psychodynamic orientation to psychotherapy by emphasizing a more "scientific" model to help people recover from their problems. This is part of the ever-changing evolution of psychotherapy, and has had a significant impact on its development.

Chapter 7
The Therapeutic Alliance

There are many reasons that drive people to seek out psychotherapy. Some people are anxious and find that they cannot stop worrying. Others may feel stuck, depressed and sad, and find it hard to motivate themselves to move forward in their lives. Many people have experienced overwhelming trauma and end up with symptoms that can be ascribed to post-traumatic stress disorder (PTSD), such as nightmares, self-isolation or out-of-control anger, that push people away from them. Some prospective clients have trouble connecting with others and enter psychotherapy to find out how they can find a partner and be in a loving relationship because they are lonely. Others need help addressing their emotional pain and anguish that has led them to addictive activities. These may include compulsive overeating, too much alcohol consumption and other compensatory activities, though these behaviors only address their persistent symptoms and emotional pain rather than the underlying cause.

I believe that too many people are juggling so many responsibilities that it is often difficult to hit the pause button and simply reflect on what is most important in their lives. Showing up to work every day to put in their eight hours or more is demanding and often stressful, even if the work is fulfilling. Coming home after a day of work to a partner (who is also often working) and children who need a healthy dinner and help with homework can be exhausting, leaving little time for oneself. There are bills that must be paid, emails to respond to, and perhaps even exercise as part of one's self-care regimen. It just goes on and on with the relentless demands of twenty-first century daily life. We all negotiate our responsibilities the best we can, but for many these day-to-day obligations take their toll. Whether one chooses to unwind and relax at the end of the day with television, YouTube music videos, alcohol or reading a good mystery novel, it is often the case that these cumulative daily responsibilities exacerbate underlying relational and intrapersonal unresolved tensions.

We are fortunate to have numerous resources available when we decide we need some help. Most full-time jobs provide medical insurance that covers outpatient mental health services. This means that we can call our primary care physician's office for an appointment to receive a prescription for changing our brain's neurochemistry to help alleviate persistent anxiety or depression. Doctors are often all too willing to oblige.

We can also ask for a referral to a psychotherapist, or even seek out a therapist on our own that health insurance will cover. The question is what's the better choice—medication or psychotherapy? Ingesting a pill once a day is certainly more convenient. In our too-busy lives it saves time over spending an hour or more with a psychotherapist, whether it is through a telehealth appointment in front of our computer or actually taking the time to drive to a therapist's office. The growing trend seems to favor the convenience of taking medication. While this may provide relief from acute symptoms of anxiety or depression more quickly and conveniently, it's important to recognize that medication alone will likely not address the root causes of the presenting problem. It's also important to recognize that medication may come with potential side effects and risks.

Is it actually worthwhile to meet with a real person to problem solve one's more daunting personal issues? That depends. Even if

CHAPTER 7

a good friend provides you with a glowing recommendation for a therapist, it is the chemistry between therapist and client that to a large extent determines the potential for a successful outcome. But what exactly is this chemistry?

Essentially, this is about feeling that you have a good fit with your chosen therapist. It has been referred to as the therapeutic relationship or therapeutic alliance. Quite a lot of research has been done about this, since there are many who believe that this alliance is the foundation for positive therapeutic outcomes. While one might characterize this as an artificial or surrogate relationship, unlike those that we typically form and maintain in our everyday life, it is unique in that it is impartial and allows a client to be fully honest and self-disclosing without the fear of judgment and criticism.

It is not uncommon for people to have been subjected to the pain and shame of judgment and criticism during their formative years. For many, that is all they know, so it is hard to imagine being in a relationship without being shamed and put down. For these reasons and many others, the therapeutic alliance can be very healing. This has been determined to be true regardless of the particular therapeutic model that the therapist has been trained in.

Ongoing research reflects that some therapists are better than others and achieve consistently better outcomes because of the way they occupy the therapeutic relationship. Current evidence shows that one's good fit with one's therapist is the most durable predictor of successful therapeutic outcomes of any factor ever studied. When evaluating therapeutic outcomes, clients don't focus on specific psychotherapy models or methods, but consistently account for their positive changes due to the relationship cultivated with their therapist. Every psychotherapy model addresses the process of change within its own theoretical framework, but more and more evidence points to the strong therapeutic alliance as the cornerstone of successful outcomes.

This is regardless of the diagnosis assigned to the client.

Interestingly, these underlying dynamics remain the same, even when evaluating the effectiveness of antidepressant medications.

> Patients' improvement with medication or placebo was found to be more related to the impact of the particular psychiatrist providing the medication (or the placebo) than to the treatment itself. The most effective psychiatrists helped their patients more using placebo than did the less effective psychiatrists who treated their patients with an antidepressant.[33]

This leads me once again to consider whether psychotherapy is more effective than medication. As I discuss in Chapter 9, most psychiatrists believe that medication is more effective at alleviating anxiety, depression and a host of other mental health issues. This of course is based on their professional training and the fact that psychiatrists by and large spend their ten-minute appointment times with patients prescribing and reviewing medications. This is what they are taught in medical school, as the large pharmaceutical companies continue to market their products and influence the psychiatric profession to promote the psychopharmacological approach. It has understandably become their therapeutic bias.

Within the psychiatric community, there is agreement that a combination of cognitive behavioral therapy (CBT), antidepressants and anti-anxiety medications has been shown to be helpful. Yet the research I have reviewed shows that psychotherapy is actually more effective than medications, and that adding medications does not significantly improve outcomes compared to psychotherapy alone. The American Psychological Association writes that

> psychotherapy even works better in the long-term and is more enduring than medication. In fact, not only is it more cost-effective, but psychotherapy leads to fewer relapses of anxiety and mild to moderate depression than medication use alone—so much so

that Norwegian Health Authorities have issued new guidelines concerning treatment of mild to moderate depression and anxiety, stating that psychological interventions, not medications, should be applied first.[34]

Why is this? One prominent professor of counseling psychology who teaches at the University of Wisconsin, Dr. Bruce Wampold, believes that both customized treatment approaches and the therapeutic relationship play significant roles. According to his research, successful therapeutic outcomes emerge from therapist-client collaboration.

> However, there are common elements of effective psychotherapies. For example, there are hundreds of studies that show that a purposeful collaborative relationship between a therapist and the patient—what we call the therapeutic alliance—is related to therapeutic progress. This relationship holds for all types of therapy. The therapeutic alliance is critical even in medication treatments for mental disorders. The most important aspect of effective therapy is that the patient and the therapist work together to help the patient reach their goals in therapy.[35]

Ongoing research continues to provide evidence that successful outcomes in psychotherapy are directly linked to the positive experience and success of the therapeutic relationship. Researchers have identified three common themes connected to the therapeutic alliance. These include the affective bond between the client and the therapist (i.e., good ongoing rapport), the collaborative nature of the relationship, and the client's and therapist's willingness to agree on the treatment goals.[36]

Much of the current emphasis on the therapeutic alliance emerged from Carl Rogers having developed a person-centered approach to psychotherapy (see Chapter 6). He realized that more than specific interventions, the therapeutic relationship is central to successful client outcomes. This approach is the key to meeting the client where he or she is. He believed that unconditional positive regard is required in order to support clients with any diagnosis, generating the deep interpersonal connection necessary not only for establishing and maintaining ongoing rapport, but for clients to feel deeply listened to without any judgment.

The profound impact of early familial dynamics on trust and interpersonal relationships reverberates deeply. For individuals who have grown up in environments marked by judgment, rigid parental expectations and rejection, the journey toward trusting others—and even just feeling comfortable around others—is often daunting. In effective psychotherapy, the therapeutic alliance serves as a crucible for exploring and transforming these deep-seated patterns of relating. Through the supportive and nonjudgmental presence of the therapist, clients have the opportunity to experience what healthy relating truly feels like. They can safely explore their fears, insecurities, and hidden shame without fear of rejection. For many, this is a revelation that gives them the chance to cultivate trust, authenticity, acceptance and vulnerability in their interactions with others.

The experience of discovering healthy and honest interpersonal relating within the therapeutic context can be profoundly healing and transformative. It offers clients a glimpse into the possibility of forming genuine connections based on mutual respect and a willingness to trust. As they incorporate these newfound insights and skills into their everyday interactions, clients typically experience profound shifts in their relationships and overall well-being.

Ultimately, one's psychotherapy experience is not just about resolving specific symptoms or issues; it's about fostering ongoing self-awareness and the capacity for authentic connection that extends far beyond the therapy room. This becomes the gift that keeps on giving.

Chapter 7

I am convinced that the most powerful and healing aspect of psychotherapy is the experience of discovering what healthy relating is really about. It means that a person is finally able to drop their social persona and discover what a trusting, authentic relationship feels like. The wariness and caution of being around others slowly begins to subside, supported by an accepting and reliably empathetic therapist. This begins to erode the self-devaluing beliefs that many clients have internalized from dysfunctional family upbringings. I believe the therapeutic alliance is the most important component in the therapy process, enabling clients to finally dream about possibilities they had buried or marginalized. To deeply connect and honestly engage with another person is not only profoundly healing—for many, it is transformative. To feel free to fully be oneself and acknowledge one's gifts, however unusual or unique, is truly a blessing.

So many therapists these days take trainings to learn a new technique for their therapeutic toolbox. They tend to overlook the value and power of focusing their attention and energy on creating a safe container for healing and transformation to occur. This is exemplified by the following quote from Carl Rogers:

> In my early professional years, I was asking the question, How can I treat, or cure, or change this person? Now I would phrase the question in this way: How can I provide a relationship which this person may use for his own personal growth?[37]

While there is increasing evidence that psychotherapy can be effective, it is certainly not the case that it works all the time, and it seems not to work for everyone. A new client must feel safe and comfortable with disclosing his or her insecurities and fears to someone who is initially a total stranger. This trust is always tested to varying degrees over the course of the therapy, and the ease with which it develops determines whether a good fit with a new therapist is something that easily and organically emerges.

I need to point out that there is always an underlying paradox that confronts a newly emerging therapeutic alliance. This is about unspoken resistance to be open and available to a total stranger whom the new client is asking help and healing from.

As discussed in Chapter 1, defense mechanisms are unconscious adaptations to protect oneself from the potential hurtfulness of others and to insulate oneself from an overwhelming experience. Defense mechanisms play a role in the therapeutic relationship. For example, clients may rationalize reasons for why a person responds in the way that they do. Some people use *rationalization* to try to explain their behavior with logical reasons, even when these explanations are not at all true. Some clients are very effective at throwing others off with *intellectualization* because of the way their mind works. While initially impressive and sometimes off-putting, it is meant to distract and redirect others from getting too close to the client's emotional vulnerabilities. Some clients have learned to *dissociate* in their relationships as a way to dull and protect their vulnerable feelings. Since emotions are based in the body, being partially checked out ("spaced out") is an effective defense mechanism for shielding one's sensitivities from powerful emotional states such as shame or anger. Being spaced out provides a way to not be fully present in relationship with others. In a supportive and trusting therapeutic alliance, clients learn to let go of their various defense mechanisms in order to retrain themselves to be fully and authentically present with another person. This is what represents a good fit with a therapist.

The intervention(s) that a psychotherapist chooses to employ is another important ingredient for maintaining a good fit in the therapeutic alliance. Interventions derive from theoretical models whose underlying assumptions have been supported by consistently successful therapeutic outcomes. These also represent the interests and inclinations of the particular psychotherapist.

For many years during my own career, I was learning and

implementing process-oriented psychology interventions. This is a model that emphasizes acting out disaffected inner parts and expressing internal feeling states, emerging images and somatic sensations in a very extroverted manner. Its emphasis is on psychodrama and while it is active and engaging, people who are shy and introverted often find this to be difficult. I used this model for ten years and personally found it to be challenging, engaging and rewarding. I taught my clients how to participate in this by supporting them to act out internal repressed parts of themselves. I enjoyed this tremendously and developed a large client base that continued to grow over the years. Yet this was not right for everyone, as some people prefer a more measured, talk therapy approach that tends to be more cognitively and behaviorally based, reflecting on one's behaviors and beliefs. After ten years of facilitating process-oriented groups with clients from my private practice, my interests and emphases changed as I discovered the energy psychology approach, a world apart from processwork.

While this was part of my professional development, not every client is interested in working with their essential energy system, since this approach is so different from traditional psychodynamic talk therapy. I take time to speak to prospective clients over the phone before setting up an initial appointment to explain that this is a very different paradigm for mental and emotional healing. I explain that this model uses tapping on the acupuncture meridian system and stimulating the body's energy centers or chakras to balance one's essential energy system. This in turn balances one's emotions, modifies unhelpful beliefs and alleviates physical tensions in the body. For people who have been referred to me from satisfied clients or have experienced acupuncture or Reiki, there is usually an immediate buy-in. But for many others who have no experiential background in this, it simply sounds too foreign. In these cases, I provide a short list of local therapists whose emphasis is traditional CBT talk therapy that is more in line with what they imagine therapy to be like. This is all about ensuring that there is a good fit from the beginning so as not to try to force or persuade prospective clients to go somewhere they are not interested in or comfortable with.

To a large extent, therapeutic interventions must also be a good match for what clients imagine they want. Basically, therapists adopt psychotherapy models they have an interest in and believe in. I am reminded of a training I took decades ago in eye movement desensitization and reprocessing (EMDR), a well-researched trauma reduction technique that involves moving a wand or one's hand from side to side in front of a client's face while they visually track the movement and internally review a traumatic event. Many clients who engage in this approach report successful outcomes in depotentiating old trauma-generated persistent symptoms of distress. Yet for me, this technique seemed overly mechanistic and prevented me from experiencing a state of flow and rapport with my clients. While I never negated its effectiveness, EMDR was not a good fit for me—I did not pursue it because I felt it minimized the therapeutic relationship. My belief then as now is that for psychotherapy to be effective for the client, the therapist and the interventions need to fit well together. When a therapist is congruent about this it comes through in the therapeutic relationship.

I am frequently surprised when I read completed intake forms that ask prospective clients to list previous therapy experiences. Among those who have been in therapy before, many write down that they tried it for several months with a particular therapist but never felt they got anywhere and that nothing changed. I don't question them further on this but realize that for various reasons they did not experience a good therapeutic alliance and thus kept looking. This is the way it should be. New clients need to interview the therapist and feel comfortable in all the ways I have described so that they feel they have a good fit with the therapist. This includes the personality of the therapist as well as their approach. Regardless of whether the therapy consists of CBT, EMDR, Jungian dream analysis, or any other approach, when the client feels respected and heard, and thus is willing to readily participate in a collaborative therapeutic relationship, a successful outcome is to be expected.

Another significant element contributing to a good therapist–client fit is reflected by the underlying values that each therapist brings to the therapy session. Prior to the beginning of the coronavirus pandemic in March of 2020, psychotherapy was predominately conducted in person in a physical office. This was the norm going back all the way to Freud in the early 1900s. Suddenly, everything changed with the initial lockdowns that required meeting with clients over the phone or in front of a computer screen for what is now called telehealth or telemedicine. A primary reason I chose to pursue this profession is because I wanted to go deep into the therapeutic relationship through connecting with people in person. From the very beginning of my career, I have truly enjoyed the experience of being with another person in an emotionally intimate setting. This reflects my personal value of deep relating and by 2024 clients were beginning to trickle back into my office. I feel grateful that we can choose to once again meet in person.

Yet for younger digital natives who grew up with a smartphone and a tablet, navigating the world from in front of a screen has become part of their daily operating system. While I have fond memories of browsing in bookstores and going into big box stores to purchase holiday gifts, younger clients in their twenties and thirties have become accustomed to ordering everything online without the inconvenience of having to drive to a store and survey the merchandise in person. This is an enormous cultural shift that also reflects how people are relating to each other now. Can a prepandemic therapist like myself somehow overcome this most significant cultural and age gap to carry on psychotherapy digitally? Is the cultivation of the therapeutic alliance just as strong now as prepandemic? Can it also be as satisfying as it was for me and many others prepandemic?

For many of my established clients who know me well and like to check in every month, it is more convenient for them to call me from their phone or meet with me over Zoom than having to drive to my office. I willingly accommodate them, but this way of conducting a therapy session is not really what I signed up for. I am hopeful that the lingering fears from the pandemic will dissipate so we can regularly meet in person once again. In fact, there are many clients who much prefer to meet with me in person because physically being in the same space with me feels more emotionally intimate. This is all about the special nonverbal energy that flows between us that makes therapeutic presence so very special and healing.

The therapist's personal and professional development have enormous implications for how they conduct the psychotherapy session. This in turn affects and influences the therapeutic relationship. From the many years I have been facilitating psychotherapy sessions as well as training other therapists to learn my Dynamic Energetic Healing™ (DEH) model, I have developed a number of core beliefs that have become internalized and are now a part of who I am as a psychotherapist. For example, I expect that positive changes are likely and that clients will achieve a positive therapeutic outcome.

Because DEH is so different from conventional psychotherapy approaches, many if not most of my new clients experience cognitive dissonance, since I am personifying a new paradigm within the larger psychotherapy world. While it remains true that most clients new to psychotherapy have certain beliefs and expectations (based on what they have seen in movies and television shows), my approach appears to be outside of the bounds of traditional talk therapy. While we certainly talk a great deal during sessions, working within an energy-based therapeutic paradigm for generating long-lasting personal change frequently confuses clients, at least initially. As a consequence, previous assumptions about therapy become challenged and destabilized, opening up and broadening clients' receptivity to new possibilities that had previously never been considered.

An important aspect of this approach comes through as I share a great deal of my in-the-moment perceptions—I am modeling for clients how they must learn to trust their own internal perceptions within the context of relationship. This is so important because many clients were not given the safety and support to trust their own internal experience during their formative years. On the contrary, they were told by controlling parents that their own perceptions of reality were wrong. As a consequence, trusting themselves and their personal experience was regularly invalidated.

Because I am a process-oriented therapist, I hold an expansive unified field of attention. This unified field incorporates varying levels of awareness. Not only do I pay attention to *what* the client is telling me but *how* they communicate to me. Building rapport with clients is more effective because I am an active listener and in various ways convey back to them what I have heard them say so they feel understood and acknowledged. I teach and encourage my clients to trust their own internal perceptions by sharing with them what I am experiencing and perceiving, thus tacitly giving them permission to feel more accepting of their own internal experience, all within the context of the therapeutic relationship. Eventually, clients learn to trust themselves because there is no one criticizing them. As a consequence, they slowly become more self-empowered, self-referential and self-accepting. In this way, clients heal the parts of themselves that they had unknowingly devalued through the negative trance imposed on them from their family of origin, which then became reinforced through their interactions with others.

The therapeutic alliance, characterized by trust, presence and mutual respect, serves as the very foundation upon which healing and growth can occur. Within this supportive relationship, clients feel empowered to explore their innermost thoughts, feelings and experiences, knowing that they are met with empathy and acceptance. This way in which I inhabit the therapeutic relationship thus erodes old dysfunctional interactional patterns that were reinforced over time. It is exciting to witness barriers dissolving and clients' deep distrust of others begin to shift, as this more innocent and intrepid part of them reawakens.

In Part 2, I will describe core shamanic practices and how over the years I have integrated this ancient healing model into the modern Western psychotherapeutic context. Because energy psychology is the operational framework from which Dynamic Energetic Healing™ emerges, core shamanic practices have seamlessly integrated into the way I work with clients. Energy psychology orients to more subtle and ancient approaches to healing the mind, body and spirit. Though literally thousands of years old, the use of the yogic chakras (as the collection centers of the subtle life-force energy that circulates within us) along with the acupuncture meridians (that course through our body affecting us physically and emotionally) are healing practices that are remarkably effective. And yes, their adapted application to contemporary psychotherapy is remarkably effective for addressing anxiety, depression and PTSD-related trauma. Add to that the orientation to the human biofield and thus you have what is referred to as the human vibrational matrix.

Now that acupuncture treatment is frequently covered by standard health insurance plans, the efficacy of addressing and accessing this subtle life-force energy, often referred to as chi, is becoming more accepted as a mainstream medical treatment. The key concept here is *subtle energy*.

So much of what therapists are called on is to help their clients experience greater connection in contrast to feeling separate or alone. The therapeutic alliance can foster greater connectedness when there is trust, mutual respect, attuned presence and understanding. In my experience, it is at the very core of what generates successful psychotherapeutic outcomes. The therapeutic alliance is profound and engaging. It is this deep relationship that facilitates and creates healing.

CHAPTER 8

"LOBOTOMY GETS THEM HOME"

The history and evolution of treating mental illness in Western Europe and America reveal a complex and often troubling past. Understanding the history of mental health treatment requires a look back to the mid-twentieth century, when options for addressing mental illness were severely limited. Societies struggled with the challenge of caring for those with mental health issues, particularly those who found themselves without a home or family support. Before the 1950s, a wide range of individuals whose behavior strayed from what was considered acceptable in polite society were confined to institutions known as asylums. This included people with schizophrenia or psychosis as well as the sexually deviant and the destitute. Asylums were chaotic and overcrowded; the conditions within them were far from therapeutic, often exacerbating the patients' suffering rather than alleviating it. These institutions struggled to provide adequate care, largely because there were no effective psychiatric medications available to manage patients' symptoms.

During the mid-twentieth century, the fields of psychiatry and neurology began to explore the human brain for biological solutions to mental illness. While psychotherapy and talk therapy remained the preferred methods for those who could afford such treatments, the dire need for alternative solutions for the severely mentally ill and financially destitute led to the development of more radical approaches.

Enter the era of psychosurgery, with the transorbital lobotomy, colloquially known as the "ice pick" lobotomy, becoming one of the most controversial approaches. These experimental psychosurgery treatments arose from a societal imperative to address the growing visibility of mental illness and the lack of adequate care facilities. The emergence of such drastic measures reflects the desperation and limited understanding of mental health during this time. This procedure, which involved inserting a sharp instrument through the eye socket to literally destroy parts of the brain, gained popularity as a quicker, less expensive treatment for those deemed severely mentally ill.

The history of lobotomy began when Dr. Walter J. Freeman (1895–1972), a neurologist and psychiatrist on the medical faculty of George Washington University, began promoting his theories of brain dysfunction being the cause of mental illness. Several innovative approaches to treating mental illness emerged.

> By the mid-1930s he had introduced several new therapies for mental patients at GW Hospital: insulin shock therapy, metrazol shock therapy and electroconvulsive therapy. All of these treatments were intended to fight psychiatric disease by subjecting patients to chemicals or jolts of electricity that might disrupt unhealthy neural activity in the brain.[38]

In 1935, Freeman attended a conference in London where he listened to a presentation by a Yale researcher discussing how chimpanzees' behaviors changed after undergoing surgical damage to their frontal lobes. They subsequently became passive and inactive.

In 1936, another conference attendee, Portuguese neurologist Egas Moniz, began applying these surgical techniques on mentally ill patients. It was Moniz who applied the term *psychosurgery*, or *psychiatric surgery*. He believed that surgically severing the neural connections between the thalamus (believed to be the seat of human emotions at the time) and the prefrontal lobes of the brain would prevent the intense and overly emotional influences of the thalamus from negatively influencing his patients' thinking. Moniz's initial lobotomy surgeries were performed by drilling a hole in his patient's skull and injecting alcohol into their brain. This was intended to destroy the neural fibers and connections that connected the frontal lobe to other parts of the brain, in particular the thalamus.

Walter Freeman was intrigued by Moniz's work, and it wasn't long after that he and James Watt (another American neurologist) began performing lobotomies even though Freeman was not a certified surgeon. In 1937, they made "nine cores in the white matter of each frontal lobe" on their first patient.

> They adapted Moniz's technique to create the "Freeman-Watts technique" or the "Freeman-Watts standard prefrontal lobotomy," in which a surgeon drilled holes in the patient's skull, then inserted and rotated a knife to destroy brain cells, targeting connections between part of the prefrontal lobes and a region in the thalamus, which is a grey-matter structure toward the center of the brain.[39]

Psychiatrists internationally explored and utilized this surgical technique. It wasn't too long before an Italian psychiatrist named Amarro Fiamberti evolved a more facile technique that would no longer require a traditional surgeon, operating room or even anesthesia.

> The technique involved using an instrument called an orbitoclast—a long, slender instrument modeled after an ice pick—which the physician would insert through the patient's eye socket using a hammer.

> They would then move the instrument side-to-side to separate the frontal lobes from the thalamus.[40]

Over the next two decades, surgeons throughout Europe and America lobotomized tens of thousands of people, many of whom had no idea what to expect. As Freeman perfected this technique, his protocol became standardized. Using an electroshock therapy machine, he would render his patient unconscious with several jolts of electricity. After their convulsions stopped, Freeman would lift the patient's eyelids to insert an instrument similar to an ice pick (called a leucotome) through a tear duct. He would then vigorously tap a surgical hammer several times to sever the bone. After inserting it about an inch and a half, he would then move the sharp tip, grinding it back and forth to separate the tissues connecting the frontal lobe from the thalamus. His son Frank, who was twenty-one at the time, was invited to observe his father performing the procedure on a patient. He recalled that it only took six or seven minutes and that fracturing the orbital plate was quick and easy.

> Indeed, the original ice pick used for the first transorbital lobotomy came from the Freeman family kitchen drawer. "We had several of them," says Frank, cheerfully. "We used to use them to punch holes in our belts when we got bigger."[41]

At that time, treatment options beyond talk therapy were scarce, and Freeman often positioned lobotomy as the only effective solution for desperate patients and their families.

The prevailing view was that severe mental illness could not be resolved by psychotherapy alone. It was Freeman's conviction that lobotomy was the most helpful psychiatric approach to address persistent depression, schizophrenia and other mental illness. He performed lobotomies on children as well as adults.

Walter Freeman and his proponents of lobotomy operated under the belief that mental illness stemmed primarily from disorders within the brain. Their narrow focus on the brain ignored the significant sociocultural factors such as dysfunctional family dynamics, poverty and income inequality, which we now understand as substantial contributors to mental illness. This approach proved especially harmful to returning veterans from World War II, many of whom suffered from variations of post-traumatic stress disorder (PTSD) without adequate recognition or treatment. Lobotomy, seen as a brain-based solution, often exacerbated their suffering by destroying their personalities without addressing the underlying issues.

Predicting the outcome of lobotomy surgery was virtually impossible, making it a hit-and-miss approach. Many patients and their families faced uncertainty and risk, with the surgery often resulting in life-altering consequences. This uncertainty underscores the experimental and ethically fraught nature of lobotomy during this period, highlighting the need for caution and thorough consideration in medical interventions.

The side effects of lobotomies were profound. A significant number of patients faced severe consequences, often slipping into a persistent vegetative state. They became unaware of their surroundings, struggled with basic bodily functions like bladder control, and lost the ability to feed or care for themselves. The surgery compromised personal initiative and independence, to the point that the personality of many individuals seemed to vanish. After the surgery, patients often sat unmoving for hours and needed assistance to eat and use the toilet. Remarkably, Freeman stated that these post-operative changes in behavior were not only therapeutic but acceptable. He interpreted the indifference and mental dullness that patients exhibited after the surgery as the intended outcome for taming the overly strong neural impulses generated from the thalamus. He believed that the mentally ill were too self-aware and had a tendency to obsess, which was caused by an overactive thalamus. Lobotomy reduced or eliminated this tendency by effectively quieting the thalamus.

Freeman kept a record of the 3,439 lobotomies he carried out over the course of his career. While approximately 14 percent (490 patients) died from the surgery, Freeman nevertheless trumpeted lobotomy with his motto "Lobotomy gets them home."[42] He was completely convinced in the efficacy of the approach and traveled across the country, teaching psychiatrists in fifty-five hospitals how to perform the surgery. Because of the dire situation in state mental hospitals and veterans' hospitals, officials and administrators welcomed Freeman to teach their staff doctors. After one or two days of demonstrating and training staff doctors in lobotomy surgery that typically lasted only about ten minutes, Freeman encouraged doctors to start using the procedure.

Dr. Walter Freeman's conviction was so strong that he advocated for the procedure to be accessible and straightforward, to the extent that doctors performing it did not require certification in surgery. This approach positioned lobotomy as a quick outpatient procedure, further popularizing it despite the significant risks involved.

Administrators at state mental hospitals saw a notable benefit in the lobotomy procedure, as it often resulted in a more subdued patient population. They observed that their facilities became quieter and safer for both the staff and other patients, with a significant reduction in disruptive behaviors and loud outbursts. Consequently, many lobotomized individuals were eventually discharged and returned to their family's care. Those who stayed in the institutions were found to be more manageable.

Between 1936 and the late 1950s, an estimated 40,000 to 50,000 Americans underwent lobotomy. This period saw a broad application of the procedure, to the extent that it was used to address not just severe mental illness but also behaviors deemed problematic or undesirable by family members. Notably, some husbands brought their wives to state mental institutions for lobotomies, seeking a solution to what they perceived as troublesome behavior, such as being too assertive or insufficiently submissive. Similarly, parents frustrated with their children's truancy or defiant behavior viewed lobotomy as a solution to enforce obedience, bypassing less invasive interventions. This practice underscores the controversial and often criticized aspects of lobotomy's history. In addition, during this era alternatives like marital counseling or play therapy for children had not yet been developed as viable options. This lack of accessible, noninvasive treatments contributed to lobotomy's appeal as a quick fix for a range of behavioral issues, reflecting broader societal tendencies to prioritize conformity over the well-being of individuals.

> Before the introduction of antipsychotic drugs or the popularisation of psychotherapy, the lobotomy was touted as a miracle cure for anything from schizophrenia to postnatal depression—and not just in the United States. Neurologists in the UK are estimated to have carried out 50,000 variants of the operation, until the late 1970s.[43]
>
> Children, women and the severely mentally ill were especially vulnerable to being lobotomized without their knowledge. In Sweden, where over 4,500 lobotomies were performed between 1944 and 1966, most of the patients were women. Parents, husbands, and doctors were able to order lobotomies without asking the person whose brain would be dismantled.[44]

Lobotomy's role in the context of Western psychotherapy extends beyond its medical intentions, serving as a tool for social control during its peak usage. Following lobotomy surgery, some patients experienced a reduction in emotional reactivity, which was considered fortunate as they appeared calmer than before. This phenomenon wasn't limited to the confines of state mental hospitals or to treating individuals with severe mental illnesses, as depicted in cultural touchstones like *One Flew Over the Cuckoo's Nest*. The procedure was also used to enforce conformity to societal norms.

Freeman's actions reflect a time when the boundaries of medical practice, ethical standards and patient rights were markedly different from today, highlighting a period in psychiatric treatment where the desperation for effective interventions led to the adoption of radical and often harmful methods.

This aspect of lobotomy's history highlights the procedure's use as a mechanism for imposing rigid norms and controlling behaviors deemed undesirable, casting a shadow over its legacy in psychiatric treatment and underscoring the importance of ethical considerations in medical practices.

One contemporary alternative to lobotomy was chemical shock therapy. In November 1940, Charles F. Read published the article *The Consequences of Metrazol Shock Therapy*.[45] He reported his findings of the possible negative consequences experienced by 320 schizophrenic patients at least one year after having received this chemical shock therapy treatment.

> Vertebral fractures were numerous in the past, possibly 20–30 per cent. However, 50 patients checked after their treatment in 1940 show no fractures.... Pulmonary tuberculosis developed in 25 patients, 8 per cent of all those treated ... Myocardial damage and a tendency to hypertension occurred in a relatively small number of patients.... Clinical evidences of damage to the central nervous system were suggestive but questionable.... However, more than 43 per cent of those with a psychosis duration of less than 3 years had improved greatly, whereas in the group of longer duration only 13.2 per cent improved.[46]

This chemical therapy had been widely used for the treatment of schizophrenia, psychosis and depression. Its intent was to induce convulsions in patients, but many ended up with severe injuries. Metrazol was withdrawn by the Food and Drug Administration in 1982 because it was too dangerous and largely ineffective.

It wasn't until 1954, with the introduction of Thorazine, an antipsychotic drug approved for treating schizophrenia, that a significant change in the treatment of mental illness began to take shape.

The introduction of Thorazine represented a breakthrough in mental health treatment, offering a glimmer of hope for more effective and humane care. For the first time, there was a pharmacological tool that could help manage the symptoms of schizophrenia, reducing the need for ongoing confinement and offering patients a chance at a better quality of life. This development marked the beginning of a new era in mental health care, shifting the focus from institutionalization to more compassionate and individualized treatment approaches.

Psychopharmacology rapidly evolved, with a strong emphasis on biological, brain-based approaches to treating mental illness. This approach has become the predominant treatment worldwide, including in the United States. However, it has also led to unintended consequences, including the widespread biochemical addiction to these drugs and their potent side effects.

At around the same time—the mid-1950s—lobotomy lost favor within the psychiatric community. Awareness of their profound and detrimental side effects grew, prompting concerns among medical professionals. One significant issue was the realization that many practitioners performing lobotomies lacked neurosurgical expertise. Additionally, there was mounting evidence that doctors administering lobotomies were not consistently reporting the negative outcomes and severe side effects associated with the procedure.

As the medical profession became increasingly aware of these shortcomings, skepticism surrounding the efficacy and safety of lobotomy grew. This shift marked a turning point in psychiatric practice, as attention shifted toward alternative treatments and a more critical evaluation of surgical interventions for mental illness.

The psychiatric community largely views Thorazine and its descendant powerful brain-altering medications as the best option for alleviating symptoms of depression and other mental and emotional issues. Professional marketing of these psychopharmaceutical drugs mirrors Walter Freeman's enthusiastic promotion of lobotomy, albeit with different methods. However, despite their widespread use, questions remain about the long-term effects and consequences of these heavily prescribed medications. The next chapter will delve into these issues, exploring the unintended consequences and challenges associated with the widespread use of psychopharmacology in modern psychiatric treatment.

CHAPTER 9
THE PSYCHOPHARMACOLOGICAL REVOLUTION

Psychotherapy models offer a wide range of approaches, each with its particular underlying theoretical assumptions. All therapy models can be useful and helpful for some people, but not everyone will be helped by using any one approach. The preference and bias of clinicians often stem from their training and supervisory experiences in specific therapeutic methods. For instance, certain therapists advocate for focused hyperventilation techniques, such as Stanislav and Christina Grof's Holotropic Breathing. They argue these methods can address birth trauma and other deep-seated traumatic blockages believed to underlie many issues. However, not every client is comfortable with or open to hyperventilation.

Then there is Jungian therapy, which emphasizes dream analysis and the exploration of dream symbols. This approach resonates well with individuals who frequently remember their dreams. This raises a question about its effectiveness for those who don't recall their dreams. Could it still offer the same level of help?

Another method currently gaining attention is emotional freedom techniques (EFT), often now referred to as tapping. Rooted in energy psychology and traditional Chinese medicine practices, EFT, which involves acupressure tapping, is touted by some therapists as a powerful tool for reducing trauma. Yet it is not universally accepted or used by the vast majority of therapists. Some are hesitant about or uninterested in exploring acupressure tapping as a way to help clients alleviate anxiety or depression simply because it appears to be so different from what most people expect to take place in a psychotherapy session.

In essence, while the variety of therapeutic approaches available can be beneficial, the effectiveness of each is significantly influenced by an individual's openness, beliefs and personal experiences. This underscores the importance of matching therapy methods to the unique needs and preferences of each client.

Although some individuals may actively seek out a specific type of psychotherapy, it's common for many to simply look for someone to talk to, often without a clear awareness of the therapist's background or the particular model of therapy they practice. As a result, a significant number of psychotherapists gravitate toward employing variations of cognitive behavioral therapy (CBT), given its broad applicability and relative ease in establishing initial rapport with new clients.

When clients arrive for an initial session bearing the weight of old traumatic residue that manifests as post-traumatic stress disorder (PTSD), panic attacks, or chronic and persistent dissociation, the effectiveness of traditional talk therapy must be called into question. While graduate schools and many psychotherapists advocate for the efficacy of talk therapy, its limitations become apparent in the context of deep-seated trauma.

Trauma and PTSD often embed themselves not just psychologically but physiologically, altering the way the brain processes information and how the body responds to perceived threats. For individuals grappling with such conditions, simply talking about their experiences typically does not reach the depth required to initiate significant healing. This is where specialized trauma-informed therapies come into play, offering more nuanced and effective approaches.

Chapter 9

Strategies like eye movement desensitization and reprocessing (EMDR), somatic experiencing and energy psychology are intended to address the root causes of trauma, helping clients to process and integrate traumatic memories safely. These methods often focus on and incorporate bodily awareness and self-regulation techniques to help individuals re-establish a sense of safety in their bodies, something talk therapy alone typically lacks the depth to achieve.

Moreover, the therapeutic community is increasingly recognizing the importance of a holistic approach to trauma, one that encompasses the mind, body and emotional terrain of the individual. This includes recognizing the role of neurobiological changes generated by trauma and employing techniques that directly address and ameliorate these changes.

While conversational therapy has its place in the therapeutic landscape, treating trauma and PTSD effectively requires a more comprehensive toolkit. Therapists must be equipped with specialized trauma-informed approaches that go beyond traditional talk therapy, addressing the complex interplay of psychological and physiological effects of trauma to facilitate healing and recovery.

But what happens when clients come in for an initial session and they are carrying old traumatic residue that falls under the category of PTSD, which may generate panic attacks or chronic and persistent dissociation? Is talk therapy as useful as graduate schools and most psychotherapists lead us to believe? When it comes to treating trauma and PTSD, I think not.

Engaging in such emotionally intimate self-disclosure requires a commitment to personal growth, emotional honesty and vulnerability. However, it also necessitates financial resources, as therapy is a professional service often costing $150 or more per session. While health insurance that covers mental health services can make therapy more accessible for many, the costs can quickly add up, especially since insurance often limits the amount of mental health treatment covered. Short-term therapy might offer some relief for those struggling with job-related anxiety or a relationship breakup but it often falls short of providing the comprehensive healing needed when there is deep-seated trauma.

In my professional experience, most individuals dealing with depression or anxiety first seek help from their primary care physician, who is frequently keen to prescribe psychopharmacological medications. When the presenting symptoms persist and the patient returns to their primary care physician, they are often then referred to a psychiatrist so their medications can be fine-tuned.

The preference among many psychiatrists for combining CBT with medication highlights a conventional treatment bias for treating mental health issues. Nonetheless, the commitment required for ongoing CBT—spanning time, money and energy—makes it a formidable path for many. Given these considerations, it's understandable why the prospect of taking a daily medication may appear more appealing to those suffering from emotional distress, despite the potential benefits of a more integrative approach to treatment.

The American Psychiatric Association published the third edition of its *Diagnostic and Statistical Manual* (DSM III) in 1980. As a result, it became widely believed in the medical community that depression and other major mental disorders were brain illnesses caused by chemical imbalances, and that psychiatric drugs could help fix these imbalances. The publication of the DSM III set off a remarkable expansion of the use of pharmacological interventions in the United States and other developed countries.

Psychotropic drugs are potent chemical agents that modulate the levels of neurotransmitters in the brain, such as dopamine, serotonin and norepinephrine. Speaking specifically of antidepressants, SNRIs are serotonin and norepinephrine reuptake inhibitors that were first introduced in the 1990s. They work by blocking the reabsorption or reuptake of the neurotransmitters serotonin and norepinephrine. Selective serotonin reuptake inhibitors (SSRIs) are currently the most commonly prescribed type of antidepressant. SSRIs are theorized to improve how neurotransmitters use serotonin. They include Citalopram (Celexa), Escitalopram (Lexapro), Fluoxetine (Prozac), Paroxetine (Paxil), and Sertraline (Zoloft).[47]

> Prozac and its kin . . . were first discovered in 1972. They address one hallmark of depression: low levels of the molecule serotonin, which neurons use to signal one another. By preventing a protein called serotonin transporter (SERT) from absorbing the serotonin back into neurons that release it, the drugs boost serotonin levels in the junctions between cells.[48]

To be clear, these are psychoactive drugs. As such, they typically induce complex, varied and often unpredictable results.

All of these medications operate under the assumption, albeit unproven (as is discussed later in this chapter), that a chemical imbalance in the brain underlies conditions like depression and anxiety, and that these imbalances can be rectified through drug intervention.

Psychotropic drugs are typically prescribed by psychiatrists, psychiatric mental health nurse practitioners or primary care physicians. In rare cases, clinical psychologists may also have prescribing privileges.

In Dr. Peter Kramer's 1993 book, *Listening to Prozac*, he muses on the medical, philosophical, psychotherapeutic and societal ramifications of antidepressants, Prozac in particular. He comments on numerous patient case histories to illustrate what he describes as the surprising transformational changes that Prozac engenders. To wit,

> When one pill at breakfast makes you a new person, or your patient, or relative, or neighbor a new person, it is difficult to resist the suggestion, the visceral certainty, that who people are is largely biologically determined. I don't mean that it is impossible to escape simplistic

biological materialism, but the drama, the rapidity, the thoroughness of drug-induced transformation make simplicity tempting. Drug responses provide hard-to-ignore evidence for certain beliefs—concerning the influence of biology on personality, intellectual performance, and the social success—that heretofore we as a society have resisted. When I saw the impact of medication on patients' self-concept, I came to believe that even if we tried to understand these matters complexly, new medications would redraw our map of those parts of the self that are biologically responsive, so that we would arrive, as a culture, at a new consensus about the human condition.[49]

It is alarming to realize that psychiatry, with its reliance on brain-altering medications, has become the predominant approach to addressing mental health issues not only in the United States but throughout the world.

Despite concerns about overreliance on medication and potential side effects, prescriptions for psychiatric drugs across all classes continue to rise steadily.

Over 40 million Americans have been taking psychotropic drugs for mental and emotional complaints. These numbers continue to increase as the pharmaceutical companies find more and better ways to market their drugs. While big pharma drug reps have been marketing these companies' pipeline of drugs directly to doctors for years through their office visits (often by providing free samples and other inducements), one can now see them advertised directly to consumers in magazines, over the radio and in television commercials.

According to a survey taken in the United States in 2013, "One in every six adults reported taking a psychiatric drug, such as an anti-depressant or a sedative."[50] According to science reporter Benedict Carey who researched this topic in 2018 and published his findings in *The New York Times*, "Some 15.5 million Americans have taken antidepressants for at least five years. The rate has almost doubled since 2010, and more than tripled since 2000."[51]

Prozac, in particular, gained rapid popularity after its FDA approval in 1987, specifically for depression. In January of 1988, Eli Lilly and Company began its marketing campaign and it became an international blockbuster drug. Annual sales in the United States reached $350 million within the first year. International sales eventually reached a peak of over two and a half billion dollars a year.[52]

As I have mentioned, the antidepressant Prozac, the first SSRI, was touted as a wonder drug, and since 1988 our society's use of antidepressants and other psychiatric drugs has exploded. I find this continuing increase in the use of these medications ominous and alarming. This expansion has included dramatically increasing the use of psychiatric drugs globally.

Mental disorders have become a significant public health problem throughout the world.

> According to the statistics of the World Health Organization, about 1 billion people in the world suffer from mental illness. Mental disorders contribute substantially to the global disease burden. They are a leading cause of disability worldwide, accounting for a significant proportion of years lived with disability. Common mental disorders, such as depression and anxiety disorders, often contribute more to the disease burden than severe mental illnesses like schizophrenia and bipolar disorder due to their higher prevalence.[53]

As a consequence, over the past 20 years, there has been an ongoing effort to "globalize" mental health care, which has led to the increased use of psychiatric drugs in these less developed countries.

To reduce the rising burden of mental disorders around the world, the Lancet Commission on Global Mental Health and

Sustainable Development "declared a need to *increase* psychiatric services globally, which would include an effort to reduce the cost and improve the supply of effective psychotropic drugs for mental, neurological, and substance use disorders."[54] The commission goes on to say that while the intention to reduce mental health disorders is an important public health goal, they also expressed concern that moving forward with this plan may actually *increase* mental health disorders throughout the world. This appears to me as oxymoronic!

This is, in fact, what has happened. There has been an expansion of psychiatric services globally over the past thirty-five years, which has led to a dramatic increase in the use of antidepressants and other psychiatric drugs. At a public health level, this approach has not worked. An article in *World Psychiatry*, in fact, acknowledges this failure.

> [D]ata from 1990 to 2015 were reviewed from four English-speaking countries: Australia, Canada, England, and the U.S. These data show that the prevalence of mood and anxiety disorders and symptoms has not decreased, despite substantial increases in the provision of treatment, particularly antidepressants.[55]

Antidepressants and antianxiety medications continue to be among the leading prescription drugs not only in the United States but around the world.

Since primary care family physicians are the ones who usually meet with depressed patients first, they have become quick to prescribe these drugs for a host of patient complaints beyond depressed mood. Dr. Joseph Glenmullen is a clinical instructor in psychiatry at Harvard Medical School and has a private psychiatry practice. Glenmullen's research has borne out that primary care physicians are writing about 70 percent of the prescriptions for Prozac, Zoloft, Paxil and Luvok, which at the time of the publication of his book in 2000 were the most widely prescribed antidepressants. *Prozac Backlash* offers a critical look at the enthusiasm for and widespread prescription of SSRIs since their introduction, questioning both the efficacy and safety profile of these drugs based on available research and clinical observations. Glenmullen elaborates with the following:

> To the already long list of conditions treated with the drugs were added anxiety, obsessions, compulsions, eating disorders, headaches, back pain, impulsivity, sexual addictions, premature ejaculation, attention deficit disorder, and pre-menstrual syndrome. Serotonin boosters are all-purpose psychoanalgesics, not just "antidepressants," which was merely the first application for which they were approved.[56]

Dr. Peter Kramer coined the term "cosmetic psychopharmacology" to describe the use of powerful psychopharmacological drugs, which were initially developed to help individuals manage inner and outer stressors.[57]

This reality highlights a concerning trend: the escalating use of psychiatric medications. However, when these medications complicate or worsen the initial issues they were intended to address, patients are often referred to psychiatrists. Psychiatrists are seen as experts in manipulating the neurochemical intricacies of these pharmaceuticals in relationship to their patients' neurochemical pathways.

Reflecting on how the psychiatric community has a pervasive bias and reliance on the use of psychiatric drugs, Professor of Clinical Psychiatry at Weill Cornell Medical College, Dr. Richard Friedman, writes that

> "American psychiatry is facing a quandary: Despite a vast investment in basic neuroscience research and its rich intellectual promise, we have little to show for it on the treatment front." Echoing the concern

that we are an overmedicated world when it comes to psychological disorders, he notes that even the newer and supposedly better new drugs are no more effective than the old ones. Almost all (95%) of the federal dollars spent on mental health research go to drugs, not psychotherapy, in clinical trials.[58]

In the past, psychiatrists often engaged in longer consultations with patients akin to psychotherapists today. However, with the advent of managed care and insurance-imposed caps on mental health reimbursements, psychiatrists now often conduct brief, ten-minute medication checks, enabling them to see more patients and generate more revenue. This is simply the current reality. This shift toward efficiency has largely been facilitated by pharmaceutical companies seeking to maximize profits.

The financial implications cannot be ignored. The pharmaceutical industry, along with the medical professionals who prescribe these medications, benefit financially from the continued widespread use of antidepressants. This reality may create a conflict of interest, where the financial gains associated with high prescription rates overshadow the commitment to patient well-being and the principle of "do no harm."

While the ease of access to psychiatric medications may seem convenient, it also underscores the need for a critical examination of the broader societal and economic factors shaping current mental health treatment. The reliance on medication as a primary mode of intervention raises questions about the balance between pharmaceutical interventions and more holistic approaches to mental health care. I discuss this issue further below.

Schizophrenia and Antipsychotics

The changing outcomes for schizophrenia in developing countries provides another example of the perils of exporting Western ideas about psychiatric diagnosis and treatments to other parts of the globe. In the decades before 1990, the World Health Organization (WHO) conducted two studies that compared outcomes for people with schizophrenia in three developing countries (India, Nigeria and Colombia) with outcomes in the United States and five other developed countries. In each study, the WHO found that outcomes in the developing countries were better—so much so that the investigators concluded that living in a developed country was a strong predictor that a person diagnosed with schizophrenia would not have a good outcome.

> One of the big differences between developing and developed countries was that patients in the developing countries used antipsychotic medications only for short periods, while those in developed countries used them long term. Only 16 percent of patients in the developing countries took antipsychotics long term.[59]

> About twenty years ago however, pharmaceutical companies began marketing atypical antipsychotics around the world. The results of that effort are now becoming clear. In a recent study funded by Eli Lilly, in which patients with schizophrenia in thirty-seven countries were maintained on antipsychotics for three years, the better outcomes in the developing countries disappeared. They were now as poor as in the developed countries.[60]

Some mental health disorders may show temporary improvement with alterations in neurotransmitter levels, but the long-term implications and efficacy of these medications remain subject to ongoing debate and research.

While medications can offer short-term relief, they were not primarily intended for long-term use and can pose real danger for individuals relying on them indefinitely. However, according to the available research, most individuals who reported using psychiatric drugs said they used the medications long term. The researchers found that 84.3 percent of adults filled three or more prescriptions for psychiatric drugs in 2013 or reported that they had started to take the drugs in 2011 or earlier. Long-term psychiatric drug users filled an average of nearly 10 prescriptions for the drugs in 2013.[61]

Research letter co-author Thomas Moore of the Institute for Safe Medication Practices called the rates of psychiatric drug use in some populations "extraordinary." He added,

> To discover that eight in 10 adults who have taken psychiatric drugs are using them long term raises safety concerns, given that there's reason to believe some of this continued use is due to dependence and withdrawal symptoms.[62]

Most clinical trials for these drugs last only a few weeks to a few months, whereas in real-world practice, patients may be on these medications for years or even decades. This gap in the research leaves both prescribers and patients with incomplete information about the long-term dangers of psychiatric medications and their management strategies, including the use of drugs like Ozempic to manage side effects.

It lies with the prescribing doctor to inform the patient what the potential negatives are and how long the patient should expect to be on the drug. Unfortunately, prescribing doctors seem to minimize the long-term side effects largely because "even the longest rigorous studies of antidepressants' safety and efficacy have followed patients for only a couple of years."[63]

Glenmullen's *Prozac Backlash* has played a significant role in bringing attention to the concerns surrounding the long-term use of SSRIs and other psychiatric medications. His critiques focus on the dangers and long-term side effects of taking psychiatric drugs.

> Neurological disorders including disfiguring facial and whole body tics, indicating potential brain damage, are an increasing concern with patients on the drugs.... With related drugs targeting serotonin, there's evidence that they may affect a "chemical lobotomy" by destroying the nerve endings that they target in the brain. And startling new information on Prozac's precipitating suicidal and violent behavior has come to light.[64]

Many of these popular antidepressants also come with sexual side effects. For many people, these problems caused by their medications can be managed. Yet more than 50 percent of patients who take SSRIs report various problems having sex. "They include low levels of sexual desire or arousal, erectile dysfunction, pleasureless or painful orgasms and loss of genital sensitivity."[65] Some people experience these sexual side effects right after starting their antidepressant and find that they gradually resolve on their own. Consequently, many doctors recommend that their patients try to wait it out over a period of several months to determine if and when these side effects will completely resolve on their own. However, it is reported that only 10 to 20 percent of these patients experience complete resolution by trying to wait it out.

> One common way to manage sexual side effects is to try another S.S.R.I. Research suggests that certain drugs such as Zoloft and Celexa, come with a higher

likelihood of sexual problems. Switching drugs, however, means enduring a trial-and-error period to find what works. If a patient is otherwise doing well on an S.S.R.I., a doctor may be hesitant to drastically change the drug regimen. Instead, the doctor might recommend adding an additional drug to the mix that could help counteract the sexual side effects.[66]

Here is but another example of how contemporary psychiatrists experiment with their patients' brains, albeit with chemicals rather than the ice pick. Nonetheless, there are numerous reports of patients who stopped taking their antidepressants yet continue to suffer with low sexual desire and the sensation of numb genitals that continue for years.

Although antidepressants may provide a small benefit over placebo for the short term, there have now been a number of studies concluding that these drugs increase the risk that a person will become chronically depressed over the long term. Researchers have dubbed this drug-induced worsening "tardive dysphoria," meaning that antidepressants are causing a biological change that often leads to persistent dysphoria, a state of profound unease or dissatisfaction.[67]

In addition, one of the risks of taking an antidepressant is that it can trigger a manic reaction. When this occurs, the individual may be diagnosed with bipolar disorder, which is seen as a more serious illness than depression. A large study done by Yale investigators found that taking an SSRI antidepressant more than doubles the risk that a depressed person will convert to bipolar disorder.[68]

Weight Loss Drugs

In December of 2023, Oprah Winfrey announced that she was taking a new weight loss drug that was helping her lose weight, addressing a challenge she has battled with for decades. The drug is Ozempic, which contains the core ingredient called semaglutide, approved by the FDA in 2017 to treat diabetes. With Winfrey's disclosure and personal endorsement, these drugs have become overnight sensations.

> According to Axios, Zocdoc, a portal that allows people to book doctor visits online, "saw a 30 percent spike" in appointments for patients seeking semaglutide drugs after Winfrey acknowledged taking [the] medication.[69]

As another example of how pharmaceutical companies earn millions of dollars on their most popular drugs, the Danish company Novo Nordisk that makes this drug has earned so much money that it had "exceeded the size of the Danish economy."[70] These drugs have been on the market for less than six years and consequently, the risks for long-term use are currently unknown. When journalist Jessica Grose of *The New York Times* called and spoke to Arthur Caplan, the founding head of the division of medical ethics at the New York University Grossman School of Medicine's department of population health, she was told that in general,

> there are very few "long-term registry studies of the sample of the population" because they're expensive and there are few incentives for drug companies to do them. "You have also situations where you don't want to find adverse events if you're the manufacturer because you want to keep selling" and it's a liability. "So they're not saying they won't do it or couldn't be forced by the F.D.A. to do it, but they're not rushing to do it on their own," he said.[71]

> Now Ozempic is being prescribed by psychiatrists as yet another drug for users of antipsychotics and some antidepressants to add to their daily drug regimen in the hopes that their weight gain from their current drugs can be better managed. This is just another example of the *prescribing cascade* that happens when "drug-induced side effects are viewed as a new ailment and treated with yet another drug that can cause still other side effects."[72]

It is usually not spoken about that long-term use of psychotropic medications becomes biochemically addictive. The brain's chemistry actually changes, often to the point that many people are unable to get off of their medications because of the plethora of unanticipated biochemical and emotional reactions.

This creates a dilemma—one that forces us to confront a challenging paradox within the psychiatric medical community. On one hand, antidepressants can offer some relief for many people struggling with depression and anxiety, potentially providing a lifeline for those in acute distress. On the other hand, the growing body of evidence regarding the difficult, sometimes harrowing withdrawal experiences begs a critical examination of the motivations behind their prescription and the long-term management of mental health.

But some psychiatrists may downplay the severe withdrawal symptoms associated with antidepressants, perhaps aiming to bolster their argument for the necessity of these medications as a primary tool in psychiatric treatment. As a result, millions of Americans who rely on psychiatric drugs may be unaware of the potential for debilitating, long-lasting withdrawal effects, even when tapering off under medical supervision.

When applied to the more than 45 million users of antidepressants in the United States, the implications are shocking.

Yet prescribing doctors continue to promote the benefits of increasing serotonin levels to address depression.

According to psychiatrist Peter Breggin,

> when many patients try to stop taking their drugs, the withdrawal syndrome produces such torture-like emotional and physical reactions that they think they need to keep taking the medication to control their "mental illness."[73]

Cosci and Chouinard reported that the various withdrawal symptoms include

> hypertension, seizures, stroke-like symptoms, amnesia, agitation, fear, anger, aggressive behavior, hallucinations, delirium, and suicidal thoughts… The longer antidepressants were taken and the higher the dose, the more severe and prolonged the withdrawal symptoms are likely to be.[74]

Others have reported that the unanticipated biochemical and emotional reactions include unprovoked rage, emotional lability and persistent electrical zapping in their brain and nervous system that suggests the brain has been permanently altered. Some sources call this "discontinuation syndrome."

In 2019, the United Kingdom began informing prospective patients about the long-lasting and severe risks involved in trying to get off these psychotropic drugs. This was initiated after the Royal College of Psychiatrists sounded the alarm. They began advising doctors who prescribe these medications that patients should know about the withdrawal risks before accepting a prescription.

> The Royal College website lists antidepressant withdrawal symptoms that include nausea, dizziness, loss of coordination, sleep problems, difficulty concentrating,

headache, the feeling of electric shocks in the body's limbs and head ("brain zaps"), mood swings, anxiety, panic and depression.[75]

Researchers James Davies and John Read reviewed 23 studies that looked at withdrawal from antidepressants. Their 2019 study found that more than half (56 percent) of patients suffered from withdrawal symptoms, almost all of whom (46 percent) rated the symptoms as severe.[76]

Unfortunately, for the 77 million Americans taking psychotropic drugs in 2020, there are no scientifically validated guidelines issued for how to prevent the common withdrawal symptoms. This is now becoming increasingly evident for all classes of psychiatric drugs.

As a consequence, patients *and their prescribing doctors* may be hesitant to initiate or follow through with discontinuing antidepressant use, even when patients have shown significant improvement. This reluctance can result in prolonged medication use that was neither desired nor intended, perpetuating the cycle of dependency.

New research indicates that long-term users of antidepressants are confronted with the increasingly likely prospect of being unable to quit after using them for a sustained period of time.

> A research team in New Zealand, led by Dr. Dee Mangin of McMaster University, conducted a clinical trial in which subjects who had been on an antidepressant for at least two years, with one-third of them taking the drugs for more than five years, had their dosages slowly reduced and found that some people's symptoms were so severe, they could not stop taking the drugs.[77]

The physical dependency that can develop with long-term use of psychotropic drugs poses significant challenges when attempting to discontinue them.

A study by psychiatrist Tom Stockmann et al., published in 2018 in the *International Journal of Risk & Safety in Medicine*, analyzed withdrawal symptoms reported on an internet forum and found that the average duration of withdrawal symptoms when discontinuing SSRI antidepressants was 90.5 weeks—roughly a year and nine months—and for SNRI antidepressants it was 50.8 weeks.[78]

Psychiatrists who are choosing to minimize the horrific withdrawal symptoms they are wholly aware of may be doing so in an effort to support their argument that antidepressants are necessary as the primary tool in their psychiatric armamentarium.

But the result is that the millions of Americans who rely on psychiatric drugs may be unaware of the potential for debilitating and long-lasting withdrawal effects, even when tapering off under medical supervision.

The ethical responsibility of the medical community is to prioritize patient health and safety above all else. This includes being transparent about the potential for withdrawal symptoms and dependency, offering comprehensive support for those looking to taper off medication, and exploring alternative treatments that address the root causes of mental health issues rather than just their symptoms.

It's vitally important to raise awareness about the potential risks and complexities associated with long-term medication use and withdrawal, as well as to provide individuals with the support and resources they need to make informed decisions about their mental health treatment journey.

While one might expect psychiatrists, who prescribe these medications, to be more cautious and circumspect when initiating treatment, the potential challenges of discontinuation are often not adequately discussed with patients up front. Consequently, patients may find themselves trapped in a cycle of long-term medication use, with little hope of being able to discontinue these "mood brighteners" without experiencing significant and often overwhelming withdrawal effects.

It is essential for patients to have access to comprehensive information about the potential challenges of long-term medication use and withdrawal, empowering them to make informed decisions about their mental health treatment journey. Yet, I fear that the psychiatric community will continue to promote the virtues of these medications as the best and most expedient solution to ameliorate depression and other mental health issues.

The decision by the United Kingdom to prioritize patient education about withdrawal risks also underscores the importance of ongoing monitoring and support for those taking psychotropic medications. For patients who choose to start these medications, it's crucial to have a clear plan in place for monitoring their effects, managing side effects, and eventually, if desired, safely discontinuing use under medical supervision.

Overall, the United Kingdom's approach could serve as a model for other countries, emphasizing the need for a more informed, cautious, and patient-centered approach to prescribing psychotropic medications. This could lead to a significant shift in how mental health care is delivered worldwide, with a greater focus on patient autonomy, informed consent, and the exploration of a wider range of treatment options.

In my many years of practice, I have encountered numerous clients who have tried to get off their meds on their own but found it too painful to overcome the side effects of withdrawal. Many of them go onto internet forums to better understand the struggles of others who have not been able to get off their medications only to give up, feeling discouraged by the daunting nature of their experiences. This is more common than most people are aware of. Many of them then come to me asking if I can help them to get off their medications. Often, I work collaboratively with their naturopath if they have one since traditional medical doctors are typically prone to prescribe additional medications to help their patients deal with the onerous side effects of being on the drugs they prescribed in the first place.

The widespread use and acceptance of antidepressants

underscore the need for greater awareness and discussion surrounding the potential risks and limitations of these medications. It's essential for patients to have access to comprehensive information about the potential challenges of long-term medication use and withdrawal, empowering them to make informed decisions about their mental health treatment journey. Yet, I fear that the psychiatric community will continue to promote the virtues of these medications as the best and most expedient solution to ameliorate depression and other mental health issues.

As we have seen, the initial promise of psychopharmacology was to correct supposed chemical imbalances in the brain. Over time, however, it's become clear that mental health disorders are far more complex, involving genetic, environmental, and psychological factors that cannot be fully addressed by medication alone.

This trend toward the "medicalization" of mental health is understandable when considering the accessibility and convenience of obtaining psychiatric drugs from primary care providers for conditions like depression or anxiety. Unlike therapy, which requires time and financial investment over multiple sessions to address underlying issues, taking a daily pill covered by health insurance is comparatively straightforward, often becoming a routine part of one's daily regimen along with one's daily vitamins.

But it is clear to me that if somebody is unhappy or anxious about what is going on in their life, it is essential to find out the larger context from where these so-called mood disorders originate. Psychotherapy provides an opportunity to utilize the human relationship, supported by trained therapists, to explore and resolve the underlying causative reasons for the problem state. So many mental health disorders originate from a fractured human connection. Supportive environments such as psychotherapy can be very effective in helping clients restore their connection with other humans. Creating a supportive environment through the psychotherapeutic alliance creates the space for clients to feel understood, validated and accepted, which can be transformative in itself. Through empathetic listening, validation of emotions, and collaborative exploration, therapists help clients navigate their challenges and develop healthier ways of relating to themselves and others. Moreover, simply taking a daily pill rarely if ever identifies the origin of the disconnection from others. Mutually supportive relationships are key to maintaining good mental and emotional balance.

Despite this, many are hoping that the continuing experimentation on people's brains will yield consistent positive healing results without the notorious, frequent side effects. So far, in real-world results, nothing much has changed. This scientific bias continues to minimize *the person in the environment*. One can rightly argue that it is the influence of one's environment that generates the onerous mental health disorders that continue to plague our collective mental health.

These considerations regarding psychotropic medications call for a balanced approach where medication is but one tool among many in the treatment of mental health issues, chosen with careful consideration of the individual's unique circumstances and their needs, and with a transparent discussion of potential outcomes.

It's crucial to recognize that medication alone does not address the complex interplay of biological, psychological and social factors contributing to mental health disorders. Comprehensive treatment approaches that incorporate psychotherapy, lifestyle modifications and social support remain essential for promoting holistic well-being and recovery.

CHAPTER 9

> **Drugs versus Cognitive Behavioral Therapy**
>
> In my experience, most individuals dealing with depression or anxiety first seek help from their primary care physician, who is frequently all too willing to prescribe psychopharmacological medications. These can stabilize the initial emotional upheaval, enabling patients to function in their daily lives. Yet, research from institutions like the University of Pennsylvania and Vanderbilt University has shown that sixteen months of cognitive behavioral therapy (CBT) not only proves to be more cost-effective, but also more effective in preventing depression recurrence compared to antidepressant medication alone.[79]
>
> The preference among many psychiatrists for combining CBT with medication highlights a broader understanding of treating mental health issues effectively. Nonetheless, the commitment required for ongoing CBT—spanning time, money, and energy—makes it a formidable path for many. Given these considerations, it's understandable why the prospect of taking a daily medication may appear more appealing to those suffering from emotional distress, despite the potential benefits of a more integrative approach to treatment.

This chapter discusses how neurobiological researchers have continued to seek answers and remedies to solve mental illness. The dominant pharmaceutical companies are largely responsible for this research and development of drugs that change the brain's neurotransmitters, along with marketing the newest versions of these drugs to consumers. While this research has been focused on introducing new versions of neurochemicals that change how the brain functions, there has also been increasing research in the field of genetics with the intent to possibly supersede these drugs' effectiveness. Billions of dollars have been allocated in pursuit of this endeavor.

In 2022, Dr. Thomas Insel, who was the director of the National Institute of Mental Health (NIMH) from 2002 through 2015, wrote a book reflecting on his experiences studying the neurobiology of emotion. He is a psychiatrist and neuroscientist by training. During his tenure as Director, he was instrumental in allocating $20 billion in federal money for research in neuroscience and genetics. This was a sharp turn in the focus for the NIMH from previous emphases on behavioral research in mental health. His book entitled *Healing: Our Path from Mental Illness to Mental Health*, describes the many failures of our mental health system, "including the ineffective delivery of care, the gutting of community health services and the reliance of police and jails for crisis services."[80] During his time at the NIMH, Insel championed basic research in genetics and neurobiology with the hope that this deeper inquiry would yield new awareness of long-held secrets into how the human brain is linked to mental illness and disease. This emphasis was largely about the neurobiology of disease.

There have been critics of Insel's oversight of the NIMH during those years. Dr. Allen Frances, a professor emeritus of psychiatry at Duke University School of Medicine in 2014 signaled that the NIMH was

> Betting the house on the long shot that neuroscience will come up with answers to help people with serious mental illness . . . (In 2022, he commented that) The end result of these last 30 years is an exciting intellectual adventure, one of the more fascinating pieces of science in our lifetimes but it hasn't helped a single patient.[81]

Ongoing research into the relationship between mental illness and genetics is continuing. Most of these researchers are continuing to seek answers that they hope genetic research will soon reveal, although none will predict how soon these answers will become available.

One might ask why his ongoing research is important. Even though the billions of dollars spent in genetic research have not yielded the hoped for results in the quest to relieve mental and emotional suffering, the belief that mental illness is fundamentally the result of biological neurochemical imbalances is yet another example of the deeply held bias in the medical community—the bias that ignores the ongoing impacts of the person in the environment.

Since pharmaceutical drugs have not adequately resolved mental illness, then research exploring possible genetic influences can perhaps find the holy grail of this issue. There are so many variables that must be considered when discussing mental health, including unsatisfying jobs and careers, income inequality, and a lack of community resources that can support families and individuals who are in crisis. When individuals cannot adequately live their day-to-day lives without fear of ending up on the streets, a psychiatric drug is not the answer. Moreover, too many Americans are barely managing to keep up with rising costs. To elaborate,

> Homelessness in the U.S. jumped 18.1% this year, hitting a record level, with the dramatic rise driven mostly by a lack of affordable housing as well as devastating natural disasters and a surge of migrants in some regions of the country, federal officials said Friday. More than 770,000 people were counted as homeless in federally required tallies taken across the country during a single night in January 2024, the U.S. Department of Housing and Urban Development said in its new report. The estimate likely undercounts the number of unhoused people given that it doesn't include people staying with friends or family because they don't have a place of their own. That jump comes on top of a 12% increase in 2023, which HUD blamed on soaring rents and the end of pandemic assistance. The 2023 increase also was driven by people experiencing homelessness for the first time.[82]

Whether it is the development of new psychiatric drugs or ongoing research into the possibility of discovering genetic links to mental illness, sufficient monthly income that pays for one's health insurance and necessary expenses may be the most important predictor of ongoing health and well-being. When people fall into feelings of despair due to an inability to clothe and house their families due to lack of income, more needs to be considered than mood brighteners. In the meantime, the emphasis on creating new psychiatric chemicals as medicines for people suffering from mental illness continues down the same path.

Before I close this chapter, I would like to quote a prescient warning from author Aldous Huxley:

> There will be in the next generation or so a pharmaceutical method of making people love their servitude and producing dictatorship without tears, so to speak, producing a kind of painless concentration camp for entire societies so that people will in fact have their liberties taken away from them but will rather enjoy it because they will be distracted from any desire to rebel by propaganda or brainwashing, or brainwashing enhanced by pharmacological methods. And this seems to be the final revolution.[83]

Huxley viewed this as a societal issue in which the wealthy and ruling classes would find more "covert" ways to control the working classes through pleasurable distractions. After all, if an individual is working for a large corporation preparing packages of products to deliver all over the country with hardly enough time during the day to eat a proper lunch and take restorative breaks, along with earning minimum wage, it is understandable that feelings of depressed mood and hopelessness will be the end result accompanied by chronic exhaustion. Since workers are often required to take random drug tests in order to keep their jobs, psychiatric drugs have provided them with a way to

CHAPTER 9

change their brains and pass the test. As I learned during my years studying Ericksonian hypnosis, trance states create a narrowing of focus and greater attentional absorption. Leave no doubt, psychopharmacological drugs are currently creating and promoting omnipresent altered states of shifting moods. Whether the intent is controlling the masses or creating ever more corporate profits for the pharmaceutical corporations, the end result is a trend that I find most alarming.

Yet even as more and more people get psychopharmacological treatment for mental health disorders, the number of adults on government disability due to these "brain-based disorders" has more than tripled since 1987. The number of children ending up disabled by psychiatric disorders has increased more than 30 fold during this period.

> In 1955, there were 355,000 adults in state and county mental hospitals with a psychiatric diagnosis. During the next three decades (the era of the first generation psychiatric drugs), the number of disabled mentally ill rose to 1.25 million. Prozac arrived on the market in 1988, and during the next 20 years, the number of disabled mentally ill grew to more than four million adults (in 2007.) Finally, the prescribing of psychiatric medications to children and adolescents took off during this period (1987 to 2007), and as this medical practice took hold, the number of youth in America receiving a government disability check because of a mental illness leapt from 16,200 in 1987 to 561,569 in 2007 (a 35-fold increase).[84]

This makes me wonder why such dramatic increases have occurred, and all of this was prepandemic. Is it the state of our world (that has always been chaotic), or could it be that the people choosing to take these drugs (recommended by their doctor) are changing their neurochemistry in ways that the developers of these drugs could never have anticipated? This appears to be the case—this psychiatric experiment continues as the use of these medications gains more and more traction worldwide.

Regarding the role of psychopharmacological treatments, it's a nuanced issue. On one hand, these medications can offer some relief and functionality to many individuals who would otherwise struggle to manage their conditions. On the other hand, the long-term effects of altering brain chemistry with these drugs are not fully understood, and for some, the side effects and withdrawal symptoms can be debilitating, potentially contributing to disability.

This same correlation is seen in country after country that has adopted widespread use of psychiatric drugs and in particular, the regular use of antidepressants. These countries have all seen sharp increases in impairment and disability due to mental disorders. What a cruel irony that these drugs are being promoted worldwide as the most effective way to address mental health issues that are related to depression and anxiety.

Chapter 10
Psychotherapy Outside the United States

People throughout the world are confronted with existential challenges every day, regardless of their nationality or ethnicity. Our basic needs must be accounted for regardless of our country of origin. In my experience, some of the most common issues that people (who are not psychotic) seek therapy for include marital and relationship challenges, anxiety, depression, dealing with loss, loneliness, poor self-esteem accompanied with negative inner self talk, post-traumatic stress disorder (PTSD), and trauma from all varieties of abuse and violence. If you have ever had to deal with any one of the above issues you know the seriousness of their impact on your mental and emotional life. While many of us may never think about how people in India or Brazil deal with these issues, the mental anguish, emotional pain and dysregulation feel just as terrible and disorienting no matter where in the world one lives. Yet the cultural values and attitudes of each country influence to a large degree the acceptance of psychotherapy to address mental health issues.

Throughout the United Kingdom, citizens seeking mental health treatment are afforded several options. Many people seeking the help of a psychotherapist get a referral from their family physician to get on the waiting list of the National Health Service (NHS). Typical wait times until a first appointment are frequently between six and twelve weeks, and the allowance is for up to twelve sessions. There is no cost to the client for the psychotherapy and counseling itself through the NHS, but those who are in a mental health crisis often choose to go the pharmacological route, at least while waiting for an initial appointment. Therapeutic treatment options include psychodynamic psychotherapy, which explores early family history; cognitive behavioral therapy (CBT), which emphasizes what a person is thinking; and marital and family therapies.

Should a prospective client choose to work with a privately employed therapist (that is, one who does not bill through the NHS), the cost varies from £120 to £180 (roughly $170 to $250) for a fifty-minute session.[85] From 2014 to 2019, I was invited to London each summer where I taught my Dynamic Energetic Healing™ model to psychotherapists from throughout the United Kingdom and Western Europe. While there were just a few who worked for the NHS, the rest of them were private practitioners managing to stay very busy. Their disclosures corroborated the fee schedule mentioned above.

In France, clients who go to their family physician for anxiety or depression can be referred to a qualified psychotherapist for a limited number of sessions. France's state health insurance will typically pay for most of the cost, often augmented by any private health insurance the client may have through their work. If someone wants to see a psychiatrist, the state health insurance will pay for a ten-minute appointment for medication at no charge to the client.[86] For those who wish to meet with a private practitioner, the cost ranges from €77 to €132 (roughly $90 to $160) per fifty-minute session.[87] The most widely recognized psychotherapy model in France is psychoanalytic or psychodynamic oriented.

In many ways, France and the United Kingdom are similar to how the United States deals with mental health needs. With the exception of Medicare and Medicaid, insurance coverage in the United States is primarily through one's employer. Those with no health insurance pay out of pocket for private practitioners or less expensive community mental health clinics, if they can get an appointment. These are Western countries with a well-established acceptance of the need for psychotherapy, but the situation is very different when one considers non-Western countries such as Mexico and Brazil.

While there is growing acceptance of psychotherapy in Mexico, those who live outside of the large urban centers are still suspicious of therapy. Mexico does not provide any government-subsidized therapy services, and as of 2019 private insurance companies were not covering psychotherapy. There are some hospitals, public institutions and even colleges that offer psychotherapy services for a minimal fee of approximately $2.50 per session, while private therapy clinics may charge upwards of $100 per session.[88] CBT tends to be the major therapeutic modality in Mexico.

Similar to Mexico, Brazil is accepting psychotherapy slowly, with many people preferring to confer with their community religious authorities such as their local parish priest. This is not surprising considering the strong Catholic and spiritual orientation of many of its citizens. Beyond that, psychoanalytic approaches are widely practiced in Brazil.

Psychotherapy in China is fairly new to its many citizens. Steven Vinay Gunther is a practicing psychotherapist in Shanghai. He has explained that acceptance of the need for psychotherapy has grown significantly over the last fifteen years, especially through the venue of popular workshops. Individual psychotherapy is just starting to gain some acceptance. Therapy workshops can be as small as twenty people or as large as hundreds of participants. These workshops vary in price, with daily fees of 1429 to 2858 yuan, the equivalent of $200 to $400 per day. For those who seek out private individual therapy, the costs can vary widely with fees from $30 per hour up to $400 for more experienced therapists.[89]

George Hu, PsyD and his wife are second-generation Chinese-Americans, but have always felt a desire to reconnect with their Chinese heritage. After working for five years as the program coordinator for outpatient services at a clinic in Fremont, California (doing both clinical and administrative work), Dr. Hu began using social media such as LinkedIn to find a new job in China. He eventually found a position and in 2016, he and his wife moved to Shanghai. He was offered the job of chief of mental health at Shanghai United Family Pudong Hospital. In the clinic, Hu mostly provides CBT and treats issues including anxiety and family problems. He reports that many Chinese people still consider mental illness shameful, yet the demand for psychological services is growing because the country is still being affected by globalization and the various cultural shifts that followed the Communist revolution years ago. "Almost everything psychologists know was developed and tested on Western populations from start to finish," he says, suggesting that even basic concepts such as attachment theory may not hold in China. "We need to back way up and start re-asking some of these questions that our field has thought to be fundamental. This is a fascinating place to be as these questions are being asked and answered."[90]

In India, the situation is completely different. Vandita Dubey is a clinical psychologist who acknowledges that even in the larger cities, there is still a stigma attached to seeking help from a psychotherapist. She says that in India there is no regulatory or licensing board requirements for psychotherapists and therefore "Many practitioners of therapy in India have no professional training or may have done a one-year distance program in counseling, at the most."[91] She says that because psychotherapy is so new and mostly met with skepticism, there is a mishmash of different approaches including CBT, psychoanalysis, and past-life regression coupled with hypnosis. Due to these various factors, many Indians looking for help with depression and anxiety assume they will be given medications to address their concerns. This is an excellent example of the challenges of importing Western psychological models in a country where there is still a great deal of emphasis on many different and revered ancient spiritual traditions. These religious and spiritual traditions continue to define the ethos of a multi-ethnic and religio-spiritual heritage that is centuries old. Insurance rarely covers psychotherapy so clients usually pay out of pocket for time with a therapist. Typical costs range from $7 to $45 per session.[92]

Overall, it has become clear to me that attitudes and direct access to psychotherapy are often very different from country to country. The examples I have provided in this chapter reflect a slow but growing acceptance that outside of the United States and Western European countries, Western psychotherapeutic services are gradually being adapted and beginning to gain greater international credibility.

With the rise of postpandemic virtual access along with growing telehealth medical and mental health services, many clinicians are now making themselves available to an international clientele. Prospective clients who live in countries where Western psychotherapy is either shunned or simply not widely available now have access to Western clinicians via services such as Zoom. For example, countries such as Australia, Colombia and Spain recognize psychologists licensed in the United States to provide services, providing the client's country does not have any additional training or licensing requirements.[93]

While the numbers of participating clinicians may be small for now, the influence of Western psychotherapy continues to grow, largely due to the increasing online presence of psychotherapists willing to reach beyond their local borders to embrace the real needs of interested clients far beyond their local jurisdiction. While there is no real substitute for in-person therapy, one has to admit that our universal interconnectedness is now reflecting the availability and influence of Western psychotherapy far beyond our local borders. This truly is shrinking our world and bringing us closer together.

Chapter 11

Cross-Cultural Psychotherapy Considerations

The many psychotherapy models that are currently embraced throughout the world do not always reflect the culture of the society where they are engaged. A central question to consider is whether the psychotherapy models that have originated in the Western Eurocentric experience can be adapted to non-Western cultures without substantially changing their underlying theoretical assumptions. While there are well over four hundred psychotherapy models throughout the world, it remains the case that just "a few theoretical orientations of Western origin among all seem to dominate psychotherapy practice."[94]

It is important to think about different societies and their use of psychotherapy as reflected by their unique cultures.

> Culture is shared learned behavior and meanings that are socially transmitted for purposes of adjustment and adaptation.... It is represented internally (i.e., cognitively, emotionally), by values, attitudes, beliefs, epistemologies, cosmologies, consciousness patterns, and notions of personhood.[95]

Because people from different cultures and traditions experience the world based on their own upbringing, social norms and societal expectations are significant determinates for what behavior is considered abnormal. Additionally, collective attitudes that often define a particular culture influence not only what is agreed upon as mental illness, but also the willingness to consider receiving psychotherapy.[96]

These cultural issues have a profound effect on various psychotherapy approaches. As an example, Avasthi claimed that

> the fact that diagnosing mental illnesses being substantially based on "listening" means the treatment process is inevitably affected by the interviewer's and client's communication skills, personalities, sociocultural beliefs, and interpretations.[97]

In an ideal world, psychotherapy models and treatment interventions would conform to the culture in which the client is being treated. This is unfortunately not always the case. Most researchers will agree that in today's world, it is the United States that predominates the profession of psychology. As a consequence, developing countries import Euro-American psychotherapy models that are not always in sync with the cultural values and customs of the importing country. This can be problematic when what is defined as normal or abnormal is embedded in Western psychotherapy models.

Diagnostic criteria and treatment interventions are often at odds with developing cultures and traditions. As one example, many Muslim people tend not to embrace Western psychotherapy approaches to mental health because the field of psychology is considered a secular science that does not include the spiritual dimension of the human experience. While this does not mean that Western psychotherapy would not be helpful to Muslims, in practice those who do sign up for psychotherapy tend to be only those who agree with its underlying values and techniques.

Listening to and dialoging with a psychotherapist is part of a verbally interactive approach to addressing mental health issues. But what about those prospective clients who live in cultures where people tend to be more internalized and less verbal as a cultural orientation? Uzoka noted that

> in Africa, where the traditional healer discretely collects information on the patient's background from the patient's family, communicates with "higher forces" over long silences during therapy, and ultimately is the one who carries the burden of verbalization and assumes an active role, emphasis on the communicativeness of the patient may hinder therapy's effectiveness.[98]

Moreover, we must consider the emphasis on individualism that is pervasive in Euro-American psychotherapies. Author Melody Beattie wrote a seminal book on this topic in 1986 called *Codependent No More: How to Stop Controlling Others and Start Caring for Yourself*. Codependency has become part of the fabric of American psychotherapy as an important theme, as clients are directed to focus on their own needs before orienting to the needs of others. (This can also be referred to as self-care.) Rather than regularly deferring to others, at the risk of completely losing oneself in a relationship, the literature on codependency continues to remind readers about the importance to orient to their own needs first.[99] Kumaraswamy spoke to this issue in regard to the Malay culture:

> For example, he claimed that a certain dependence on parents is normal in Malay culture and efforts by a mental health professional to have the client gain independence in Western standards would bring the client more harm than good.[100]

While this may make sense when we consider a non-Western country such as Malaysia, it continues to be made clear by researchers that even in the United States, people who come from non-white origins and those who do not identify with mainstream American culture report that quite often, their own psychological needs are not being addressed by Western psychotherapy approaches.

> According to a meta-analysis across 65 studies conducted by Smith, Rodriquez, and Bernal (2011), as the number of cultural adaptation elements increases so does the effectiveness of the treatment.[101]

What I find so interesting is how cross-cultural research continues to bear out how mental health professionals in various countries around the world acknowledge how important it is to include "traditional healers" in their treatment protocols. This makes perfect sense, since traditional healers and shamans worldwide play an influential role in the maintenance of cohesive communities. If Western-based psychotherapy is to be helpful beyond its Western context, including community shamans as part of the treatment team is an important consideration.

As every effective therapist knows, maintaining rapport with clients is one of the most important foundations for successful outcomes. If clients with a non-Western worldview are told that their shamans are part of their treatment team, consistently better mental health outcomes are likely to ensue. This is an important acknowledgment that traditional healing models (which are many thousands of years old) still play an important role in maintaining the health and well-being of the local citizenry. Integrating contemporary research-based psychological knowledge with centuries-old traditional healing approaches could be the genesis of taking the best practices of both worldviews. It just may be the case that this integration will engender more effective and widespread acceptance of Western psychotherapy throughout the world.

With all the upheaval and collective trauma borne of warfare, income inequality and mass migrations due to changing climate and political unrest, effective and approachable mental health approaches are essential. Truly considering the multicultural values and needs of any non-Western culture within the world of psychotherapy strikes me as a more realistic and balanced approach to supporting prospective clients within the larger psychotherapy context.

The United States is truly a multicultural melting pot with immigrants from throughout the world. The same may be said of the United Kingdom as well as other Western countries. With growing awareness of the need for a more integrative psychotherapy approach, more people will become available and willing to enter into a deep and emotionally intimate therapeutic relationship in order to restore their healthy mental and emotional balance.

PART 2:

INTEGRATING SHAMANIC STRATEGIES IN DYNAMIC ENERGETIC HEALING™

Chapter 12
Sacred Imagination, Psychotherapy and the Living Earth

We live in a multidimensional reality. Without getting into the propositions suggested by quantum physicists, we can say that humans inhabit many different dimensions. Poets and fiction writers know this. Scientists researching different areas of knowledge, such as oceanography and astronomy, know this. Indigenous societies have known this for thousands of years. When mystics try to relate their unusual experiences of being spiritually moved by their unique interior perceptions, many people become inspired and, at the same time, wonder what these unusual life-changing experiences are all about.

Traditional Newtonian and quantum physicists relate to our expanding universe in ways that most of us have difficulty understanding. Sending spacecraft like the James Webb telescope a million miles into deep space requires the skill set of astrophysicists who can calculate complex mathematical formulae that most of us have a hard time relating to.

Physicists spend their time dealing with the nature and properties of matter and energy: light, gravity, radiation, magnetic fields and how the structure of atoms impacts our planet and other celestial bodies. Many nonphysicists find all of this to be abstract and difficult to appreciate and understand. Many of us do not understand the language of physics, but this does not diminish the impact of physics in our daily lives.

Similarly, many anthropologists are flummoxed by how indigenous peoples accumulated their knowledge of the healing capabilities of native plants. Most assume it was through trial and error over long periods of time. Yet if you were to ask native people about how their *vegetalistas*, whose specialty is plant medicines, acquire their remarkable knowledge, they would all tell you the same thing: their personal and cultural knowledge of how plants provide healing derives from nonordinary encounters with the numinous. These experiences include spontaneous visions, dreams and direct communications from the plants themselves.

Honoring the spirit of tobacco

> What is especially striking is that the medicinal uses for plants that nonindustrial people were taught during these experiences correspond nearly perfectly to the medicinal actions of the plants that have been identified through science.[102]

This type of knowledge acquisition is unfamiliar to most of us in the West. When we dream, we might acknowledge to ourselves how strange and interesting a particular dream symbol is, and we might even bring our dream to a Jungian psychotherapist trained in dream analysis. We might characterize a high production dream as a curiosity and wonder about it as it slowly fades from our awareness. This is because modern industrialized people typically do not value dreams except as inchoate stirrings from our unconscious.

In our tech-oriented, information-based society, we typically have too many emails and texts to deal with to give our dreams their due. We have become so preoccupied by information overload that our interior life has largely become marginalized, if not atrophied.

The core issue here is that differing epistemologies that discuss how we know and make sense of our relationship to reality tend to be baked into our cultural zeitgeist. The Eurocentric operating epistemology is rational-scientific; everything can be separated and analyzed. But preindustrial indigenous orientations to our world and the universe assert that *there is an underlying unifying force that is sacred and permeates all things.* This includes plants and animals, including ourselves, as we are just another aspect of the sacred. Thus, when we embrace this epistemology, we are able to communicate with all living things.

These are two very different understandings of how we are related to the universe and how we are able to interact with the world. The University of Sheffield in the United Kingdom describes this in the following way:

> Epistemology is the **theory of knowledge.** It is concerned with the mind's relation to reality. What is it

for this relation to be one of knowledge? Do we know things? And if we do, how and when do we know things? These questions, and so the field of epistemology, is as old as philosophy itself. Answering these questions requires considering the relationship between knowledge, truth, belief, reason, evidence and reliability. It requires considering the different psychological **routes to knowledge,** including different processes of reasoning—logical and scientific—introspection, perception, memory, testimony and intuition.[103]

The Eurocentric rational-analytic biases ascribe to the preindustrial indigenous orientations labels that include

> unscientific, irrational, unreasoning, or illogical. Such thoughts and perceptions, it is assumed, have less value, are based on improper assumptions about the nature of reality, and are therefore something to be discounted, dismissed, degraded.[104]

Let's return to talk about dreaming for a moment. What do you make of your dreams? Have you ever awakened from an engaging and high production dream, layered with complexity and images that rivet your attention, only to find that within minutes the memories of your dream have vanished like a plume of smoke? Have you ever wondered why and how you dream in technicolor with figures and inner voices that surprise you as fantastical scenarios unfold?

Dreaming is one of the most mysterious functions of our brain. Freud characterized dreams as the royal road to the unconscious, and Jung gave considerable importance to the processing and analyzing of the dream figures and archetypal symbols in dreams as the way out of neurosis. Yet for many psychotherapists who use cognitive behavioral therapy (CBT), as well as the psychiatric community, the meandering and elusive nature of the dreaming unconscious is largely irrelevant. Perhaps for the philosophical materialist all sources of inner wisdom, information, advice, or visions—all perceived entities, voices, and images—are simply mental constructions, the expressions of neuronal fireworks at that, and probably deranged fireworks at that.[105]

However, throughout the centuries, humans have deeply pondered the meaning of our dreaming process. As behaviorism began to lose its influence, a client's interior subjective experience reemerged as valid and valuable in the eyes of psychotherapists. Troublesome outer behaviors can be scientifically measured and extinguished through operant or Skinnerian conditioning (at least in theory for the behaviorist camp), but psychotherapists began anew to appreciate how important the inner world of clients is for addressing and transforming persistent traumatic residue while honoring the client's personal experience.

There are traditions and intentional practices of lucid dreaming throughout the world wherein the dreamer learns how to keep a part of his or her egoic consciousness present through auto-suggestion just before falling asleep. This is a way to *consciously* connect to and enter into one's dreams. Of course, this is understood as taking place within the mysterious and fertile unconscious mind, at least as defined by Western psychology going back to Freud.

I assert that all of us are *dreaming* all the time, often imagining having a conversation yet to be experienced (i.e., mental rehearsal), or fantasizing about what to make for dinner or what foreign country to travel to for our next vacation. This qualifies as dreaming while awake, as these internal and often unconscious preoccupations take us away from being completely present to our ongoing experience. Various meditation practices are designed to mitigate this ongoing dreaming process so we can be more present to ourselves, moment to moment, in order to live our lives more intentionally. Yet as we internally focus on these imagined scenarios, we are choosing to participate in an aspect of being human that is integral to who we are and how we negotiate our day-to-day reality. When we read fiction and become immersed in a fictional story, we step into a dreaming state that pulls up deep into an imaginary human created universe.

> "We read a few words at the beginning of the book or the particular story, and suddenly we find ourselves seeing not words on a page but a train moving through Russia, an old Italian crying, or a farmhouse battered by rain." We enter a dreamworld, we forget ourselves, our conscious mind sleeps.[106]

People who enjoy getting lost and immersed in good fiction have many different genres to choose from. These include mystery, western, romance, horror, fantasy and science fiction, among many others. Reading fiction exercises and expands the imagination. For example,

> Books such as *The Lord of the Rings* seem so real, the dreaming so like personal dreaming, the meanings and struggles so basic to what it means to be human, that millions of people find something in it. It becomes great fiction.[107]

This predisposition for how we operate in the world is an expression of our survival-based, ordinary reality internal operating system that, for the most part, runs on autopilot. This is a universal human propensity. We also have the ability to consciously partner with this uniquely human capability and more deliberately bring it into our daily life, nurturing the vision that is driven by our passion. As Albert Einstein once said, "Imagination is everything. It is the preview of life's coming attractions."[108] This reflects our uniquely human imaginative faculty that is our creative power. It fosters innovation, originality and creative vision.

A powerful form of imagination is visualization, especially that which arises from deliberate exercises in guided imagery. It has been noted that for those who use guided imagery, mood-enhancing neurotransmitters such as serotonin are increased, producing pervasive feelings of well-being. This is also one of the positive consequences of the shamanic journey, since most people who journey describe vivid imagery of hidden realms in *nonordinary reality* (NOR) rich with detail that continues to resonate within for many hours and even days following the journey. When done on a regular basis, one is able to stay upbeat and feel happy with deep feelings of gratitude and awe.

There continues to be excellent ongoing research that supports the healing impacts of imagery. Elite athletes repeatedly use imagery via mental rehearsal prior to their events with great success. Psychotherapist Belleruth Naparstek has written extensively about the power of imagery. She has discovered over time that clients with significant post-traumatic stress disorder (PTSD) benefit enormously from daily imagery exercises as part of their healing and recovery.

> In fact, the imagery is taken in primarily through the right hemisphere, by way of primitive, sensory, and emotion-based channels in the brain and nervous system, using our capacity for sensing, perceiving, feeling, and apprehending rather than our left-brain thinking, judging, analyzing, and deciding.[109]

Long-term research has corroborated that using imagery as a psychotherapeutic strategy for ameliorating the effects of PTSD and trauma facilitates healing. It is multilayered and cumulatively impacts the dysregulated nervous systems of clients who have been traumatized. Typically, the healing effects of guided imagery require repetitive listening over time. This can be done in the therapist's office and then in the privacy of one's home. Once recorded, a customized guided visualization can be used as a self-care and self-healing strategy. There are also many guided visualizations available online now for specific maladies.

> Imagery has been found to reduce anxiety and depression; lower blood pressure; reduce cholesterol and lipid peroxides; speed up healing from cuts, fractures, and burns; cut blood loss and length of hospital stay in surgery patients; beef up short-term immune function; reduce pain from arthritis and fibromyalgia.[110]

It is significant that visualization and imagery exercises elicit strong emotions through multiple channels of perception, much like a shamanic journey. As one becomes increasingly absorbed in the depth and complexity of a shamanic journey, many people become deeply emotional and often report that their heart opens in an unanticipated way. This is both from the *power* being absorbed from one's compassionate spirits and the way the imagery is impacting one's nervous system.

Where do our new ideas and possibilities come from? How is it that by staying present with a powerful inner vision layered with emotional nuance we can bring this imaginative visioning into concrete manifestation? It is the nexus between the unfathomable mystery of creation and the human mind. *Our awareness and perception of Spirit and the Divine are essentially mediated through the human imagination.*

How does shamanism fit into this schema and how is it relevant to the psychotherapy context? Shamanism can be understood as the path to becoming proficient in intentionally accessing our *sacred imagination*. It is a way of being and of experiencing this awe and wonder through disciplined practice, negotiating and discovering ancient means of ecstatically interacting with the universe. This is in counterpoint to the role that socialization imposes on us to conform to the prevailing cultural belief system and to the doctrine that is reinforced in our various religious traditions. Believing in something and choosing to internalize church doctrine on faith is something else altogether.

Chapter 12

> Cultural conditioning is like bad software. Over and over it's diddled with so that it can just run on the next attempt! But there is cultural hardware, and it's that cultural hardware—otherwise known as authentic being—that we are propelled toward by the example of the shaman ... Shamanism therefore is a call to authenticity.[111]

Shamanism can be described not only as an animistic orientation to life, but as a series of time-tested techniques that facilitate the connection to spiritual beings through the intentional shamanic visionary journey. These journeys are accomplished through the shifting of one's consciousness in order to enter into the dreamlike NOR, where one learns to cultivate ongoing relationships with compassionate spirits in order to stay *power-filled* with concentrated life force. This is nourishment par excellence. It is through our intentional and cultivated imaginative visioning that the sacred shamanic journey populated by compassionate spirits unfolds. Other than what is known as *active imagination* through the efforts of Carl Gustav Jung, I am unaware of a Western psychotherapy model that accesses this *other reality* as the template from which profound healing results.

The suffering borne by human beings who mostly live in a conditioned reality orientation needs more than active listening by an attentive therapist. As we cultivate relationships with the spiritual beings in NOR, who are often regarded as helping and compassionate spirits, we discover that they instruct, protect and guide us. In so many ways, they also bless our everyday experience. This experience may sound fantastical and wishful thinking, yet these practices are reported to be over 50,000 years old by anthropological research and artifacts. They are innate to our species, as they are universally shared human traits developed by early indigenous peoples who had no technology and thus required other means to enhance their survivability.

Shamans discovered that their connection to personal helping spirits provided effective ways of healing and helping their communities. While traditional shamans provide numerous services, including divination, healing of the mind and body, herbal remedies and the removal of negative energies acquired from others, contemporary people who have learned how to apply these methods as healthcare advocates and healers are best described as *shamanic practitioners*. Whether shaman or shamanic practitioner, *the healing realm where the work is done is that of the soul.* While it may be said that I am servicing my clients as my own psychotherapeutic community, it would be inappropriate to label myself a shaman since I have not grown up in an indigenous community embedded in a multi-generational tradition of sacred ceremonies and rituals.

Anthropologist Dr. Michael Harner is widely regarded as being responsible for a revival of shamanic practices in the West. He began teaching students and close friends basic shamanic journey techniques when he was a professor of anthropology in the 1970s. At the time, he could not have imagined the widespread embrace of what he came to describe as *core shamanic practices*. Through his continuing research and ongoing personal interactions with indigenous shamans throughout the world, he discovered that roughly 90 percent of indigenous shamanic practices worldwide are based on a solid core of key elements among nearly all indigenous cultures. These common features have been practiced throughout the world, from Siberia to North and South America as well as throughout Western Europe, Asia, Africa and Australia. In 1980, Harner's seminal book *The Way of the Shaman* was published.[112] This followed his extensive fieldwork with two indigenous communities in the 1950s in South America (the Jivaro and Conibo people). During his fieldwork, he was invited to participate in their ceremonies. While he was deeply invested in the demands and responsibilities of academia, his experiences with these tribes disassembled his Western biases about the nature of reality. He learned that there are other dimensions that can be accessed that provide profound healing and revelatory experiences. As anthropologists Jeremy Narby and Frances Huxley have remarked,

> Shamanism is grounded in self and subjectivity while science has a method that seeks to rise above the researcher's subjective self. In many ways shamanism is an autology, or the study of self, while science is a heterology, the study of others.[113]

Throughout human history, the shaman has been regarded as the master dreamer. The shaman learns how to intentionally dissociate an aspect of his or her consciousness in order to enter into another dimension of reality, now often called NOR. While in this shamanic dimension, the shaman is able to maintain conscious awareness and stay focused on specific tasks while at the same time interacting with beings who inhabit this nonordinary realm. It is lucid dreaming par excellence—intentional, unscripted and intrepid as process unfolds. Mythologist Joseph Campbell speaks to this shamanic dreaming process by alluding to the hero's journey.

> The dreamer is a distinguished operatic artist, and, like all who have elected to follow, not the safely marked general highways of the day, but the adventure of the special, dimly audible call that comes to those whose ears are open within as well as without, she has had to make her way alone, through difficulties not commonly encountered.[114]

The shaman negotiates this realm through focused, disciplined intention and expands his or her consciousness through direct revelation (unmediated by others), interacting with extraordinary beings called compassionate spirits. These beings are engaging, wise and filled with the *power* to heal. At times it strikes me as surprising and mysterious that these spirits are always available and willing to help. *It is a profound mystery that you and I can choose to participate in.*

Through my engagement in NOR, I am able to support my clients in overcoming old and persistent challenges that conventional psychotherapy has been unable to sufficiently address. The dream world and the spirit world merge as the cognitive distinctions between them collapse. Shamanic journeying is a subjective experiential exploration of the numinous. It is available to everyone—it is available to you. Michael Pollen reflects on this after experiencing his own nonordinary experiences.

> This I think, is the great value of exploring nonordinary states of consciousness: the light they reflect back on the ordinary ones, which no longer seem so transparent or so ordinary. To realize, as William James concluded, that normal waking consciousness is but one of many potential forms of consciousness—ways of perceiving or constructing the world—separated from it by merely the "filmiest of screens," is to recognize our account of reality, whether inward or outward, is incomplete at best.[115]

In these transpersonal realms, the shaman participates in *visionary experiences*. His or her cultivated relationships with and connections to compassionate spirits are accompanied by the experience of *power*. This *power* is generated from the shaman's forged connection to his or her compassionate spirits. It provides for *power-filled* transformation and healing for the shaman and the person who the shaman is journeying for. The shaman absorbs this concentrated *power* through his or her phenomenological connection to compassionate spirits.

When I journey, the experience is often like getting plugged into an electrical power socket of high voltage life-force energy. I become significantly energized, so much so that I have learned I dare not journey in the evenings as I will be unable to sleep due to the vibrating *power* and energy surging through me. Mythologist

Chapter 12

Joseph Campbell speaks to this through the archetypal lens of the hero's journey.

> A hero ventures forth from the world of common day into a region of supernatural wonder: fabulous forces are there encountered and a decisive victory is won: the hero comes back from this mysterious adventure with the power to bestow boons on his fellow man.[116]

Mercea Eliade (the eminent historian of religion and philosopher, in his seminal book published in 1951, *Shamanism: Archaic Techniques of Ecstasy*) describes the shaman as "the great master of ecstasy."[117] This is because the universal energy and *power* coursing through the shaman is so pure and concentrated that it is often experienced ecstatically by the shaman in their journeys and ongoing relationship with their compassionate spirits.

I have been using the term "shamanic journey," but what does this mean and what is the mechanism through which these journeys take place? The vehicle through which the shaman does her work is universally identified as percussive or sonic drive. This is generated through rhythmic and mesmerizing drumming, clicking of sticks or rattling (sometimes singing or ecstatic dancing is used). Initially, Harner thought that it was only through psychotropic plants used in shamanic cultures (such as ayahuasca, a recipe of a tropical vine and bark, or psilocybin, a species of mushroom) that the visionary experience was generated. It later became clear to him through his research that this was not the case at all.

> It was becoming obvious to me that throughout the world, percussion sound, most notably by drumming, was far more widely used than psychedelics by indigenous shamans. It was difficult to accept the possibility that the shamanic use of the drum could profoundly alter one's state of consciousness…. Gradually, my cross cultural reading in shamanism forced me to

conclude that shamans in most of the world's cultures did not ingest or use psychotropic plants in order to change consciousness.[118]

Harner continued his research on how shamans were able to shift their consciousness in order to initiate the visionary journey experience without psychotropic plants. He determined through research and personal experimentation that a consistent and monotonous beat between 205 and 220 times a minute was the proper range of repetitive drumming.

> This conclusion was a major personal discovery, for it meant shamanic spiritual experiences could no longer be dismissed as simply due to the effects of drugs. Indeed, the implications were enormous, as they suggested that drums and drugs were different doorways to the same spiritual realms.[119]

As he continued his research, Harner discovered that the Sami ("Lapp") people of northern Scandinavia call the drum literally "a thing out of which pictures come" (gavadas).[120] He began to call the altered state generated by the "auditory driving" the *shamanic state of consciousness*. As his excitement grew, he continued to research the mechanism of drumming for creating the shamanic state of consciousness. He came across a publication written by a psychiatrist, Wolfgang Jilek,

> who had studied the therapeutic effects of the shamanistic Spirit Dances of the Salish Indian people of British Columbia and Washington. He and a colleague found that the Salish deerskin drums were predominantly beaten four to seven times per second during shamanistic initiation procedures. He noted that this was in the theta-wave EEG frequency range, a range that "is expected to be most effective in the production of trance states. This was faster than the

tempo range I had found effective for journeying, but both practices shared a loud, monotonous beat."[121]

The shaman learns how to intentionally dissociate an aspect of herself and, through unwavering intent accompanied by her helping spirits, is directed to a particular locale in the nonordinary worlds. One might say it is applied consciousness alchemically derived through focused intention. In many ways this is truly an archetypal journey into the nonordinary realms where everything is alive, magical and available to interact with. To reiterate, this is a realm of consciousness where everything is permeated with spirit—*it is the realm of soul*. Navigating this realm requires letting go of a conventional-reality orientation that we are accustomed to operating in and that most people believe is all there is. One must be prepared to suspend one's disbelief and allow process to unfold without the usual censoring and ongoing critiquing by our analytic thinking mind. Core shamanic methods connect the shaman or shamanic practitioner to deep archetypal experiences that are both ancient and filled with *power*. When this infusion of healing energy is conveyed or transferred from the shamanic practitioner to the client, profound psychotherapeutic change occurs and consciousness is transformed.

Cross-culturally, over 90 percent of shamanic indigenous practices have demonstrated that these spiritual realms reside within three arenas: the lower world, this middle world that we live in and the upper world. This is called the shamanic tripartite universe. The shamanic practitioner through the aid of percussive drive shifts her consciousness so that she creates a very unique and particular trance state. This shift enables her to remain consciously focused and engaged throughout her interactions with compassionate spirits who occupy these realms.

The shamanic journey is an apt name for the shaman's experience as it reflects an ongoing process that unfolds moment by moment. This is in many ways analogous to how Joseph Campbell describes the archetypal hero's journey. It is all about shifting and transforming one's consciousness, enabling the journeyer to explore new spiritual worlds and interact with the beings who occupy these realms. This is the spiritual aspect of self that every one of us possesses. It is an integral part of our neurology and our humanity. This state of intentionally generated trance is an alteration of consciousness wherein one narrows one's attention to exclude other thoughts and stimuli in order to focus on the particular journey experience as it ecstatically unfolds. The drumming or rattling is the driving engine that keeps the journeyer pressing ever forward. There are times when the journeyer experiences herself merging with the consciousness of a power animal or anthropomorphic teacher, briefly embodying the compassionate spirit with its unusual qualities. Shamanic teacher Tom Cowan describes it this way:

> The shaman is a master of escaping the mind-body matrix that characterizes ordinary consciousness and entering the shamanic or nonordinary states of consciousness. In this dreamlike state the imaginal realm reshapes itself, creating a placeless, timeless field in which the shaman can participate in the consciousness of other creatures.... Journeying reshapes the imaginal realm, and consciousness becomes geographied; it becomes the spirit world in which the shaman will travel.... Once the shaman's consciousness has shifted, its inner structure has reshaped itself, and the shaman participates in the consciousness of another animal, plant, or object.[122]

Many years ago, I participated in a fire walking ceremony. While the oak logs in the center of the circle burned down into glowing hot coals, our group repeatedly chanted in a particular way for upward of two hours. During this time, I was dealing with my fears and doubts about walking barefoot across a 30-foot diameter circle of glowing hot coals. When the time came for me to walk across them, I was both uncertain and confident that I could do this without getting my feet burned. I remained determined and focused as I prepared to walk across the glowing hot coals. I succeeded and felt relieved and proud of myself, since there were several people in our group who ended up with painful burns under their feet and toes. With sufficient intention, focus and collective support for successfully negotiating this challenge, I had generated a particular state of trance enabling me to accomplish my intended task. Unlike the very real risks of walking barefoot over hot burning coals, I have never had any negative experiences during my shamanic journeys into the nonordinary realms.

On a purely practical level, it would be prudent to ask how I integrate these visionary and transpersonal practices into a Western-based psychotherapy setting. It is a fair and important question. In fact, it is the basic thesis of this book. Just because the origins of these shamanic strategies predate Freud (and our Western approach to contextualize mental and emotional problems into a neatly tied box within which the unconscious mind pulsates) and are, in fact, many thousands of years old, does not imply that they are obsolete. To the contrary, these approaches are just as effective now as they have been for millennia. This is because journeying into these dimensions is a natural, time-tested human ability and inclination.

I am not suggesting that Western psychotherapy's embrace of the role of the unconscious mind (as the underlying foundation for prolonged neurosis including PTSD) is necessarily dubious. Moreover, I understand this as an intellectual construct based on a theory that a part of us remains hidden but nonetheless operative (often referred to as that which lies below the tip of the iceberg). I do not intend to argue the value or validity of trying to access the unconscious mind as I too have been trained to relate it to the source of our dreams, often as repressed trauma and "unfulfilled wishes and desires." Western psychotherapy has been largely about mining the contents of this mysterious aspect of ourselves, a deeply hidden interior universe that acts on us, most often without our consent or awareness. While dreams that emanate from the depths of our unconscious *happen to us*, predominately without our consent, shamanic journeying occurs when we decide to take a particular action, and with focused intention, initiate the incursion into the nonordinary realms.

While much has been learned about the value of exploring the unconscious over the last 120 plus years since Freud began writing about this phenomenon, historically speaking, it pales in comparison to the many thousands of years during which shamans have been interacting with the spiritual components of the living Earth and the many numinous realms. Most therapists who have been trained in graduate programs accept this construct of the unconscious mind as the essential underlying inner mechanism from which many if not most of our persistent problems originate. Strictly speaking though, this is a relatively new and emerging theory of attempting to heal the emotional and psychological pain that impacts human lives. Nevertheless, Western psychology and psychiatry make every attempt to prove its value through evidence-based therapies that rely on replicative studies in order to prove its efficacy. Yet because of its relatively nascent emergence since Freud in the early twentieth century, it is actually quite easy to question its efficacy in helping millions of people make significant changes to their dysphoric states and moods.

> As long as we stay ensnared in hoary dualistic conceptions that oppose mind or spirit to body, there is no hope for a unified view or for a unified approach to therapy. The medical establishment will insist that only science can know. But that is not a view supportable by science; it is not a scientific view; it is an ideology.[123]

Dynamic Energetic Healing™ (DEH) stands out among other energy psychology models because of its emphasis on

CHAPTER 12

the psychospiritual component of the human experience, and on how spiritual resources are solicited and integrated into the transformative change process that occurs with clients. *What exactly are spiritual resources?* If you ask ten spiritually sensitive people it's likely you will receive ten different explanations. For the Tibetan Buddhist, spiritual resources may be accessed through becoming identified with a specific deity through meditation. For a Christian, spiritual resources are frequently made available through one's faith in and commitment to the loving heart of Jesus Christ through prayer. For indigenous peoples and shamanic communities, spiritual resources are more literally embedded in all aspects of life on this living Earth, because those with this particular worldview not just believe but personally experience that everything is filled with and embodies the energy and *power* of Spirit.

I refer to myself as a shamanic practitioner because I have developed the skill set and willingness to move into the unknown dimensions of NOR, enabling me to recruit the help of compassionate spirits with whom I've cultivated relationships over many years. This *other reality* can only be accessed when one has the willingness and the courage to disassociate from our consensus reality beliefs. One must be available to the unpredictable and train oneself to be comfortable and flexible working within the unknown as each shamanic journey unfolds. It is within these nonordinary forays that spiritual resources become accessible.

Many decades ago when I was reading Carlos Castaneda's books, I was struck by what Carlos's teacher Don Juan explained to Carlos about consensus reality:

> Our normal expectations about reality are created by a social consensus. We are taught how to see and understand the world. The trick of socialization is to convince us that the descriptions we agree upon define the limits of the real world. What we call

> reality is only one way of seeing the world, a way that is supported by social consensus.[124]

For Don Juan, reality is only a description that the majority chooses to agree upon. This suggests that reality is much more fluid than most of us choose to consider. Another way to frame this is from Jungian psychologist Dr. Arnold Mindell, who developed process-oriented psychology and with whom I studied for ten years. He has remarked that our everyday reality is what most of us have unconsciously agreed is the only way we humans negotiate the world. Because most people don't question the epistemological underpinnings of the dominant culture, our reality orientation tends to be narrowly focused, one of the hallmarks of trance. "Consensus reality which reflects ordinary reality is the most seductive of all trances."[125]

From my years of training in and understanding hypnosis, anything that is repeated over and over without an opportunity to challenge or dispute *becomes our reality*—it becomes embedded into our default cognitive operating system. Every therapist who orients to a psychodynamic model knows the power of family systems to impart and imprint certain beliefs, roles and values through repetition and reinforcement over time. After centuries of Western colonization supported by a Eurocentric religious foundation, most people do not question consensus reality, and thus our mental health system is determined and restricted by this collective unchallenged agreement.

Subtle energies are always with us. What I refer to as *subtle energy* is what indigenous peoples may describe as *power* or *medicine*. This is the world I inhabit and share with my clients. How do I work with clients who are stuck in the consensus reality trance? It's really not a problem. Many new clients are referred to me from a friend of theirs who has worked with me in the past or may currently be working with me. These new clients come in with a positive expectancy of excellent therapeutic outcomes, and they are immediately more open to this unconventional approach. If after meeting me and hearing about my therapeutic approach in more detail they decide they would prefer to work with someone conducting a traditional talk therapy experience, I have colleagues that I can refer them to.

I am introducing new clients to a psychotherapeutic paradigm that includes energy psychology and kinesiological muscle testing as the underlying therapeutic framework. Over time, clients become increasingly available to consider a more fluid self-identity that is not necessarily wedded to the Western-based belief systems that they have come in with. Once clients are comfortable with the muscle testing/energy checking and accessing their *energy body*, shamanic interventions are easily assimilated.

The biofield component of the energy body

A Foot in Both Worlds

Clients are surprised at how quickly positive changes occur, even as it takes some time for their consensus reality belief system to loosen its grip so that prior expectations of simply talking out problems begin to adjust and shift. At a certain point in the DEH therapy process, clients become open to and available to their own hero's journey to healing.

CHAPTER 13
FRONTAL OCCIPITAL HOLDING AS THE VEHICLE FOR SHAMANIC HEALING

Introducing a client to work in a therapeutic environment accessing subtle energies using an energy psychology paradigm is both challenging and rewarding. It is important to note that clients who come in for psychotherapy are not expecting shamanic healing with rattling, drumming and ceremonies. Additionally, many need to be educated about the strategies that are implemented when using an energy-based approach. I no longer need to rattle or beat a drum in order to access and bring forth the *power* of my compassionate spirit helpers to help my clients heal. I use a technique called frontal occipital holding.

While the client is sitting in a chair, I stand by their side and make gentle contact with their forehead with one hand and the back of their head with my other hand. (For a more detailed description, see my first book: *Dynamic Energetic Healing: Integrating Core Shamanic Practices with Energy Psychology Applications and Processwork Principles*.) I then direct the client to think about and reflect upon the issue we are addressing. Meanwhile, I quietly recite to myself an invocation to call on the Great Spirit for help. I ask for the most loving, healing, powerful, benevolent energies or compassionate spirits to come in me and through me to help this client achieve their healing results. I open myself up to anything that comes into my awareness, and within seconds, images and impressions begin to reveal themselves as a detailed, compressed-time shamanic journey unfolds before my inner vision.

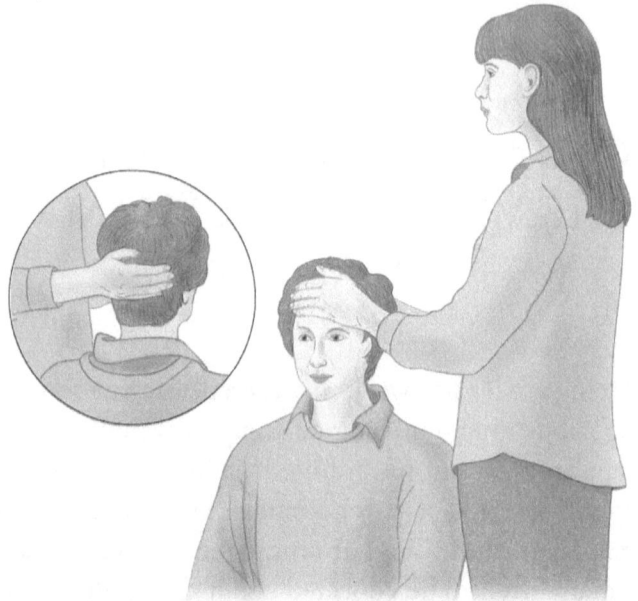

Hand positioning for frontal occipital holding

Perhaps the best way to describe my internal experience is to say that I consciously enter the shamanic dreamtime experience as I follow the exploits of my helping and compassionate spirits doing their healing. This is truly participating in what the ancients referred to as the Great Mystery. Typically, this procedure takes two to three minutes, as I internally observe one or more of my helping spirits perform their healing interventions in nonordinary reality (NOR). For example, they may remove a dark energy intrusion or perform a soul retrieval and return a split-off part of my client's vital essence that was lost long ago as a consequence of an old trauma. Through many years of rigorous training and practice, I am able to move in and out of the dreamtime experience, essentially psycho-navigating between this consensus reality and NOR on behalf of my client.

CHAPTER 13

Shamanic intercession during frontal occipital holding

As a consequence of the constraints imposed by the Covid-19 pandemic, nearly 75 percent of my individual psychotherapy sessions are now remote over Zoom. Therefore, I have had to adapt in order to successfully implement my unique approach to psychotherapy. One adaptation was integrating remote muscle testing. This includes selecting the best energy-based intervention to keep the healing process moving forward. It also includes muscle testing the client to determine the results of each intervention as it relates to the therapeutic objective within the larger overall therapeutic intention.

I mastered remote energy testing prior to the pandemic because there have always been occasions when in-person preliminary muscle testing indicated that my client was not sufficiently hydrated to muscle test further, regardless of how much water the client was ingesting. The test for hydration is the first requirement of the behavioral applied kinesiological muscle testing process. Thus, when a client cannot demonstrate becoming sufficiently hydrated, I cannot proceed with the physical muscle testing without getting skewed results. Over time, I determined that non-local or non-touching energy checking was required while standing several feet across from the client in my treatment room in order to elicit accurate feedback. Invariably, the energy checking determined that the dehydration reading reflected that there was subtle negative energy (SNE) in the client's energy field. This SNE tries to confuse and redirect me from identifying its presence. At first, I found this very strange. I eventually realized that the SNE needs to stay invested and incorporated within the client for its own mysterious agenda. It becomes veiled as a way to prevent its discovery.

Most clients come in sufficiently hydrated. If they do not, a few sips of water is all that is needed for the muscle test indicator to determine we can proceed. But when dehydration continues to be problematic, it quickly becomes apparent that this is a red flag identifying SNE in the client's energy field. Once this is determined, it is easy enough to identify what formulation of SNE is present (such as an energetic intrusion, for example), and what interventions are best suited to release it. As a consequence, I have trained myself to reliably muscle test over Zoom or even during telephone sessions with the same degree of accuracy as in-person muscle testing. I had to make this same adaptation in order to use frontal occipital holding over Zoom or telephone.

The classic guidebook on muscle testing, *Your Body Doesn't Lie*, was written by psychiatrist John Diamond in 1979 after he had studied with Dr. George Goodheart (1918–2008), who developed muscle testing as a chiropractor. Diamond began applying these techniques to his patients and further developed his technique that he labeled *behavioral kinesiology*.[126] This involves gently pushing down on a person's extended arm, challenging the deltoid muscle when one's arm is extended as the client considers a question asked. Over time, as I developed greater intuitive and energy-based sensitivity, I was able to trust the muscle testing at a distance that became *energy testing*, as I was now testing the information fields in my clients' *energy body*. This is not special to me as I have taught this to many DEH trainees during the 19 years of my training program. Diamond was not only innovative; he was highly sensitive. He began to realize that many physical and emotional problems start at an energetic level.

> I have come to believe that an illness starts as a problem on the *energy level*, a problem that may exist for many years before it manifests itself in physical disease.[127]

As he continued to research and develop behavioral kinesiology, he discovered that everything that we interact with has its own unique energetic signature. Certain foods such as sugar always weaken an individual when muscle tested. Certain fabrics such as synthetic clothing like polyester versus cotton or wool also consistently weaken people when muscle tested. He elaborates with the following:

> Behavioral kinesiology uses the basic testing techniques of applied kinesiology, but focuses on the factors in the patient's surroundings and life-style that are raising and lowering body energy. Many of the factors that lower energy are products of the technological revolution: the poisons and noises in our environment, the overrefined and unnatural foods we find on the supermarket shelves, the synthetic fabrics from which so many of our clothes are made. Other factors are individual habits or tendencies, such as posture, ability to handle stress, and human relationships.[128]

It is always surprising to new trainees learning muscle testing how placing a small, unmarked bottle of liquid bleach in their hand always tests weak. This is also the case when directed to think about a frightening or traumatic event they have experienced when being tested. This is because our *energy body* is interacting with the noxious substance as well as the toxic memory, certain heavy metal music or negative thinking about a current news event. It does not require a great leap to learn to trust one's remote *energy checking* once one understands experientially how the behavioral kinesiological muscle testing consistently provides accurate feedback when done correctly and consistently.

When the muscle testing selects frontal occipital holding as the highest priority energetic strategy, I ask my client to focus internally on the particular issue we are addressing (which has already been identified through the muscle testing). Meanwhile, I imagine and visualize my client sitting in the chair as I stand by its side with my hands held upright in the position of actually placing them on my client's head, just as if she were sitting there. I keep my hands in position throughout the entire frontal occipital holding process as I call for help from whichever helping spirit emerges in my shamanic inner visioning. Within seconds, images appear and a comprehensive shamanic journey on my client's behalf begins, albeit in a compressed time frame that typically unfolds in two to three minutes. I hold the space for my helping spirits to come forth and perform their healing. Being able to proceed in this way is a testament to the intelligence of the compassionate spirits—they have adapted in this non-local way of servicing my clients with their healing powers.

There is no drumming or rattling, only the unfolding events of the healing journey that has adapted to the needs of the current situation. I feel into the events unfolding, and frequently find my body twitching and jerking in response to the *power* being funneled through me as I hold the space for and observe the actions of my helping spirits. Often, I exhale deeply several times during the procedure as I feel the SNE being expunged.

Chapter 13

While the vast majority of my clients come to me for energy-based psychotherapy that includes using frontal occipital holding, occasionally a client requests a traditional shamanic journey without any of the muscle testing. This is when I take out the rattle and do a twenty to forty-five minute traditional journey that I narrate to them as they take notes. When these journeys are complete, we discuss what ensued to determine if a follow-up appointment is warranted.

While using the frontal occipital holding intervention, the healing outcome occurs in NOR but is immediately experienced by the client in our everyday ordinary reality. Thus, any emotional reactivity is mostly bypassed even as the resolution of the problem state occurs. Working in this way is truly a wonder. Muscle testing follows each intervention to determine and corroborate the degree of resolution of the problem we were addressing. Typically, clients experience immediate relief as mind-body-spirit balance occurs.

While most indigenous shamans keep their journey experience to themselves, I have discovered how valuable it is to share my journey with my client. The imagery I describe makes a deep impression and stays with the client long after the session is finished. Just to be clear, there are two phenomena that are occurring during and immediately after implementing frontal occipital holding. First there is the spiritual and/or energetic healing that occurs through the connection made and subsequent infusion of the *power* that is generated by the compassionate spirits in the journey. Second, there is the conscious awareness of physical and emotional shifts that immediately and sometimes gradually follow the frontal occipital holding that clients experience. As an example, I may see the serpentine-like intrusion tightly wrapped around the client's throat being released and transmuted by a particular helping spirit. This might reflect an aspect of old psychotoxic residue absorbed by the client being forced to suppress their emotional pain. This is an example of the most profound outcome of shamanic healing, for it immediately mitigates the client's symptoms. Moreover, there is deep value in sharing the imagery I have seen in NOR because the imagery stays with the client long after the session. This reinforces the power of the healing release through indirect hypnotic suggestion.

After the client leaves the office, their process of internally reviewing the healing imagery I have shared recruits a different part of their brain and thus creates a transient altered state that the client is able to reflect upon much longer than would be the case with a mere conversation. This typically generates an internal preoccupation as the client repeatedly goes over the imagery described during our energetic connection from the frontal occipital holding. While the healing has already occurred, the client's subsequent internal review process supports a deepening integration of what has been experienced during our therapy session.

After the energetic or spiritually-based healing component has been completed, the client is stimulating her own creative unconscious self-healing processes to deepen her response potential for more complete and long-lasting trauma resolution. This is an example of a profound shift in the consciousness of a client: over-identification with the victim archetype is immediately mitigated. As a consequence, eliminating the underlying source of the outward symptoms quickly resolves the presenting problem.

After sharing my journey experience with the client, we discuss the ramifications of what an intrusion wrapped around her throat represented. We wonder aloud why this absorption of psychotoxic energy from a particular individual occurred and what this represents about the client's relational dynamic with that person. We discuss how the client may have felt disempowered to such a degree that her energetic boundaries became too porous, setting her up for this psychotoxic energy absorption. I ask her about this person being the personification of a *dream figure* she grew up with, and whether an old family psychodynamic is now repeating itself in her current life.

Chapter 13

To experience a compressed-time shamanic journey wherein the healing occurs very quickly provides us with lots of time to reflect on and discuss how this loss of personal power happened and what needs to change in order to prevent its recurrence. So, even as I use energy-based strategies, there is ample time to process and discuss any underlying dynamics that led up to this intrusion. People new to this energy-based approach may presume that because the word *energy* is so frequently used to describe the mechanics of this approach, it is incompatible with traditional talk therapy or cognitive behavioral therapy (CBT). In reality, this energy-based approach generates all kinds of questions from both the client and the therapist, leading to rich and unexpected discussions, often revealing insights that spontaneously materialize.

Because shamanic journeying is based on a different epistemological foundation, discussions include new ideas and considerations that would not emerge within a conventional CBT approach. As a consequence, I believe that clients are able to expand their thinking to be more "out of the box" when considering these new and innovative possibilities.

From my personal clinical experience, four primary issues stand out that I am confronted with day in and day out. While there are parallels to Western psychological understandings and interpretations of these problem states, shamanic perceptions of dis-ease and various forms of malaise emerge from thousands of years of experience that tend to be recurring themes. These are described as *loss of personal power, soul loss/soul stealing, psychotoxic intrusions* and *earthbound spirit attachments*. Please understand that these ways of addressing and describing personal disturbances and dis-ease come from a very different way of relating to and being in the world, accompanied by healing approaches that to many readers will seem strange and foreign. This emphasizes that there are different approaches to mental and emotional healing than what we have been taught through more than a century of Western Eurocentric bias.

The particular jargon used in my discussions with clients is to a large extent part of the shamanic tradition. As a consequence, it is important to check your own personal reality biases so you can be open and available to this different paradigm and approach to healing the mind, body and spirit. This is because shamanic healing is addressing the spiritual aspect of humans that can be described as the pervasive life force that takes on a multitude of expressions. In other words, this is about our very essence or soul.

For example, when a client complains about a constant gnawing stomach pain or a disturbing and persistent sense of depersonalization accompanied by an unknown fear, the shamanic practitioner concerns herself with the underlying spiritual cause, which is sometimes called the energetic cause. From this shamanic perspective, the exploration begins in NOR versus trying to sort things out by discussing one's day-to-day interactions through a talk therapy approach. This is not to say that these two realities are not linked—each reality affects the other. For example, identifying and releasing a psychotoxic intrusion in someone's solar plexus gives the client's physical body and mental/emotional state the chance to return to balance. This is just one example of this mutually influential ongoing relationship. But operating from a time-tested and quite different understanding of our relationship to the earth requires that shamanic investigations occur in the domain of NOR. This is the realm wherein the causal factors reside and where the solutions for healing them manifest.

Chapter 14
Power Animals and Shamanic Journeying

Frequently, the shaman will journey in order to retrieve a *power animal* for her client. In the shamanic tripartite universe, power animals are usually found in the lower world. They are perceived as any animal that we are familiar with and occasionally mythic animals such as a dragon or unicorn, each of which possesses its own unique capabilities to help and protect us. There are also zoomorphic beings that are part human and part animal. In his own shamanic journeys, anthropologist Hank Wesselman encountered and engaged with Leopard Man when he was transported into nonordinary reality (NOR).[129]

Any animal can be a power animal, and each has a unique combination of specialized features and strengths. For example, a mouse may not seem like a very impressive power animal, but consider that mice can get into very small spaces and chew through wire and other objects in order to get where they need to go. Clients frequently have biases and believe they should have a large and fierce power animal, such as a lion or a wild boar. When told that the shamanic practitioner acquired a mouse for their power animal through a power animal retrieval, clients often feel disappointed. Clients don't realize that every power animal possesses its own unique healing and protective aspects. Therefore, shamans cultivate relationships with a number of personal power animals over many years.

For instance, a mouse in NOR serving as a power animal can be a guide to the shamanic practitioner by discovering small and otherwise inaccessible entry points and gaps into caves and crevices. A mouse also has extraordinary hearing ability and is an excellent climber, an asset when walking in a wooded or jungle environment. They are also known for their excellent olfactory sense. In NOR size does not matter, since the power animal Mouse can be carried in the shaman's hand, guiding the shaman to find what is being sought through its senses of hearing and smell.

Power animals choose to bond with the shamanic practitioner during their journey, not the other way around. It is the same dynamic when the shaman is journeying on her client's behalf. Thus, when the shaman is searching for a power animal to support her client, exactly the right animal will appear and present itself to the shaman—the power animal knows what the client needs in order to augment that person's personal power.

After an initial diagnostic journey, a power animal retrieval is frequently the first journey the shamanic practitioner does on behalf of her client. Once a power animal has been located, confirmed and dialogued with, the practitioner then energetically infuses the power animal's essence into the client through her breath as a way to strengthen and augment the client's *power*. The client is then told about the features and strengths of his newly acquired power animal. He might be instructed to pay greater attention to his dreams, and even use active imagination as a way to engage his new power animal as a way to strengthen his relationship to it. Sometimes the shamanic practitioner recommends that her client acquire a small fetish of their newly received power animal and keep it with them at all times. While this requires very little from the client, the power animal's increased vibrational frequency will continue to support the client's healing, helping the client become more in charge of his life.

CHAPTER 14

If the client is unfamiliar with power animals and does not have their own shamanic practice (which is usually the case), acquiring a fetish to keep with them in their pocket or purse is one way to regularly reinforce their intent and connection with their newly acquired power animal. Going back to our example, when a client thinks about Mouse regularly throughout the day, he can pay greater attention to his outer environment by noticing the sounds and scents he encounters when out in the world. This is one way to escape the constant and relentless inner chatter—he is now partnering with his new ally in order to reorient to his day-to-day world differently. Over time the client begins to become more trusting intuitively from this evolving relationship with his power animal.

A power animal is not that different from the ancient concept of the guardian angel. Many religious traditions support the notion of guardian spirits being with us from birth. These include Judaism, Roman Catholicism and Christianity in general. What is unique in the shamanic tradition is how someone can journey for themselves and contact one or more power animals that can provide not just solace but the *power*, positive energy and actual healing to support their day-to-day life. In this way, through one's own efforts, one connects with and cultivates an ongoing relationship with a numinous being in contrast to simply having faith that one's guardian angel is present. The very process of acquiring one's own power animal is profoundly empowering. Power animals become a shamanic practitioner's spiritually intimate companion. Their roles are many and they support the shamanic practitioner's vital force and overall well-being. Anthropologist and shamanic teacher Michael Harner has often commented on the many roles the power animal plays, especially in keeping the shamanic practitioner healthy.

> The importance of the power animal goes far beyond calling for assistance. Power animals connect one to the incredible power of the universe and modulate it in a

> form that does not overwhelm the individual human. Shamans and others who have such spiritual guardians become themselves power-filled, or power-full, and stay that way as long as they remain connected to these spiritual representatives of the universe.[130]

The American philosopher and psychologist Willam James wrote about the transpersonal aspects of our interactions with the mythic and primal consciousness in his book *The Varieties of Religious Experience: A Study in Human Nature.*

> James has discovered a primal level anterior to the very distinction between subject and object. He is poised to make philosophical sense of ancient shamanic procedures in which the healers open themselves and their clients to powers of paradigmatically regenerative beings.[131]

While shamanic journeying is frequently experienced through one's inner visual perceptual channel, all of the senses are engaged. Depending on our unique neurology, seeing images, feeling body sensations, hearing sounds and smelling the scents of a jungle in NOR are all aspects of the journey experience. Many individuals discover that their interior experience while journeying is embellished through one dominant perceptional channel. So long as one is able to stay engaged in the journey and feel connected to an ongoing and unfolding experience, no one perceptual channel is better than another. This is important when journeying for a power animal. One may not visualize an emerging power animal in NOR but may hear a large feline approaching. One may then proprioceptively feel and sense the power animal rubbing against one's legs, which is common behavior for cats.

Throughout the many years I have been teaching others to journey for themselves, most people report an astounding array of interior perceptions. When I am journeying for a client or friend in-person, I narrate the journey experience in real time.

CHAPTER 14

Calling forth one's power animal

This in essence allows my client to vicariously participate by visualizing and imagining the journey in a multisensory way as I am describing it unfolding. When I journey to retrieve a power animal for a client, my narration supports the client to enter into the imaginative realm and vicariously join with me as a power animal is identified and approached. The client then enters into an altered state to become more available and open to when their new power animal is infused into them. Traditional shamans often choose not to describe their journeys—only the teachings and guidance are disclosed. However, my personal experiences with clients over many years support my decision to verbally narrate my journey as the experience unfolds. Part of this strategy allows the client to bypass the analytical left hemisphere thinking brain in order to emphasize the depth of interior experience as one becomes absorbed in the experience of *sacred imagination*.

The relationship that one cultivates with one's power animal(s) is beautiful, intimate and ever unfolding. Simply sitting next to one's power animal during the shamanic journey provides for the absorption of the animal's *power*. This is hard to convey if you have not yet experienced it. In my personal experience, my power animals and my anthropomorphic teachers occasionally merge with me at some point in the journey. When this occurs, *their power becomes my power*. It is at their initiative that this merging happens. This becomes a profound assimilation of vital force—I usually feel my physical body vibrating with their power. Harner has discovered through his multicultural research why this category of compassionate spirits is so important to the shamanic practitioner.

> The power animal, or guardian spirit, might be compared to an electric transformer or adapter that receives the immense power of the universe and modulates into a form that can be safely transmitted to a human. The immensity of the power is one of the reasons shamans work with intermediary powers, such as power animals, rather than calling upon the total universe itself.[132]

During the journey, this can be brief or last for minutes on end. I am never quite sure how long the merging is as I become so deeply identified with my power animal or teacher that I lose track of time. The experience is healing, nourishing and replenishing. Because I journey three or four times per week, this becomes a source of ongoing healing and nourishment that sustains me as I navigate my daily life in ordinary reality. This truly is a gift that keeps on giving. When the journey comes to a close, I feel energized, grateful and *power-filled*. You too can experience this should you choose to pursue this path.

In my many years of shamanic journey work, I have cultivated relationships with many power animals. Each one possesses its own particular specialty. Whenever a *soul retrieval* is indicated, Horse spontaneously emerges. When the extraction of psycho-toxic energies represented as an *energetic intrusion* is identified (usually in service of one of my clients), Panther emerges; its specialty is the transmutation of this dark and heavy energy until the intrusion is completely eliminated.

When there is an earthbound spirit that has attached to the *energy body* of my client, it is Eagle who appears as the facilitator to release the grip of the typically frightened and confused earthbound spirit. Eagle then carries the errant spirit away to wherever it next needs to go. The compassionate spirits know the territory of NOR, so I needn't concern myself about where the disoriented and frightened earthbound spirit will be taken.

When I journey to the lower and upper worlds, my power animals show up to meet me. It may be Panther in the lower world or Eagle in the upper world. Sometimes I simply spend time with them in their particular domain. Other times one of my power animals takes me to the anthropomorphic teacher I wish to meet with. For example, when Eagle takes me to meet with an upper-world teacher, Eagle and I are merged as I feel its *power* vibrating through me. This feeling persists long after the journey completes itself.

I am always grateful—and filled with awe and wonder—that these compassionate spirits are so available to support me and my clients. It is a total blessing. I invite you to consider the possibilities and seek out your own training. Your life experience will be changed forever.

CHAPTER 15
HOW SHAMANIC PRACTICES PROVIDE REPLENISHMENT

When clients come in for psychotherapy, they often feel disempowered and emotionally depleted. This is true for nearly all conditions including depression, post-traumatic stress disorder (PTSD), generalized anxiety and marital conflict. My task is to help clients restore a sense of centeredness and self-confidence, and to regain control over pressing and persistent states of malaise. Clients are vulnerable when they are confused and upset. Issues that frequently need to be addressed include compromised and insubstantial interpersonal boundaries, dissociation, unhealed and persistent trauma, a pervasive sense of powerlessness, codependency, and an overall feeling of lack of support and connection to others.

Therapists use various models and strategies to help individuals feel more in control of their lives. Whether it is cognitive behavioral therapy (CBT), psychodynamic psychotherapy, energy psychology or various forms of bodywork, the therapeutic intent is to alleviate the symptoms that are destabilizing the client and discover their underlying source so they can be confronted to stop them from recurring.

Medical researchers have developed a variety of synthesized neurochemicals for desperate patients to ingest daily in pill form to directly resolve the imbalance that they theorize is the underlying cause of the depression, anxiety or other diagnosis.

Many of these strategies can be helpful, yet (as explained in Part 1) too many of these approaches are insufficient for the healing outcomes that clients are seeking help for, particularly when unresolved trauma persists. Psychiatric medications typically do not resolve the underlying issues.

Traditional healing approaches offer very different solutions. Virtually all indigenous cultures embrace the belief that an impersonal and supernatural *power* animates all things. This belief is known as *animism*. The animating power infuses people, animals and plant life—in fact, all aspects of the natural world. It also encompasses the elemental forces of our planet including weather patterns, rivers and even inanimate objects such as mountains. In shamanic cultures, everything has a living spirit that can be communicated with. Throughout history, people have also identified certain locations that are imbued with higher concentrations of *power*. Stonehenge in the United Kingdom and certain religious sites that people are drawn to for pilgrimage, such as the Western Wall in Jerusalem and Mecca in Saudi Arabia, are examples of this phenomenon. People report feeling uplifted and even healed of the condition they came for by visiting these power-infused sites. In addition, sacred objects are believed to be imbued with *power* that many legends are based on, such as the Holy Grail.

Traditional healers and shamans across the world believe that a strong store of *power* is at the root of excellent health and well-being, as well as being responsible for the unusual powers of many shamans worldwide. There are different names for this *power* depending on local tradition and culture, but all refer to the same *power* that can be accessed and concentrated within oneself regardless of one's geographic location.

The early Hawaiians and Polynesians referred to this *power* as *mana*. The Hindu yogic tradition calls this force *prana*, while traditional Chinese medicine refers to it as *chi*. While the names

CHAPTER 15

Absorbing power from the spirits of nature

are culturally dependent, this is the same life force that animates all things. People over the centuries have learned how to collect it, store it and circulate it for personal balance, ongoing health and healing. Many advanced practitioners have even learned how to concentrate it and emit it for the healing benefit of others.

For over two decades I was a practitioner of Kundalini yoga. I learned that through specific breathing techniques such as breath of fire and various meditations, I could intentionally collect and concentrate prana for extraordinary well-being. I have also learned a form of Qigong called Soaring Crane. The practice of Qigong typically involves movement exercises that stimulate one's chi so that any blocks to this circulating subtle energy are released. This keeps the acupuncture meridians or channels open and free flowing, allowing the chi to move through the body without obstructions. Through practicing Qigong over time, one accumulates increasing stores of chi; this provides robust physical and emotional balance along with increasing mental energy and well-being. Chinese medicine doctor Roger Jahnke, who teaches and writes about Qigong: describes the importance of this powerful animating force:

> For your whole existence, according to Chinese tradition, from before your birth through this present moment and into your future, you always have been and always will be infused with the essential unifying feature of the universe—the Qi. It is never not present, you are swimming in it. It bathes you, internally and externally, constantly fueling, cleansing, healing, rejuvenating, and enlightening you.[133]

He elaborates on one of the central tenants of Qigong:

> The ultimate Qigong goal is to plug directly into the force that runs the entire universe.... Through Qigong, you can purposefully create a direct channel into an unlimited field of ever-present nourishing resources. The origin of this energy is the universe itself—the sun, the earth, the boundless field of potential (sometimes called the quantum field). The same astounding resource that regulates the seasons, causes plants to grow, and creates stars and galaxies is available to each of us. This resource is Qi.[134]

The tradition of Qigong articulates the need to refuel and replenish oneself as an everyday intentional practice. Daily practice is encouraged in order to be regularly replenished and fully present so as not to become depleted physically, emotionally and mentally. While the practices of Kundalini yoga and Qigong support replenishment, adherents of these traditions believe that prana/chi is an impersonal manifestation of the universal revitalizing energy. In shamanic practices, partnering with compassionate spirits through ongoing relationships provides for a different experience of absorbing *power* because *these are personal relationships that deepen over time.*

When I journey to a particular teacher, I bring specific questions and concerns to be addressed. (I must first set my intention for what I want to inquire about or get help with). I have profound conversations in my interactions with my compassionate spirits and I am given wise counsel and infusions of *power*. My teachers may talk with me or instruct me through different and unusual experiences that take place in locations within a particular teacher's domain. I am sometimes introduced to a particular plant whose spirit will support me in my everyday life, provided I take the time to cultivate an ongoing relationship with it through ritual or ceremony that I am instructed to conduct. Other times, I may journey for the benefit of my clients or family who need support at the physical or emotional level. Sometimes I perform a soul retrieval for a client to redress soul loss (of vital essence) from an old trauma. If a client is feeling weak and disheartened, I perform a power animal retrieval in order to augment their personal *power*. This will give them the added strength to confront what they were avoiding.

These and other techniques within the shamanic practitioner's skill set provide clients, friends and family members with *power* in order to better navigate the challenges of our everyday normal consensus reality. While the *power* I describe may be the same animating life force that is accessed in Qigong and Kundalini yoga, the relationships that are developed over time in the shamanic journey are rich and complex. These foundational relationships are cultivated over time with wise and compassionate beings that will remain available in the nonordinary realms whenever I need to consult and partner with them.

A Foot in Both Worlds

Absorbing power from one's power animal

Shamanic practitioners discover that regularly connecting with their compassionate allies in the nonordinary realms provides for increasing cumulative stores of *power*. The more one journeys to interact with one's special helpers, the more *power* one accumulates to support staying *power-filled*. This prevents depletion and keeps one's vital life force bright, strong and circulating. This practice underscores that if you do not recharge your energy on a regular basis, you will eventually become depleted or develop dis-ease. This is all about maintaining health and balance. The energy you expend must be recharged and replenished to maintain a positive mental attitude and excellent overall health. Shamanic practices support this in a palpable way.

It is a well-known fact that getting a good night's sleep and eating mindfully and healthily each day provides a foundation for overall good health and sustaining energy. This greatly helps one to get through the day without ending up exhausted. Yet many people over-caffeinate throughout their day, come home physically spent and frequently unwind from the relentless demands of their workday using alcohol, internet browsing or television. For those with children, work doesn't end until the little ones are in bed. Does this day-in and day-out routine support the ongoing energy necessary to keep up with the myriad demands of a lifestyle that begs for work-life balance?

Different spiritual traditions provide their own structured approaches to enhance one's health and well-being, including various meditation teachings. Throughout the years of practicing many different spiritual disciplines, I have noticed the positive differences in my overall energy and well-being. I discovered early in college that I have a strong spiritual nature that has directed me to seek out these various practices through experiential personal discovery. It is inspiring to read about spiritual adepts and wonder how these individuals acquired their powers. But reading about how a master stimulates and mobilizes spiritual *power* for herself and others is quite different from discovering how one can generate this for oneself through various intentional practices.

I recognize that it may not be easy for you to believe or relate to my descriptions of my subjective experience and its relationship to subtle energies. On a more concrete level, if you have never tasted a freshly picked fig, my description of its texture and unique taste is likely something that will remain mysterious to you. My attempt to describe subtle energy is similar. Until you personally experience it, this subtle energy will, to varying degrees, remain academic and abstract. Nonetheless, the energetic lift I experience from my regular shamanic journey work is inspiring and physically nourishing.

I have explored and learned a great deal over the years when it comes to incorporating psychospiritual therapeutic models that access subtle energies. I only use therapeutic approaches that are effective and time tested. Shamanic healing practices certainly fall into this category. Anthropologists believe that this animistic worldview has been practiced by humans for about 50,000 years, predating all so-called traditional religious traditions. Among all of the techniques, modalities and approaches that call on and integrate *power* for the benefit of my clients, shamanic healing remains the most *power-filled* and profound. A special blessing to me is that I, too, am a beneficiary when shamanic healing is called for during the psychotherapy session. After using the frontal occipital holding strategy that opens up a passageway for the compassionate spirits, I always feel and experience the *power* that revitalizes my client as well as myself.

Over the last several decades, my sensitivity to subtle energy and the *power* experienced in shamanic journey work has continued to blossom. While mysterious, the experiences of receiving these energetic infusions have consistently been immediately enlivening and always uplifting. *These energy-based experiences are intended to be replenishing and nourishing.* These techniques are teachable, so you too can learn how to experience and interact with the compassionate spirits yourself. You can take workshops to learn how to experience the vital life force through developing relationships with compassionate spirits. The Foundation for Shamanic Studies, founded by Michael Harner, offers numerous trainings from well-vetted teachers.[135] In my Dynamic Energetic Healing™ (DEH) trainings in London, a major emphasis has been on learning to navigate nonordinary reality (NOR) through practicing the shamanic journey in a group setting.

Anthropologists study human culture by examining the archeological remains of past indigenous groups and participating in fieldwork on location when possible. They investigate the belief systems, art, hunting and gathering or agricultural practices, language, and customs of a given cultural group. Every culture creates its own constellations of beliefs, philosophy and ways of interacting with the world. Thus, the majority of people in any society tend to support and live under a collective belief system that supports their way of life. In Western contemporary life, the values of technology, ongoing economic growth and material consumption supported by fossil fuels support our everyday lifestyle.

> Practically speaking, this means that people's interpretations of the phenomena will be largely determined by their personal beliefs, philosophy, and "world hypothesis." The world hypothesis consists of the fundamental beliefs about the nature of the world and reality that underlie the life and work of a community. Most people simply take the consensual assumptions of their culture or subculture unquestioningly and interpret the world accordingly.[136]

This suggests that there are other aspects of the world that many people either are not aware of or do not have the curiosity to explore beyond the agreed-upon consensus reality.

> The domain of what we do not know we do not know is unimaginably vast and replete with regenerative potential. New possibilities, new alternatives, are sudden and perhaps shocking openings in the experienced world.[137]

This confronts the fundamental belief of shamanic healing traditions—that there is an unseen universe populated by beings who are called *spirits*. In traditional indigenous cultures, the shaman interacts with these sentient beings who exist in another dimension of reality that has come to be known as NOR. Psychiatrist Roger Walsh suggests that "Shamans are pioneers in exploring as yet poorly understood capacities of the human mind."[138] He goes on to describe how he understands spirits in the following way:

> If we are to be completely honest, we must acknowledge that even now we have not disproved the possible

existence of spirits (intelligent, non-material entities independent of the channel's mind) or their role in some channeling.[139]

The theme of this chapter has been how certain energy-based practices from different traditions, historical time periods and various parts of the world support the replenishment of the life force that enlivens and energizes us. Of all the practices I have partaken of associated with subtle energies that are outside of the mainstream belief systems, shamanic healing is the most robust, remarkable and consistent. This is demonstrated in the energetic boost I receive immediately following my engagement with compassionate spirits and in the remarkable healing that I experience after shamanic journeying. This is also the experience of my clients. Should this intrigue you, I encourage you to explore this way of being.

CHAPTER 16

MERGING AND SHAPESHIFTING—THREE PERSONAL EXAMPLES

In shamanic healing, it is the ongoing relationships with one's helping spirits that the shamanic practitioner cultivates over time that are central to successful healing outcomes. When I am journeying, my perception and experience shift back and forth from visualizing and observing experiences as they unfold in nonordinary reality (NOR) to becoming completely identified with my ally figure. When I am witnessing events unfold, I am holding the space with my attention and focus for my helping spirits to take various actions. I am fully present with my ally figures even as I visually perceive the events as they happen. It is very dreamlike. I see and feel myself moving through various experiences as my helping spirits guide and determine the direction of the unfolding.

It is important that I initiate each journey with a clear goal for what I am seeking. Once I am congruent with my intention for beginning the journey, my helping spirits take over, and our journey becomes a collaborative experience. Initially I am separate from but accompanying my helping spirit. Thus, I am experiencing the journey from a third-person perspective—I am perceiving and experiencing the journey as a companion and partner. There are other times when my interior experience shifts and I become one with my helping spirit—I experience

Merging and shapeshifting

the unfolding of events from a first-person orientation. In these latter cases I am *merged* with my ally figure—there is very little differentiation between us. To varying degrees, I profoundly feel the experience of being one with my helping spirit. This first-person experience is sometimes referred to as *shapeshifting*, since my accustomed self-identity merges with my helping spirit and I increasingly become one with my ally figure. When this occurs, I am less an observer and more intimately identified with my ally. I experience and perceive through the expansive beingness and presence of my ally.

I recall one time during my Foundation for Shamanic Studies three-year advanced initiation training when Alicia, one of the facilitators, demonstrated this to our group. She had the unusual ability to merge and shapeshift into and with her power animals. For this demonstration she went into journey while others drummed from the periphery of our circle. Within one minute, I and the rest of the group witnessed Alicia shapeshifting and perceived her transforming herself into a beautiful iridescent winged animal that was vibrating and moving around in profound beauty. It seemed so impossible, yet we were all mesmerized by this immediate transformation from human to power animal that completely took over her normal human physical identity and appearance. She was profoundly demonstrating how, with intention and strong mental focus, one can collapse the boundaries between ordinary reality and NOR. While I had read of many accounts of indigenous shamans shapeshifting as part of their repertoire, this was the first time I was privileged to witness this phenomenon firsthand. She was a skilled shamanic practitioner and we were all fortunate to have her as one of our teachers. It was an experience I will never forget.

What follows are three personal examples of how I have experienced merging and shapeshifting.

Example One: Merging with My Power Animal to Infuse Healing *Power*

For many years prepandemic, I taught numerous clients of mine the shamanic journey method as a way to augment their own personal healing. In the evening, eight to ten clients gathered in my office to learn how to integrate the shamanic healing skill set. These shamanic healing groups typically required a commitment of three to four months, meeting once a week. Once everyone felt competent in the basic shamanic journey and had acquired at least one lower-world power animal and one upper-world anthropomorphic teacher, among other tasks, we journeyed as a group for one member who lay down in the middle of the circle. Sometimes just prior to the group journey the person who volunteered to be the client would ask the group to address a specific issue that they needed help and healing with. Sometimes it was for an emotional issue, such as generalized anxiety or codependent tendencies. Other times it was for a physical malady they were struggling with. In either case the group members would trade off drumming in order to create the percussive stimulation for the rest of the journeying group.

The group members found this collective journeying experience very gratifying. When each person finished writing down their journey on their pad of paper, we would go around the circle so each member could describe their journey and provide insights to the "client."

Occasionally, I asked for a group member to come to the center of the circle but not disclose what they desired as a healing outcome. This was another wrinkle in the process. It required each neophyte shamanic practitioner to trust their helping spirit to provide diagnostic information followed by direct healing for the "client."

I should note that each person who was journeying was doing so from a distance. One can say this was remote or non-local, even though the distance was only seven to ten feet away. This has the same impact as when I am journeying for someone over Zoom who lives in Europe or Canada—distance is irrelevant when working in NOR.

On one occasion, I explained to the group that this journey was to challenge them to be open to merge with their respective helping spirit and then physically move close to the "client" in the merged state. They then had to allow their helping spirit to direct them to do whatever was necessary on behalf of the client. Often, when one of the participants volunteered to beat the drum, I was free to journey on the client's behalf as well. After just a few minutes, one of my power animals, Panther, emerged. I was directed to merge with Panther so it could guide me to facilitate the healing.

As I became increasingly identified with Panther, I was drawn to begin moving close to the client who was lying down, experiencing the graceful and powerfully muscled feline moving around the client.

CHAPTER 16

I found myself moving like a panther on all fours, sensing what was going on for this client as I was mentally asking for healing for them. Initially, I/we were drawn to his solar plexus. I was directed to place my hands just above that point, and images emerged that identified an energetic intrusion, which I perceived as a black, oily mass. Immediately I was drawn to scoop up this dark mass and throw it into the Willamette River, several miles away. This was repeated three times until all of the oily residue was removed at the prompting of Panther. Once completed, I/we continued to crawl around the client moving just like you might imagine a black panther stealthily moving. We were sensing and sniffing around the client until I felt a strong urge to place my hands on his chest just over his sternum bone. As I physically placed my hands over his chest, I felt a torrent of powerful energy moving through me that was being infused into him. After about two full minutes of Panther's *power* being channeled and infused through me, it waned and finally stopped. That was when I knew that the healing process was complete. I/we then circled around him one more time and, not noticing anything more, I returned to my place in the circle and disengaged from Panther.

It is important to emphasize that while this experience may be interpreted as transient spirit possession, it is something that occurs through agreement. Once the particular task is completed, it is the shamanic practitioner's decision to thank the helping spirit and then intentionally disengage and separate. Merging in this way is specific to a particular task and once completed, the merging must be ended. In our everyday ordinary reality it is I who must be sovereign and choose when to merge my energy with that of one of my helping spirits, for it is in ordinary reality that my day-to-day survival tasks occur and thus I must be always fully present.

When the journeying was finished and everyone had written down their journey experience, we went around the circle so each person could share their experience as it related to the "client." After I shared my experience, the participant who received the healing told me that he had been dealing with significant heart disease for the previous decade. He had one stent inserted already and was told that he would need another surgery at some point in the future. He told me that when my hands were over his chest he felt warm and even hot sensations throughout his chest, something that surprised him but that felt nurturing and positive. He had never revealed his coronary artery disease to me before. My helping spirit knew exactly where its healing energy and *power* needed to be directed for this client.

About twenty years later this individual required coronary bypass surgery to replace several occluded arteries. He survived the surgery and went through a long recovery process. His experience reminded me of the healing circle described above and the sensations of healing energy that were directed to exactly the right place. I believe that the healing that occurred that evening delayed his eventual surgery for many years. This was a confirmation illustrating the *power* and knowledge of the helping spirits when we regularly partner with them for health and healing.

Michael Harner told me that physical healing outcomes often require numerous shamanic healing journeys to create the intended result. During one of our semi-annual circles (during the three-year program that he taught), he told us about how his long-term eye disease was healed after he met with a Hawaiian Kahuna that he knew. The Kahuna had journeyed for him on four consecutive days.

Sometimes shamanic healing strategies require daily or weekly journeys to cumulatively impact the client's condition for a healing outcome. It is understood that physical manifestations of dis-ease typically build up over time, often over many years due to genetic predispositions or a cavalier lifestyle with habits that promote the physical disorder. If understood in this way, it makes sense that multiple shamanic healing journeys with a sustained focus on a particular physical disease process will cumulatively generate the intended healing result. This recognition of shamanic healing remains mysterious to me. I can only wonder what the healing outcome might have been for this client of mine if we had agreed to journey regularly with the intention to heal and resolve his heart disease.

Example Two: Sharing *Power* during a Sustained Merging

Many years ago I participated in a three-day training given by shamanic practitioner Betsy Bergstrom. The theme of the training was mediumship, something I had only read about previously and had always looked askance at. Betsy had been one of the participants in my three-year advanced shamanic initiations training given by Michael Harner. Betsy has a unique shamanic skill set that tends to focus on what she calls middle-world work. It is in this middle world that we conduct our day-to-day ordinary reality business. It is also in this middle world that shamans connect to the elements and plant spirits. Additionally, this middle-world realm that we live in is where earthbound spirits of the deceased can attach to people and cause problems for them.

After explaining the historical roots of mediumship, she called in the energies of many powerful compassionate spirits, including Saint Germain, the Egyptian goddess Isis, the Norse god Odin, and many others. As each of these beings came into our space, Betsy directed us to feel into their energy and assess to what degree we felt a strong resonance. This was new for me; I had never before been in the presence of a shamanic practitioner who was able to connect with many compassionate spirits one after another, bringing forth their energy and presence so that we could all personally experience their presence to varying degrees. I began to realize that for especially sensitive individuals, mediumship is based on the medium's ability to call in the energy and presence of the deceased who we might call our ancestors.

I felt little resonance from many of the beings that Betsy brought forth, but I had a strong reaction when the energy of

Odin was in the room. I wanted to get to know this being and find out more about him, since I felt a strong energetic connection to him. After this experiential exercise, Betsy explained that we would go into the nearby woods to find a fallen limb to use as a staff to enable us to channel *power* from our newly chosen and affiliated helping spirit to others in the room. She had some accoutrements available to embellish our staffs, such as multicolored leather strips, some attractive feathers, beads and other items. All these objects helped us get into the spirit of the activity and add our personal artistic touch to our own staff.

In some shamanic traditions, collective chanting and singing is used to journey in place of the drum or rattle. This too was a new experience for me. Betsy instructed us as we practiced singing a repetitive song, so we all became quickly conversant with it. Eventually we were to journey to connect with our newly chosen spirit ally to cultivate a new reliable and trusting relationship.

After we each became comfortable with our new ally figure, Betsy explained that out of our group of approximately forty participants, three of us at a time would climb the stairs onto the dais where there were three large seats positioned. Each of us would take our seat, holding our own staff out to our right side. The rest of the group then began singing the song over and over that we had earlier practiced so that each person on the dais could shift their consciousness and move into NOR in order to connect with their newly acquired spirit ally. Betsy then gave the three people sitting on the dais a couple of minutes to initiate and solidify our connection with our helping spirit, all the while holding our staff out to the right.

When it was my turn to occupy one of the three seats, I quickly connected with Odin and saw through my shamanic visioning Odin seated on his upper-world throne with his staff held out in front of him, emanating *power*. Very soon, people from the group came onto the dais in threes, with each person standing next to one of the three people holding their own staff.

Their task was to grasp the staff of the person seated on the dais and be open to receiving *power* being channeled through the staff. As I had never done anything like this before I was very curious to find out how this process would unfold.

Each of the three people coming onto the dais was given several minutes to grasp one of the three staffs and be available to receive *power* through the agency of the staff. I cannot say for sure how long it took for all the participants to cycle through, but it was likely about forty minutes long.

I recall how surprised I was to be able to maintain my focused attention on Odin for this entire length of time. My attention never wavered. I still remember holding the vision of sitting next to Odin in NOR (while holding *his* staff), while he was holding out his staff and radiating *power* through my staff in the large room. This was another profound experience of the merging of my energy with the energy of my helping spirit. I was surprised that I was able to experience in the first person an ongoing connection in his upper-world realm for as long as I did.

Odin and I were essentially undifferentiated in this merged state. I stayed connected to him in both the third person and first person. I was also able to maintain the vision of being seated next to Odin throughout the forty minutes; I was wearing an eye cover so as not to be distracted by outer sensory stimuli. I could feel the *power* surging through me via the staff that was now being shared and emitted to the group members who one by one stood next to me while grasping my staff.

When all the group members had cycled through, the singing stopped and we were released back to our seat in the circle. We discussed our experiences both as the staff holders and as those who came onto the dais to receive *power* through grasping another's staff.

Over time, with practice and commitment, what I have described becomes possible with surprisingly powerful healing impacts. To this day, I continue to be blessed by Odin as he frequently presents himself to me when I am using frontal occipital holding for my clients in my Dynamic Energetic Healing™ (DEH) psychotherapy sessions. He holds out his staff in NOR and his *power* courses through me to support my client. He is a most powerful and generous compassionate spirit. I am grateful to have experienced this new way of connecting and merging with this powerful being. He continues to support me as well as my clients.

Example Three: Sharing and Receiving *Power* with Arms Extended

During one session of my Michael Harner three-year advanced shamanic initiations training, we were learning how to channel *power* to several people after merging. Those of us in the center of the circle stood with our arms extended out in front of us as several people in the circle were drumming. We journeyed to merge with one of our helping spirits and stay identified with our ally as people from the circle came to stand in front of us facing away from us. I merged with my upper-world Mayan teacher and ended up putting my hands on the shoulders of five different people, one at a time, as I stood behind each of them. I channeled and infused *power* into them until they felt they were filled up.

After the fifth person disengaged from me I noticed that the *power* that had been surging through me began to wane. At this point I mentally thanked my Mayan teacher, disengaged and returned to my seat. I felt very energized. When the next group of individuals came into the middle of the circle, I was given the opportunity to have one of them put their hands on my shoulders and in their merged state, channel and infuse *power* into me. At the end of the exercise and throughout the rest of the day into the evening, I was just buzzing with energy and felt elated. That evening, sleep did not come easily—I was still vibrating with *power*. But the next morning I awakened feeling great.

Chapter 16

Many of my personal journeys involve merging with my allies to experience their *power* surging through me, often directed to parts of my body that realize significant benefit from this healing energy. There are times when at the beginning of my journeys, I merge with one of my power animals, including Dolphin, Panther, Eagle and Shark. In these merged states, I enjoy the vicarious experience of moving with them in their respective domain as I feel their *power* coursing through my body. These experiences are common for me and cumulatively healing. When I am merged with Dolphin as we move through the ocean or river, I feel Dolphin's muscular movement as it propels itself arching and jumping in and out of the water; I also feel the pure joy it embodies. When I am merged with Panther, I feel its muscular stealthy movement throughout my entire body and, for that short time, enjoy the feelings and sensations of moving in a feline manner, hyper-alert to the sounds and scents that pervade the jungle flora. It is during these merged experiences that my power animal's *power* is absorbed by me and becomes my *power* that remains with me long after the journey ends.

I feel very fortunate to have my shamanic experiences continue to evolve, as merging in these ways did not happen when I began learning the basics of shamanic journeying. Like so many aspects of shamanic journeying, one's abilities and awareness continue to evolve over time. I continue to be surprised, fascinated and grateful for the ongoing changes in awareness that evolve through my relationships with the helping spirits. These new learnings and awarenesses are testaments to the creativity and generosity proffered by these remarkable beings. I remain humbled and blessed as I now experience my life in ongoing awe and wonder.

Chapter 17
Dissociation, Soul Loss and Soul Retrieval

Psychotherapists who work with clients who are dealing with trauma are familiar with dissociation. This phenomenon is one of the many defense mechanisms used by our unconscious mind to help us deal with an overwhelming traumatic experience. When individuals dissociate, they are typically spacy and find it difficult to focus mentally and concentrate. They feel chronically tired and tend to reach for caffeine throughout their day (more than they are accustomed to) in an effort to boost their energy.

I have had many clients over the years who are chronic dissociators due to previous trauma. They tend to get too easily triggered when stimuli similar to the original traumatizing insult occur. For example, someone who grew up with a verbally abusive, angry parent may check out when his spouse gets angry with him. Until this person finds a good psychotherapist or shamanic practitioner with whom to explore and identify the roots of this problem, he will probably go through life chronically dissociating. This is because this is an unconscious response that gets triggered outside of conscious awareness. This tends to create a sense of detachment from our everyday ordinary reality. These people often feel distant and disconnected from what is happening in the moment, generating feelings of ennui. This perpetuates a significant loss of personal power, because internal resources normally available become inaccessible and are hijacked by the overexcited sympathetic nervous system.

Dissociation is a hallmark of protracted post-traumatic stress disorder (PTSD), and for these unfortunate people it typically doesn't resolve on its own. This is primarily because most people who dissociate do not even know it is happening. It tends to be a chronic condition because of the involvement of the sympathetic nervous system, which becomes regularly overstimulated and easily triggered. Out-of-body experiences and derealization (discussed below) frequently become part of the out-of-control experience that keeps happening to the dissociated person. Overidentification with the Victim archetype often ensues. Traumatized clients can feel tormented by unbidden flashbacks, nightmares and memories of the event(s) that frequently arouse the amygdala and hippocampus repeatedly. When this occurs, an alarm state re-engages and the cycle continues unchecked. It can feel like being trapped in a tortuous inner prison from which there is no escape.

> The problem for those who go on to develop PTSD is that the cycling back-and-forth, from parasympathetic to sympathetic activation, doesn't stop but instead becomes a self-sustaining neurological feedback circuit. The pattern becomes imprinted in the irritated, sensitized neuronal networks involved. What's worse, if left to its own oscillating pattern, the symptoms become increasingly entrenched, and often they worsen.[140]

What has always interested me is where that part of our consciousness goes when we dissociate. Can the split-off part be located? There are countless references in the psychotherapy literature on trauma to PTSD clients remembering floating above the scene of their abuse and just watching it happen as children. This derealization has also been reported after traffic accidents when the driver, trapped in the car, recalls observing from above as the EMTs were trying to help free him. But where does one dissociate to years after a traumatic event when ongoing PTSD has taken hold? For most therapists this is nebulous and prone to speculation. Is the dissociated part floating above the body? Is it trapped and sealed off in the unconscious mind in some hidden compartment? Has it become a split-off or autonomous part orbiting the person's consciousness like a satellite, occasionally broadcasting intrusive thought forms that disturb?

One reason that cognitive behavioral therapy (CBT) is frequently not very successful with resolving traumatic residue is because often the dissociated part carries with it information, memories and feeling states that are inaccessible through cognitive discussion and analysis. People often cannot remember important aspects of a trauma because the part or parts of them that can be helpful are no longer accessible—they have become dissociated. In the shamanic

Dissociation and soul loss

paradigm this is because the client has suffered *soul loss*.

In shamanic healing, when an individual experiences trauma and dissociates, it is considered loss of part of one's vital essence. The practitioner's task is to journey into the nonordinary realms to discover where the split-off absent soul part has ended up. The shamanic practitioner doesn't know where to look, but his allies—his helping spirits—know the territory of nonordinary reality (NOR). The helping spirit leads the shamanic practitioner to where this dissociated part ended up. This could be in the lower world, the middle world or the upper world.

Once the spirit ally has taken the shamanic practitioner to the location where the traumatized part fled to in NOR, a dialogue can be initiated between the practitioner and the part that fled the physical body. The practitioner tries to persuade the split-off part to return. Together with the practitioner's power animal, the missing part is carried back to ordinary reality and through a specific process can then be infused back into the client. This is referred to as a *soul retrieval*. The successful outcome depends on the collaborative relationship between the shamanic practitioner and his helping spirit or ally.

Shamans recognize that for many of us, there is great likelihood that our vital essence has been compromised by degrees throughout our lives through accidents, illness, surgeries and trauma. Over time, it becomes evident that as we work with our helping spirits, more and more dissociated parts of us become reintegrated as we progressively and cumulatively become more whole and complete.

The importance of resolving soul loss cannot be overstated. We all know individuals who seem aimless, wandering through their life frustrated and lost. Without the inner knowing and conviction of one's life purpose, these people often just drift and go through the motions of living without joy, passion and gratitude. This description reflects loss of personal power driven primarily through soul loss, often the result of unresolved trauma.

CHAPTER 17

Compensatory behaviors such as various forms of addiction or trying to self-isolate frequently result, compromising the person's ongoing life experience. Soul loss can be remedied if one has the willingness to consider different approaches and open up to new ideas and possibilities for wholeness that have been successfully used for thousands of years.

When I journey for a client who has unresolved trauma, partnering with one of my helping spirits yields surprising and substantive results. During my initial journey, I seek diagnostic information through the assistance of my helping spirit. Once I receive this, I next journey to acquire a power animal for my client through a power animal retrieval. My follow-up session with this client involves discussing changes that have occurred during the interim and reviewing how to stay connected to one's newly received guardian spirit.

I then explain what a soul retrieval entails and initiate the journey in search of one or more inner parts that fled as a consequence of trauma. I am clear in my intent at the initiation of the drumming or rattling music and begin narrating my journey experience in real time to my client. Sometimes my compassionate spirit takes us to the upper world, where a younger part may be found peacefully inhabiting a serene wooded area, content to be away from the person or people who generated the need to flee. Other times this split-off part may be perceived as a shattered debris field that must be collected by my power animal. There are many locations in NOR where this lost soul part may have fled to.

Once we locate it, I initiate a dialogue with this younger part. I explain to it that it is dearly missed and that it is now safe, since the abuser or abusers are gone now, allowing the more mature grown-up self to welcome this part back. I explain how important it is for both my client and for this part that fled to reunite so reintegration and healing can occur.

There are times when the soul part is reluctant to return and must be persuaded. Other times, this lost part is eager to return, reassured by the gentle beauty of my power animal, frequently Horse. Sometimes the retrieved part cannot communicate at all, such as when my power animal casts a wide net to collect the debris field that represents the many disparate elements of the vital essence that shattered.

Once my power animal has collected this lost part, Horse begins to gallop away from the particular environment as we hold on to it tightly. Many times during the same journey, Horse next takes us to another environment where an older teenage part has been hiding out. There, the same exchange will take place. I have had the experience during a single soul retrieval when several parts over different time periods of the client's life are identified and collected by Horse.

It is common for the client hearing my narration to remark afterward how profound this experience was for them. During the dialogue part of the journey, the soul part reveals comments and clues to me about the context that generated the soul loss and flight to a nonordinary environment for psychic and emotional safety. At a certain point during the journey and upon return to ordinary reality in my office, I kneel over my client lying on his back and energetically infuse through my breath the soul part(s) into his heart center. I then gently help the client to sit up at ninety degrees as I focus on the part(s) once again, infusing this aspect of his vital essence into his crown chakra. I then rattle around the client to seal in the part(s). This completes the soul retrieval.

Sometimes clients are barely aware of this integration process at their conscious level. Other times, the client becomes very emotional over a period of days or even weeks. Subsequent sessions can involve recapitulating the original traumatic context using energy psychology strategies to ensure that the client has strong energetic boundaries with his past, as well as the newly returned part that is gradually integrating. Intentionally staying in relationship with the returned inner part(s) is a most important task following a soul retrieval. This often involves active imagination exercises and daily journaling, which yield ongoing insights about the original context and conditions that created the soul flight. This is an excellent example of blending psychotherapy and shamanic healing in order to smooth the way for a complete integration of the returned soul part.

Some people actually prey on others in relationships. Sometimes they can be described as energetic vampires. While the expression *soul stealing* may conjure up thoughts of sorcery and horror movies, the reality is that soul stealing happens all too frequently. This occurs when one person in a relationship is domineering and controlling toward the other. This can also occur when one person is obsequious to the other, who happily continues to dominate. In either case, there is an obvious imbalance in the power dynamic. Often when one person is clearly dominant, the submissive one essentially gives up vital essence and loses it to the dominant individual. The result is a cumulative depletion of vital essence from one individual that is siphoned off and acquired for greater power and vitality by the dominant one.

This soul stealing is not an unusual consequence of this relational dynamic wherein one person becomes progressively weakened and the other person becomes more invigorated. The weakened person experiences soul loss through this process and thus will benefit from a soul retrieval. The dilemma is that if the person who received the soul retrieval continues in the same relational dynamic with the domineering person, it is likely that the soul stealing will persist. The way out of this is for the weaker individual to become aware of the dynamic and choose to challenge it. Comprehensive and supportive psychotherapy to help generate insight and awareness of this is warranted, given that the dynamic is likely an unconscious pattern internalized from the person's family of origin.

Being overly nice, conflict avoidant or codependent in a relationship can set up the conditions wherein soul stealing occurs.

Much has been written about codependent relationships and boundary setting in the psychotherapeutic literature, but defining it as *soul stealing* is known only in the shamanic healing paradigm. This is a good example of how the collaboration between psychotherapy and shamanic healing is warranted. Thus, effective psychotherapy needs to create sufficient insight and awareness to provide clients with useful information, enabling them to realize there are more choices available than simply continuing along in a depleting and self-sabotaging relationship.

This is another example of why shamanic healing is so important to incorporate into the psychotherapy session. When the soul retrieval and integration of a younger, traumatized, split-off inner part is accomplished, new vitality and insights emerge. Clients report that they feel more complete and more whole. With new vital energy and the accompanying internal cognitive awarenesses beginning to percolate, clients begin to perceive and appreciate their current situation more honestly. This creates shifts in their awareness that often provide much greater openness to re-evaluate their relationships with greater clarity, vitality, personal power and self-confidence. It is often a game changer.

Chapter 18

Traumatic Residue as Energetic Imprints

To understand energetic imprints, one must first be open to energy-based approaches to healing. At its very core, subtle energy is always part of our ongoing daily life. My experiences extracting psychotoxic intrusions continue to confirm how subtle negative energy imprints profoundly impact my clients.

I have discovered through decades of working with energy-based healing approaches that traumatic residue stays stuck not only in the unconscious mind but the physical body and throughout our *energy body*. These imprints of old trauma accumulate over time in layers.

Metaphorically, I am reminded of a candy called a jaw breaker. These are like very large, hard marbles with many multicolored layers of sweet candy flavors. As you may recall from childhood, you roll them around in your mouth, letting the various layers dissolve to reveal the next colored layer. Since you cannot break them apart for fear of breaking your teeth or jaw, they dissolve slowly until you have finally finished getting through each layer. The beauty and distinctiveness of this candy is that each layer is revealed incrementally (should you be curious enough to pull it out of your mouth to see what color the next layer is), until you have ingested all the sugared layers.

Old traumatic residue can be described as cumulative multilayered trauma that is much like a jaw breaker. There are energy psychology practitioners and shamanic practitioners who, like myself, have trained themselves to become sensitive to the many forms of energy circulating in and around themselves and their clients. I provide a specialized approach to helping clients rid themselves of the tyranny of distress that often presents as post-traumatic stress disorder (PTSD) with persistent symptoms that promulgate despair and untold suffering. Sometimes, targeting a particular layer of traumatic residue releases that specific imprint. Other times, addressing a symptom of persistent trauma leads us to a deeper layer of repressed trauma that then releases multiple imprints simultaneously.

The jaw breaker is a useful metaphor since traumatic events tend to become imprinted in our *energy body* until released through focused energy-based strategies. The more trauma that a person experiences, the deeper the layering process goes—additional energetic imprints create an increasingly dense repository of cumulative trauma.

Many psychotherapy models claim to be the best approach to alleviate the persistent suffering of PTSD, depression and anxiety. Some models propose that trauma is stuck in the physical body; others insist it is trapped in the unconscious mind. It is not my task here to deconstruct or criticize other therapy models, as I have already commented on the effectiveness or lack thereof regarding other therapeutic approaches. I do, however, want to briefly discuss why Dynamic Energetic Healing™, which is a combination of energy psychology approaches and core shamanism strategies, is so successful in eliminating cumulative traumatic energetic imprints.

Using kinesiological muscle testing with clients, *I connect with the energy of my client* to determine the best intervention or strategy to use. Sometimes, I direct my client to tap on the end points of a specific acupuncture meridian (called acupressure

Chapter 18

Traumatic residue stored in the energy body *and the physical body*

tapping) while internally reviewing the disturbance. Other times, I direct the client to gently move their hand back and forth in front of a specific chakra to fan and stimulate its energy while they attune to the disturbance. The client may focus on how their physical body is feeling, what they are thinking about or what feeling states become stimulated during that time. As particular pathways of the acupuncture meridian system or specific chakras become stimulated in this manner, the vital energy that was congested or blocked for years now becomes liberated. As the pathway or energy center becomes unblocked, the vital energy begins to flow once more. This creates a healing outcome as the energetic imprint (related to a particular trauma) begins to release. When this occurs, the individual starts to come into balance. Clients notice this balancing as emotions and physical symptoms rapidly begin to normalize.

The origins of these healing traditions and techniques are thousands of years old. When they are understood and used appropriately with therapeutic intent, old traumatic imprints are directly impacted. I always energy check after each therapeutic intervention so both the client and I are made aware of the degree of success achieved to alleviate the effects of old, buried trauma that became imprinted like the many layers of an energetic jaw breaker. Results are acknowledged through the client's self-report as well as through the muscle testing process. This is most helpful. Were it not for the implementation of energy checking, I would be limited to the client's self-report. However, using behavioral muscle testing/energy checking to identify the energetic origin of a trauma along with shamanic healing techniques via frontal occipital holding provides much greater detail about the extent *and underlying cause* of the imprints left by trauma. Incorporating these energy-based strategies also often gets to the very core of the traumatic residue.

Many clients who have experienced prolonged trauma are chronically dissociated. This common defense mechanism, which involves emotionally numbing oneself from feelings of overwhelm and despair is understandable, but it is very disabling. Dissociation opens the door for clients to unintentionally absorb psychotoxic energy from another person or the environment, because dissociation significantly compromises a person's energetic boundaries. This often creates a new negative energetic imprint for the person to be encumbered by. Until the *energetic intrusion* is released, it is likely that this individual will remain dissociated. This can last for decades, not just days or weeks, during which time additional layers of traumatic residue are accumulated, just like the multiple layers of a jaw breaker. What's even more worrisome is the resultant loss of personal power that promulgates ongoing vulnerability in the person's relationships.

When the compassionate spirits are recruited through the frontal occipital holding strategy, I am able to quickly move into nonordinary reality (NOR) in order to access the spiritual resources from this other healing dimension. My compassionate allies then identify specifically where in the body or the energy field the intrusion has nested, and proceed to energetically release this absorption of psychotoxic energy as I hold the space for them to do their healing work. It is often the case that my client experiences a deep physical body exhalation of something being released that they hadn't even known existed before. This is indicative of a significant negative energetic imprint that discharges completely.

Through the helpfulness and accuracy of muscle testing, I can identify the energetic origin of current symptoms that may be the result of not just one but several reinforcing traumatic incidents that have built up many layers of traumatic energetic imprints over decades. My work with clients is to diligently dissolve all of these multilayered imprints that have accumulated over their lifetime.

For example, let's imagine a veteran of a tour of duty to Iraq or Afghanistan who experienced several war-related traumas that are the *apparent* cause of his PTSD symptoms. If the presenting symptom is relentless anxiety, I still ask for the *energetic origin* of his problem through the help of muscle testing. The actual energetic origin may stem from the period when the client was six to twelve years old, when he was living with an abusive alcoholic father. These experiences are the early cumulative subtle negative energetic imprints that first need to be released so we can then get to the more recent war-related traumas that imprinted over the earlier ones. Like the metaphoric jaw breaker, we must identify each layer and work toward clearing each layer of energetic imprints until the muscle testing indicates the client has released all layers of the cumulative trauma.

Talk therapy approaches to addressing this type of cumulative trauma do not address energetic imprints, as these are not part of the traditional Western psychotherapy paradigm. It is certainly possible to review one's early life traumas through a psychodynamic investigatory approach over time. But in my experience, merely recalling, talking about and describing abuses that happened to a person in the past are insufficient to release the cumulative traumatic residue load that the client is carrying.

This is why so many clients terminate their traditional talk therapy long before their persistent anxiety or depression is healed. As a consequence, psychopharmaceutical medications are often the next therapeutic intervention. However, as I have mentioned previously, these powerful drugs do not help to resolve the underlying causes and origins—they merely address the persistent symptoms to help the client maintain some semblance of functionality. The use of medications is not healing—it is symptom management. We can do better than that, and with sensitive energy-based strategies that include shamanic intercession, clients experience the relief of being unburdened from what are often years of psychotoxic energy accumulation.

Chapter 19
Energetic Boundaries, Intrusions and Extraction of Psychotoxic Energies

Many of my clients suffer from compromised energetic boundaries. Some clients cannot keep protective energetic boundaries with just one person, such as a current partner or a parent who was particularly angry, abusive or controlling during the client's formative years. In these situations where energetic boundaries are weak and compromised, outside negative energies become more available and invasive. This is typically expressed as clients not having agency in their relationships, which often leads to codependency and feeling disempowered.

Maintaining firm and secure energetic boundaries is essential to staying self-empowered. When vulnerabilities persist due to developmental stresses, such as early attachment disorder issues (as described in Chapter 3, on John Bowlby), energetic boundaries are challenging to maintain. When we feel safe in our various environments, our surrounding energy field maintains integrity, thus protecting us from threatening outside energies. As I have described elsewhere, once I began training in energy psychology (EP) approaches to psychotherapy, I unwittingly absorbed my clients' psychotoxic energies, especially from clients who had trauma to work through. This happened because I did not yet understand the need for and value of *energetic boundaries*.

Maintaining healthy boundaries was never a problem for me before I began training in EP, but in EP the therapist's first orientation is to the client's *energy body*. Consequently, my tendency to empathically reach into my clients' energy field was causing me to absorb their upset and traumatic residue. In shamanic parlance, this absorption of outside negative energies is known as acquiring an energetic *intrusion*. It was these intrusions that led to my exhaustion. I did not know that I needed to separate energetically from my clients after each session had ended. It was only when I visited a spiritist healer in Brazil that I understood the underlying cause of my exhaustion was my weak energetic boundaries.

Since *energy* was now the emphasis and new currency when I worked with clients, I had to determine how to use my inherent strengths as a sensitive empath to gather information energetically (and thus intuitively) from clients *without absorbing their energy*. With a fresh understanding of energetic boundaries, I began to appreciate how essential it is for psychotherapists to implement certain strategies and integrate consistent energetic hygiene. This becomes even more important when considering the impact on the therapist (and the therapeutic relationship) of transference and countertransference. These unconscious projections go on during sessions between client and therapist frequently.

Transference and countertransference tend to heighten overidentification with the *dream figures* (the unconscious projections onto another person) and often linger in the psychotherapeutic context. For example, if a therapist experienced a sarcastic and demeaning mother growing up, it is likely that a female client will eventually emerge and personify that dream figure. If the therapist has not worked on herself sufficiently, the therapist will likely unconsciously react to this projected dream figure. Among other consequences, the therapist will start to feel disempowered, resentful and weakened. While this would be attributed solely to countertransference in the Western psychotherapeutic paradigm, at its root it is a too-permeable energetic boundary. This weakened boundary stems from a lack of sufficient awareness and is generated by unconscious vulnerability. Whether from countertransference or the therapist's empathic propensities, it is essential for the therapist to have robust energetic boundaries.

Some therapists have a hard time with angry and aggressive clients. Some therapists have difficulty with clients who have been repeatedly and brutally abused. The degree of emotional discomfort with particular clients largely determines whether the therapist will be able to maintain healthy energetic boundaries. The effect on the therapist can be subtle, and it is frequently caused by an unhealed part of the therapist. The degree to which the therapist maintains his or her energetic boundaries determines the extent to which he or she stays grounded and self-empowered.

Cognitive behavioral therapy (CBT) and many other talk therapy models do not take this energetic boundary issue into account because "energy" is not part of their assumptions—it does not enter into the Western approach to psychotherapy. While therapists generally do talk to their clients about setting boundaries with alcoholics and other types of threatening, abusive individuals, integrating this energetic understanding of being in relationship with clients is essential for therapists' ongoing health.

Different psychological paradigms use different theories, assumptions, approaches and interventions. While I suffered for several years with adrenal exhaustion before I knew how important it is to maintain strong energetic boundaries, in retrospect I am grateful that my journey to heal from that led me to discover and appreciate the validity and value of an energy-based approach that is what makes up the core of the EP model. Of course, my evolving awareness of the impact of subtle energy has benefited my clients, since I can now help them establish

Protection through robust energetic boundaries

energetic boundaries with their spouses, problematic parents (past and present), particular emotional energies (such as anger and guilt) and even their boss if needed. Implementing these energy-based therapeutic practices then becomes a way to support best practices and prevent burnout for the therapist.

People become disempowered for many reasons. From a psychotherapeutic perspective, these reasons may include trauma, post-traumatic stress disorder (PTSD), growing up in a dysfunctional family environment where personal physical and emotional safety was compromised, and feeling generally unsupported without any positive reinforcement. There are many nuances to how people react to abuse, neglect and the lack of emotional support, but all of these experiences generate a loss of personal power. There have been many therapeutic approaches over the years to address this, including inner child work, supportive long-term therapy, healing old shame, hypnotherapy, trauma-reducing therapies such as eye movement desensitization and reprocessing (EMDR), psychiatric drugs, and group therapy. With a caring, skilled and committed therapist, I believe that to varying degrees many of these therapeutic approaches can be helpful.

As our physical body requires nutritious food, clean air, pure water and daily physical activity to feel well, shamanic practitioners are regularly sustained by this omnipresent and mysterious *power* that is infused into them through their contact with their helping spirits. While this *power* may appear to be something mystical, in the shamanic paradigm its assimilation and absorption is to be expected for those practitioners who regularly journey into the nonordinary realms, for it is in these rarified spirit-based environments that they communicate and interact with their helping spirits from whom their *power* is received. It is through their ongoing association with their helping spirits that shamans continue to stay *power-filled*. This *power* protects them from absorbing psychotoxic intrusions from others.

Over time, shamanic practitioners become adept and proficient at gathering, storing, intensifying and, when necessary, sharing this *power* with others in need. Shamanic journeying provides for a strong and resilient immune system and generates an ongoing experience of being supercharged with vital life force. It is nourishment par excellence. Journeying into nonordinary reality (NOR) is the shaman's way to stay *power-filled*. It is also how the practitioner maintains strong energetic boundaries. The more one is filled with accumulations of *power*, the greater is one's resilience to the common stressors we are confronted with every day. You can learn to cultivate this as well.

Our skin protects us from a variety of external factors including bacteria, various chemicals, temperature imbalances and the sun's ultraviolet light. What is less widely known is that our energy field, when healthy and coherent, protects us from various energetic threats. These energetic threats can include what we all emit from powerful emotional states that include hostility and anger, anxiety and fear, shame, depressed mood, and the despair that often accompanies PTSD and unresolved trauma. When individuals are not *power-filled* and are struggling with any of these issues, they are prone to absorbing the emotional and energetic emissions from others. This is particularly true when a person is dissociated, because that creates an opening or a gap in their overall energy field that causes unusual vulnerability. Sometimes it is the intrusion itself that causes clients to dissociate as a response, and thus flee from energy in their system that is disruptive and noxious, though they know not its source.

While psychotherapists implement various approaches to help their clients overcome unhealthy mental and emotional behaviors and moods (which frequently include psychopharmacological medications), shamanic practitioners use time-tested strategies to reveal and resolve the underlying spiritual or energetic causes. This is accomplished during the shamanic journey into NOR with the help of compassionate spirits. To be clear, the shamanic practitioner is merely the conduit and the vehicle through which the connection with one's helping spirit and its *power* provide for the extraction or removal of the psychotoxic intrusion. The shamanic practitioner holds the space through her alliance with her helping spirit who is the agent that releases the intrusion. The tremendous relief clients experience immediately after the intrusion is released is remarkable. Typically, if they were dissociated, they come back into their body and feel completely whole once again. It then becomes their task to stay grounded in their body and ensure that their energetic boundaries with the particular person or individuals stay strong and constant. This becomes their therapeutic objective.

Different indigenous cultures describe or represent the energetic intrusion that is unique to their shamanic cultural tradition. For example, some shamanic traditions often perceive intrusions as darts stuck in different places in the body. Others perceive intrusions as dark, aggressive animals such as rats or snakes. Once the intrusion is identified and located in a specific area of the client's body, the shaman removes the intrusion and returns it to nature in various ways. Some shamans use a hollow bone of a dead animal to suck out the noxious energy and then spit it out into a bowl, doing this repeatedly until the intrusion is completely extracted and then dumped into a hole in the earth. Others merge with their power animal and, in the merged state, locate the intrusion, scoop it out, and throw this psychotoxic energy into the jungle or a river where it is assimilated.

While these descriptions may seem preternatural, primitive and fantastical, my personal experience corroborates this on a daily basis with clients. It continues to be my experience that when someone absorbs psychotoxic energy as an energetic intrusion, they frequently experience loss of mental focus, unusual tiredness and various expressions of emotional distress such as atypical anxiety. An affected person may complain of physical pain in and around where the intrusion has nested. All of this is indicative of loss of *power*. See the case studies provided in the next section of this book for several examples of how clients of mine have been relieved of intrusions through my shamanic healing work.

Clients often come to therapy because they have experienced different degrees of trauma in their lives. These traumatic events have often left them victimized and feeling powerless. Establishing strong, healthy energetic boundaries is all about making better choices about self-care in order to stay *power-filled*. This process often includes realistically reassessing their current relationships to ensure that there is a healthy balance of power in order to avoid the trap of codependency. It is primarily within the relational context that energetic boundaries matter most. Staying present to oneself and grounded in one's personal power remain the central key to preventing energetic intrusions.

A Foot in Both Worlds

This is the path to keeping one's personal power constant and remaining strong in the face of day-to-day challenges.

CHAPTER 20
EARTHBOUND SPIRITS

When we die, what happens to our vital essence, that remarkable and unique expression of our animating life force that is sometimes called our soul? There has been much written about and discussed throughout the centuries on this matter. Atheists believe we just disappear like a whisp of smoke—end of story. Scientists look for proof that there is some kind of afterlife; until they find it, they will be unwilling to believe that our souls continue to evolve. Various religious traditions believe in the transmigration of the soul from lifetime to lifetime. Many Buddhist and Hindu traditions believe in karma, in which our actions from previous lifetimes determine our incarnation and circumstances in our current—and future—lifetimes. Tibetan Buddhism insists that the soul of the Dalai Lama transmigrates with unbroken succession from one lifetime to the next. Curiously, the child who the Tibetan Buddhist monks identify as the reincarnated Dalai Lama always fulfills this spiritual destiny.

Shamans assert that once death comes for us, our soul leaves the physical body and continues on its journey as it evolves to wherever it goes next, perhaps to the light of oneness. However, for various reasons, some spirits of the deceased get stuck or trapped in our middle world—their progression to wherever their next destination is becomes stymied. These

A Foot in Both Worlds

An earthbound spirit

spirits become earthbound and are sometimes known as wandering or suffering ghosts.

Sometimes this occurs because of a sudden accidental death that provided no forewarning. As a consequence, these beings often don't even know they are deceased. They tend to be confused, fearful and disoriented. They search for their loved ones and are often drawn to a particular person whose light has a similar resonance to their own. They then latch onto that person's *energy body* in order to experience a secure connection as a way to alleviate their fear. Other times the spirit of a deceased person feels it is imperative to stay close to a loved one in order to protect them. Or, the spirit of the deceased may have enough awareness to wait in this state of purgatory until the loved one dies so they can travel together to wherever they go next. For example, I once identified that a client was being affected by an earthbound spirit. He said that he knew this—it was his sister with whom he had had a very close relationship. Just prior to her passing, she told him she would wait for him and then together they would move on to wherever they were to go next. I did not "release" this earthbound spirit since they had made an agreement. It remained "in his field," hovering around him but not attached to him—that would have created problems for him.

If the spirit of a deceased person attaches to a living person who becomes its host, it is not unusual for the spirit of the deceased to feel rejuvenated. The deceased spirit may also vicariously experience some aspects of the living person, such as their gratification from food or other kinds of sensual experience.

Because of its state of confusion, the deceased spirit may not even be aware that it is attached to a living person. On the other hand, the attached spirit may use its influence to encourage the living person to make choices that support the fulfillment of the spirit's own desires. (See Case Study 16: Spirit Attachment and Releasement.)

It is not unusual for the living person to notice feeling off or physically depleted in ways that conventional therapeutic approaches are unable to satisfactorily address. People with an attachment may just attribute their dis-ease to an unidentifiable virus, hoping it will run its course.

This experience of feeling drained and depleted may exacerbate a variety of preexisting illnesses that the host person is managing with the help of their daily medication. Examples of this include spikes of blood sugar or increases in blood pressure that the individual has been keeping under control. Occasionally, the living person may manifest symptoms of an illness that directly relate to the illness experienced by the deceased person before death. The host person may also become emotionally or mentally compromised as a consequence of being influenced by the spirit of the deceased.

A deceased spirit may or may not know what has happened to it. It may be unaware of its own death and status as a deceased person who is now a wandering and lost spirit. It may also be unaware of its attachment to a living person. It may even feel that the body it is attached to is its own.

But some deceased beings are aware of their state and may try to exploit the situation by actively influencing their host based on their own desires. Yet because they are experiencing things through another person, their experience is usually muted and thus is rarely satisfying. Nevertheless, the spirit that has attached to a living person may persist in its attempts to influence its host in an effort to experience vicarious pleasure and the feeling of satisfaction in sensory-based gratification. This then influences the living host to do things and act in ways that are out of character and often mystifying to the living person. The living person usually wonders what the heck has changed that has caused them to engage in new and unfamiliar behaviors. Most never suspect that this could be the result of so-called possession illness.

Once a proper diagnosis is made, it is the task of the shamanic practitioner to support their client to be rid of the unbidden spirit. At the same time, releasing the attached spirit is a most compassionate intervention—it helps the suffering spirit to move on to wherever it next needs to go.

When an earthbound spirit attaches to a living person, many problems may occur for the living person, since aspects of the deceased spirit can begin to influence the living person. The attached spirit may try to influence its host to make choices and do things that reflect what the deceased being desires. As mentioned above, it may influence their host to do the things that brought pleasure to the deceased spirit, such as participating in addictive behaviors that are uncharacteristic of the living person. This may cause mental confusion along with unusual behaviors, weird and upsetting dreams, dissociation and other issues.

CHAPTER 20

I have never encountered an earthbound spirit possessing someone in a demonic and dramatic manner the way Hollywood likes to portray them. Some religious traditions use exorcism strategies to forcefully drive out the possessing spirit, but these have always seemed to me to be misguided and traumatic for both the living person and the spirit of the deceased.

In my experience, once the being is identified, it is quite easy to release it with the help of my compassionate allies. My compassionate spirits know the territory of nonordinary reality (NOR) and are thus able to facilitate the release of the earthbound spirit from the living person and help usher it away to wherever it needs to go next. This creates a compassionate win-win outcome for both the living person and the possessing spirit.

Traditionally, this spirit releasement work of the shaman is known as *psychopomp work*. The shaman becomes the conductor

An earthbound spirit attachment

of the errant soul with the help of her spirit allies. These spirit allies become the guides for the earthbound spirit to help it transition to wherever it next needs to go. For shamanic practitioners like myself, this is not unusual and once identified is easy to facilitate. To use an analogy, many people contract cold and flu viruses when they become run down or are careless and cavalier with protecting their health. It is well understood that we are all in constant contact with bacteria and viruses, but usually we only become infected and ill when our emotional and physical resistances are weakened. Like these microbes, earthbound spirits of the deceased are invisible but they can and do affect us. Taking your health seriously and ensuring that you are *power-filled* in order to maintain strong energetic boundaries helps to prevent these beings from attaching to your energy field.

Ought we be worried about earthbound spirits? Typically, they attach to people who have experienced some kind of trauma and are dissociated. As with energetic intrusions (which I have discussed in detail elsewhere), it is when an individual is in an emotionally weakened state that dissociation initially occurs, opening up the door for uninvited energies to sneak in. Once the attached spirit is released, I make sure that my client has excellent energetic boundaries with it in particular, as well as all that encompasses NOR.

For someone who experiences an attachment for the first time, it can become frightening and unnerving to consider that this is yet another possible consequence of unhealed traumatic residue. Even a powerful fright that created an opening in one's energy field causing a dissociative response can open the door for an earthbound spirit to come through and attach itself.

Energetic intrusions and attachments happen much more frequently than most people are aware of. Fortunately, shamanic practitioners can easily remedy these troublesome energy-based problems. This is the realm of the soul, and traditional shamans have been navigating these nonordinary realms for many thousands of years. I am very grateful that I and many others now know the techniques that provide healing and balance to people beset by these subtle energy issues. Once an earthbound spirit attachment has been identified and released, both the living person and the attached spirit benefit, since each of them end up in a better place going forward. This is why the releasement process is referred to as a win-win outcome—they end up resolved of the unwarranted connection that was causing problems to both. For the living person, any exacerbations of medical issues abate, while the earthbound spirit is finally moving forward on its soul's journey. This is a most compassionate outcome.

PART 3:

CLINICAL CASE STUDIES IN DYNAMIC ENERGETIC HEALING™

Introduction to Case Studies

The following clinical case studies reflect how shamanic interventions are successfully integrated into the psychotherapy session. There are repeated themes that show up throughout these examples. As a way to help you better understand these case studies, I first want to introduce and briefly explain these themes.

My Dynamic Energetic Healing™ (DEH) model, uses behavioral muscle testing that derives from the discipline of applied kinesiology. This is a way of receiving direct client feedback by either gently pushing down on a client's arm when asking a question, or developing the required sensitivity to muscle test (also referred to as energy test; I use the terms interchangeably) at a distance, often referred to as remote or non-local testing. I have integrated this methodology into my DEH model and have been using this for over twenty years. Prior to 2020 when the pandemic started, I would occasionally need to energy test standing in front of my client without any physical contact due to confusing or inconsistent responses resulting from the presence of subtle negative energy. However, when the pandemic started, psychotherapy was conducted online either with Zoom or Skype, or over the telephone. Fortunately, I had mastered remote energy testing so my telehealth appointments were not compromised in any way.

Implementing accurate muscle testing has transformed the way I approach psychotherapy. I learned this as a part of the energy psychology model that I incrementally integrated into my psychotherapy approach. This way of working has enabled me to support my clients in a more comprehensive manner. For example, by asking for the energetic origin of a current presenting problem, the energy checking might indicate that an event fourteen years earlier is responsible. This fosters a discussion of what was occurring during that time of my client's life experience. It could be something that my client can immediately relate to as part of his or her personal history, or it could be an event that the client has completely forgotten. Either way, being able to pinpoint a specific time frame and/or significant event—frequently trauma-based—from a client's past leads to uncovering and resolving an issue that has been left festering and often buried and that has continually affected them negatively.

As I became increasingly sensitive to subtle energy when working with clients, I began incorporating muscle testing to ask for the best energetic strategies to address the particular issue we are confronting in the moment. As a result, I may direct a client to start tapping on various meridian points or stimulate certain chakra centers in order to create balance related to the specific issue. During any of these energy-based interventions, the client is attuning to the problem state or issue at hand.

I have also developed increasing sensitivity to subtle *negative* energy. This category includes different forms or expressions of under-the-radar interference patterns that tend to keep traumatic residue stuck in place. As I energy test my client, there are times when I suddenly have an *inner knowing* that there is something afoot that is negatively impacting the client's therapeutic goal or intention. It is at this point that I begin asking via energy checking whether there is subtle negative energy enmeshed in the client's problem state. The energy checking will confirm this.

Introduction to Case Studies

Then I begin using the energy checking to ask more pointed questions specific to subtle negative energy possibilities.

As you will read, I usually energy check my clients at the beginning of each session to determine if they are fully grounded in their physical body. When the muscle testing determines that a client is only 31 percent embodied, for example, further inquiry typically identifies subtle negative energy involvement. Sometimes the muscle testing identifies a client is only 15 percent embodied. This scale of embodiment is not necessarily to be understood literally, but it is a measure of how solid and congruent a client is at the moment, relating to their self-confidence in relation to the person or situation we are discussing.

Dissociation is a recognized defense mechanism that happens unconsciously as a way to evade acknowledging a difficult emotional response (such as anger) or responsibility for occupying a particular relationship. Generally, when the muscle testing scale of embodiment is on the low end, it indicates how perilous this person's relationship is to the other, with whom energetic boundaries are compromised. When someone is significantly dissociated, it affects their concentration, memory and overall physical well-being, particularly the severity and perpetuation of their physical symptoms. Through the muscle testing inquiry process, we usually discover that when dissociation is present, subtle negative energy is involved. We are then able to determine the energetic origin of a particular event(s), which provides meaningful insight into what is usually some kind of trauma. Once the negative energy is discharged, clients typically spontaneously return to being fully grounded in their body and sigh a deep sigh of relief.

These case studies describe how certain categories of subtle negative energy create problems for clients. You will read about different formulations of subtle negative energy, how they are identified through the muscle testing process, and how I am able to help my clients release these formulations. As a prelude to reading these case studies, I want to review what some of these formulations are and how they are addressed successfully.

These subtle negative energy formulations derive from the core shamanic healing paradigm. As discussed earlier, this approach to experiencing life on our planet is a nature-based animistic orientation. It is nonrational, and thus it requires a different way to interact with and understand being on our planet. As it is animistic, the underlying principle asserts that everything is filled with this animating life force and has its own spiritual intelligence and expression. However, because it is soul-based versus rational-analytic, one who is shamanically trained perceives things differently.

Our everyday normal reality is based on a general consensus about what is true. Core shamanic practices transcend this agreement; they take place in nonordinary reality (NOR). Shamans and shamanic practitioners learn how to negotiate both of these epistemological approaches to knowing what is true. Shamanic practitioners like myself learn how to move back and forth between these two intersecting realities, since each one impacts the other. People who know nothing about core shamanic approaches tend to label this soul-based approach in various ways. These characterizations may include simply being made up, magic or witchcraft. These descriptions are made because shamanic practitioners have a foot in both worlds. Michael Harner characterizes this in the following way:

> While the work of shamans encompasses virtually the full gamut of known spiritual practices, shamanism is universally characterized by an intentional change in consciousness (Eliade's "ecstasy") to engage in purposeful two-way interaction with spirits. Its most distinctive feature, which is not universal, is the out of body journey to other worlds.[141]

While shamanism is frequently characterized as the oldest healing approach on our planet spanning many thousands of

Introduction to Case Studies

years, it is so different from our scientific and industrialized everyday reality that most people simply do not have any familiar reference points to latch on to.

The beings who inhabit this other reality are referred to as spirits. They are intelligent, creative, sentient, and primarily compassionate. Spirits take on many different forms endowed with powerful healing capabilities. They elicit powerful healing outcomes when asked to help by shamanic practitioners, who learn how to partner with spirits to generate various healing outcomes.

I use two primary methods to enable the removal of the subtle negative energy. One method is the formal shamanic journey accompanied by drumming or rattling that I have described earlier in the book. In these journeys into NOR, I begin with a very specific goal and seek out my helping spirits to assist me in accomplishing my therapeutic outcome. Typically, this takes between fifteen and forty-five minutes. The other method is when the frontal occipital holding intervention is called forth through muscle testing. I have already described this as a compressed-time shamanic journey that typically takes two to three minutes while I stand to the side of my client, making gentle contact with their forehead and occipital ridge at the back of their head. This can also be done non-locally as I have described in Chapter 13.

In addition to using the two approaches above, I also often incorporate energy psychology strategies to help remove resolve subtle negative energy. For instance, if someone has an energetic intrusion located in their throat center, stimulating that energy center by having them move their hand back and forth in front of the throat while thinking about the issue at hand often precedes the frontal occipital holding in order to more easily facilitate the removal or extraction of the intrusion.

The following case studies are accounts of clients who had very different problems. Anthropological research has confirmed that over the millennia, shamans have developed a comprehensive skill set in order to service and support their communities by addressing these problems and others. Over time with training, commitment and practice, contemporary shamanic practitioners are learning to acquire these many time-honored capabilities. The shamanic practitioner's skill set and tasks include the following:

- Divination as a way to consider possible future choices
- Diagnosing and treating the spiritual cause of illness, both emotional and physical
- Soul retrieval to address *soul loss* and chronic dissociation
- Power animal retrieval as a way to support and augment a client's personal power
- Cultivating long-lasting relationships with anthropomorphic and animal spirits
- Extractions of *psychotoxic intrusions*
- Releasing *earth-bound spirits* of the deceased that can attach to a living person
- Psychopomp work to assist the dying and dead to cross over during their transition
- Cleansing of an inhabitable space of negative energies (e.g., hotel rooms)
- Bringing forth ancestral spirits for help, healing and guidance
- Connecting with various spirits of the natural world for protection and *power*
- Releasing lingering traumatic residue, including post-traumatic stress disorder (PTSD), anxiety and depression
- *Spiritual dismemberment* for deep personal cleansing and purification
- Strategies to stay *power-filled*

As you will see, I have chosen to include case studies that showcase a number of these skills.

Introduction to Case Studies

Energy checking is used throughout each session to identify energy psychology strategies to implement. While these case studies emphasize frontal occipital holding, many other energy-based strategies are frequently incorporated. These involve tapping on acupuncture meridians or fanning in front of chakras while the client is thinking about the specific issue. It continues to be my experience that when subtle negative energy is identified through the muscle testing process, various subtle negative energy formulations that I have previously described in detail suddenly become available to confront. These case studies include addressing earthbound spirits (including ancestral spirits), intrusions (including collective intrusions), and soul loss and soul stealing. I have even included some personal experiences when I was contaminated by collective intrusions that created significant physical distress.

In most cases, compromised energetic boundaries set up the conditions that allow these different formulations of subtle negative energy to embed themselves in clients. This can be the result of unhealed trauma, dissociation or unusual collective fear, such as during the beginning of the pandemic and subsequent lockdowns. While we have all read about areas of the world where mosquito-borne illnesses proliferate and infect thousands of people, nothing in our lifetime measures up to the global pandemic that killed millions of people and whose virus continues to circulate with changing variants. Nevertheless, with accurate muscle testing and the availability of shamanic intervention, all of these disturbances can be released including what I describe as collective fear that manifests as collective energetic intrusions.

Over the last three decades I have taught many clients how to experience the shamanic journey for themselves. The most effective format was when I facilitated small practice groups over a number of consecutive weeks. Remarkably, clients learned this journeying skill fairly easily. It was always helpful for each member to share their journey experiences in the group circle as it reinforced each participant's own forays into NOR. It did not take long for each client to overcome their self-consciousness and allow themselves to just go with their experiences, accepting whatever unfolded without self-criticism.

As one begins to journey shamanically, a common response is that of heightened feelings of love and connection with all beings and the natural world. This experience of the opening of the heart is at the core of shamanic journeying. Everything tends to come alive with great alacrity in the nonordinary realms, eliciting feelings of appreciation and love that many people tend to compartmentalize due to the demands of our unrelenting survival-based lives.

As Process unfolds in the journey, excitement, wonder, revelation and surprise all coincide to uplift the journeyer. This is in stark contrast to the constricted emotional responses that often follow trauma, whether it be a single incident or trauma that is cumulative as a result of ongoing emotional or physical abuse. While everyone reacts to trauma in their own particular way, there are common responses that restrict and inhibit people emotionally. These can be multilayered and include physical and interpersonal reactions that make up the many lingering symptoms of trauma that develop into persistent PTSD. Talk therapies such as cognitive behavioral therapy (CBT) can often result in clients becoming retraumatized, since many therapists believe that painstakingly recapitulating every aspect of the traumatic event(s) generates eventual healing. Many therapists trained to specifically address trauma have a different understanding of how to approach its treatment.

Cleveland area psychotherapist Linda Gould, L.P.C.C., says:

> Oftentimes in trauma, healing cannot be completed because traumatic experience becomes locked in various areas of the brain. We don't work trauma through by just talking about it. Talking is primarily a left hemisphere activity. In order to complete the healing process, a traumatized person must first access the limbic system and the right hemisphere of the brain,

INTRODUCTION TO CASE STUDIES

where images, body sensations and feelings are stored. By activating this area of the brain and accessing the stored images, body sensations and feelings, a person is able to attach meaning to them and move this traumatic material to more adaptive resolution.[142]

The shamanic journey generates a multisensory experience of rich and vibrant imagery accompanied by body sensations through the absorption of *power* and via profound feeling states that are typically unanticipated. In our everyday world of global warming, gun-related massacres and ongoing species extinctions, shamanic healing becomes more important than ever before. In particular, the heart-opening imagery that unfolds as one journeys into the dimensions of NOR heightens feelings of love, gratitude, and connectivity with the larger world. The shamanic journey is an especially potent producer of these mood-enhancing neurotransmitters, given the upbeat and often euphoric feeling states that ensue. Given our daily menu of discouraging news, shamanic journeying for ourselves and our clients becomes more important than ever. Once again, I encourage you to seek out a reputable teacher or organization with many years of journeying experience in order to discover these extraordinary and ongoing benefits that are just waiting to be had.

While many of these case studies may appear strange and unusual, they are emblematic of subtle negative energy disturbances that I address nearly every time I interact with clients. I say nearly every time because as clients recover from old trauma and begin to maintain strong energetic boundaries to stay *power-filled*, their vulnerability related to energetic intrusions and attachments diminishes. Eventually, clients learn to stay present to themselves and stay empowered.

I trust you will find these case studies fascinating and inspiring.

Case Study 1:
Animal Earthbound Spirit Attachments

In my many years of supporting clients through shamanic healing approaches, this case study stands out to me as unique. While I have learned over the years that it is not unusual for the wandering and disoriented spirit of a deceased person to attach itself to the energy field of another person, this client taught me something new.

Several years ago, Julia came to my office mourning the loss of her beloved pet. She was so bereft that she could not stop grieving. By her own admission, she is a "dog person." For all of her adult life, she has had dogs as an integral part of her family. She explained that she had other dogs die but this time she just could not get over it. Her most recent dog died at the age of 16, quite old for a large Samoyed. She wanted some assistance to overcome her loss, as she acknowledged that ever since her dog's death she had never quite felt the same. She wanted to come to terms with her loss so she could move on and simply live her life without constantly crying and thinking about her beloved long-time companion. At it happens, I also have Samoyeds and thus understood her emotional attachment to her beloved former companion.

She told me she just felt stuck in this ongoing, overwhelming grief that was interfering in her life. Her emotional pain was just getting worse and she was deeply depressed. She needed help to come to terms with her loss and be at peace. This was her singular therapeutic intention.

As I initiated my muscle testing, I identified that she was, in fact, carrying some traumatic residue that she had not yet been able to release. One of the issues I was quickly able to discern was that she was only 20 percent in her physical body. Dissociation from trauma is not at all unusual. However, when it persists, one's ability to concentrate and think clearly is significantly compromised. Additionally, because of the gap in one's *energy body*, one becomes more vulnerable to subtle negative energy formulations.

As we went through the steps to restore full embodiment, the indicator for the presence of subtle negative energy emerged in the muscle testing process. Specifically, it was an earthbound spirit attachment. When I asked what the best strategy would be to release this, frontal occipital holding was called for. What I saw greatly surprised me—it was the spirit of her beloved dog that was attached to her energy field!

Earlier in the session, Julia had admitted that she just didn't want to let this family member go. She explained that this particular dog was the last of a long line of dogs that she had cherished as a companion that helped her to feel complete. As I spent more time in the shamanic state of consciousness, I saw and heard that there was a pack of dogs in the distance, barking and beckoning the spirit of her dog to join them. It became clear to me that this was her dog's ancestral pack. I was so touched because I had never before seen a dog or any animal attached to somebody's energy field; until now, it had always been the spirit of a lost or disoriented human being.

Because Julia so loved her dog and her dog was so loyal to her, Julia ended up in a situation that ultimately was not good for either her or her dog's spirit. I could see her dog's spirit, stuck and conflicted, continuously going back and forth between Julia and her ancestral pack. I started to tear up.

In my shamanic state of consciousness, I decided to intervene and convey to the dog's spirit that it really was okay to leave Julia. Eventually, and with the encouragement of one of my power animals (and good communication being generated between the attached dog's spirit and its spiritual family of the pack waiting in the background), the loyal pet disengaged from Julia's energy field and joined its companions. All the dogs became celebratory and ascended as a pack to the place they needed to go to next. It was only when I gave her dog's spirit permission to leave her person that it was willing to leave Julia's side.

In shamanic healing this is called *psychopomp work*, since I ended up being the conductor of this animal's soul. When I shared this with Julia, she was not at all surprised. She was both saddened and heartened to know that her loyal companion was initially willing to sacrifice its own personal evolution to stay with her. If you have a pet dog in your life, I suspect you will understand. After this spirit releasement had been completed, Julia spontaneously returned to being 100 percent in her physical body, as confirmed by my muscle testing.

We talked quite a bit afterward, much of it about Samoyeds. Julia told me she felt relieved and thanked me for helping. She admitted that since this was to be her last dog as she was getting into her sixties and wanted to travel without the responsibilities of caring for and having to board a dog, she was holding on to her beloved pet. Accepting its passing would mean a profound shift in her self-identity—she would no longer be a person with a loyal canine companion and, since she lived alone, her self-identity as a truly single person would be heightened. We spent the rest of the session talking about our respective experiences living with dogs. Julia admitted that while she would feel greater freedom to do what she wanted on a whim, she acknowledged that this had been a very hard adjustment.

Curiously, when I muscle tested her to determine if she had strong energetic boundaries with her former canine companion, she tested positive. Once her dog's spirit was finally released after I gave it permission to join its spirit pack, Julia was immediately released from her own push-pull relationship with her former companion. Both she and her deceased companion were finally free.

When I next asked her how she was feeling after our discussion, she told me she was still experiencing sadness but, more importantly, she felt free of the burden of guilt that had weighed heavily on her. She hadn't realized how her unwillingness to let

CASE STUDY 1

go of her dog had kept her dog stuck to her in a way that was selfish of her. She also told me she felt lighter—as if a weight had been lifted from her heart. She went on to say that she was anticipating feeling sad for some time to come but now felt certain that she could move forward into the next chapter of her life. This one session was the only time I worked with Julia, as she had received what she had sought.

Another Animal Earthbound Spirit Attachment of a Pet Dog

Over a decade later, a client named Richard made an appointment. I had met with Richard before but it had been several years since the previous time. Richard had been retired for three years and lived alone with his dog. He had decided to retire about mid-2020 as the impacts of the Covid-19 pandemic began to wear on him. Even before the pandemic, Richard was able to do his graphic design work at home. It was because of his ability to work at home that he had decided many years before to acquire a dog. It was a Boston terrier that weighed no more than fifteen pounds.

Richard bonded very quickly to his dog and discovered the joys of canine companionship. He told me that he never felt lonely because his dog was with him all the time. At least three times a day he would take his dog for a walk in the neighborhood or occasionally to a local dog park. When I asked him if he ever thought about getting married again, Richard remarked that living with his dog helped him to be free of stress and that he really did not miss being married. He told me he liked his autonomy and while he was open to a new relationship if it just happened somehow, he was very content having his dog as his constant companion.

When his Boston terrier got cancer during its twelfth year, Richard was beside himself. In spite of good veterinary care, his beloved dog died five months after being diagnosed. Richard understood that he would be grieving and had read two books about grief and loss. He tried daily journaling for a while and some guided imagery exercises he had discovered. He told me that initially they helped dull his emotional pain but after about six weeks, he felt they were no longer helpful and he just tried to get through each day. He acknowledged he was depressed and had lost his joie de vivre. He no longer went for walks in the park because that would bring up memories of being with his dog.

One day, Richard thought that writing a children's story about his dog would be a way to honor his dog's memory. Since he was a graphic designer, he felt that doing this project would stimulate his creativity and perhaps help him get back into life. But first he had to think up the story and write the text. Initially, he was very excited about his writing project. But after two days of thinking about the plot and doing some initial outlining, he was blocked. No matter how hard he tried to motivate himself to start writing, he was in too much emotional pain to generate the mental focus needed for this project. Even trying to create images and illustrated scenarios outlining the chapters through his graphic design program felt too daunting. He felt stuck and hopeless.

After a bit of discussion about his therapeutic intention, it became clear to me that Richard was still suffering from acute traumatic loss. I decided that we would start off by muscle testing for any remaining traumatic residue from the loss of his dog. The issues that tested strong included a limiting belief that he would never experience joy again, dissociation, lingering negative emotional charge characterized by sadness and emptiness, and a double bind that essentially said that while he intellectually understood the importance of resolving his loss and moving on, to do so would be tantamount to abandoning his beloved dog. He was stuck in his protracted grief.

As I continued to inquire, the indicator for subtle negative energy suddenly emerged. My muscle testing determined that this represented an earthbound spirit attachment. This attachment muscle tested as the highest priority to treat first. The frontal occipital holding was next indicated as the best intervention to use. As I gently placed my hands on the front and back of his head, I centered myself and asked for help. Very quickly, I noticed that there was an outside energy that had merged with Richard. While not initially clear, it soon became evident that this earthbound spirit was his dog's spirit. Unlike in Julia's case, in which the dog's spirit was conflicted about joining her pack or staying with Julia, this situation did not reflect to me any internal conflict. Richard's dog's spirit was merged with his own energy field since both of them wanted to stay together—there was no ancestral pack beckoning his dog's spirit to join them.

This time, the dog's spirit was uncommunicative and thus I called on Eagle to assist. As Eagle flew around us, Richard's and the dog's merged energy fields gradually separated. Soon Eagle was able to grab onto Richard's dog's spirit and carry it away to wherever it needed to go next.

When I reported my experience to Richard, he told me he wasn't surprised. He explained that their bond was something he had never before experienced and thus was very special. He expressed mixed feelings, realizing it was time to surrender to the reality of his loss and move forward with his life. He was emotionally choked up and teared up a bit but acknowledged he suddenly felt lighter than he had felt in a long time. As is sometimes the case, muscle testing indicated that all of the residual trauma spontaneously resolved, as did his dissociation. Richard was now fully grounded in his physical body. When I tested the underlying limiting belief and double bind, I found that they had dissolved too. Importantly, the muscle testing indicated that Richard now had excellent energetic boundaries with his beloved dog, even as he thanked me for helping him move forward with his life to confront his grief. He acknowledged that it would likely take some time to reconcile this loss but he was now confidant he could and would do it.

We discussed ways he could continue to honor his dog while not falling back to feeling possessive. I explained that it would always be possible to energetically pull his dog's spirit back into his own energy field if he became overly focused on holding onto the dog emotionally. I explained that this would be just as bad for his dog's spirit as his own. Finally, I came around to refer to his children's book project. I had him repeat some affirming statements, including "I am now ready to move forward on developing the manuscript that children will relate to." This and several other statements muscle tested strong.

Richard smiled. He remarked that as we were talking about this creative project, he felt some enthusiasm stirring inside of him. He realized that this would actually be the best way to honor his beloved dog and stay in relationship with him in a way that would benefit them both. After ninety minutes, we got up from our chairs and exchanged a hug. Richard thanked me and left the office. Since that session I received one email from him, again thanking me and letting me know his writing project was beginning to gather some momentum. He then said he would send me a copy of his book whenever it gets completed.

Commentary

Being a pet owner myself, I must acknowledge that our three dogs are family members that enrich my life and my wife's. When I come home from work and open the door from the garage to enter the house, I am greeted by our three enthusiastic dogs who are woo-wooing and wagging their tails in excitement. It is a wonderful way to be greeted—they are all over me and it feels like a lovefest. This is a common experience that dog owners get to enjoy day in and day out. My dogs' love is unconditional and we are always glad to be with one another.

These two case studies reflect the emotional toll that losing one's devoted dog can take. Being in relationship with our pets opens our heart, and to be without that loving companion often feels devastating. I found it fascinating that when applying frontal occipital holding and opening myself up to the world of spirit, it was the spirits of the pet dogs that were initially revealed to me, not my personal helping spirits. These experiences provided me with new awareness of the depth of our connection to our pets. Their presence in the nonordinary realms revealed and underscored to me just how profoundly we are connected to our beloved pets. It also highlighted the Buddhist doctrine of impermanence and how our emotional attachments can lead to suffering if we are unwilling or unable to accept the transient nature of life, and especially of our relationships.

It is not in our nature to easily accept aging and the gradual decline and deterioration of our physical bodies, but it is something we could all spend more time contemplating to better get to a place of acceptance. These two case studies taught me a lot about appreciating each day with our dogs and the people we love. It was only after I was able to intervene on behalf of each of these pet dogs that my clients were able to finally willingly accept their loss. This is not at all to diminish the normal grieving that is part of losing a loved one. Yet at a certain point, it is important to realize that losing a loved one is a part of life; to love is, to varying degrees, having to deal with loss. The many long-term benefits of loving another far outweighs potential loss, even as we become attached to our beloved pets.

Case Study 2:
Intrusions, Psoriatic Arthritis and a Parasitic Attachment

A client named Gerald scheduled an appointment with me to resolve a persistent medical issue. He had heard about my energy-based work from a friend and was feeling desperate, since traditional medical approaches had not worked for him. He reported that he had been reinfected by psoriatic arthritis numerous times since he first contracted a form of psoriasis when he was fourteen. Gerald was fifty-seven at the time of our initial appointment. When he was forty-four, he was working as a building inspector when he had another episode of psoriatic arthritis. He had to quit his job and endured the pain that lasted three months. After addressing some underlying limiting beliefs, it was determined that he was only 31 percent embodied; that is, he was significantly dissociated. Thus, his first therapeutic goal was to restore full embodiment. This took three ninety-minute sessions to actualize.

First, significant subtle negative energy and traumatic residue had to be addressed. I determined through muscle testing that the first energetic origin was a trauma that occurred when Gerald was a teenager. He was struggling with identity issues, since he grew up in a rigid conservative evangelical Christian milieu. These issues were cumulative and coalesced when he was sixteen.

When testing for congruency to move forward on the intention, my muscle testing indicated he had significant subtle negative energy that was embedded in the cumulative family-related trauma he had suffered. Upon further inquiry, it was determined to be an earthbound spirit attachment. Frontal occipital holding was called for. As I placed my hands gently around his head and asked for help, I saw what I call a *parasitic attachment* in Gerald's throat chakra. These beings frequently appear when someone has experienced ongoing trauma. I call them parasitic because I see them siphoning the vital energy from the client. Over time, this weakens the client by compromising their life force and promulgating significant dissociation and illness. I have determined that this type of attachment represents in NOR an analog to a person who was abusive to my client. The energy of relentless persecution *becomes* this parasitic being in NOR that torments and weakens its host. This type of entity is very different from a typical earthbound spirit that is confused and frightened, searching for comfort and connection for solace. Once I saw what the situation was, I called for help from my compassionate spirits.

Immediately, I saw that Gerald's spiritual body was in the lower-world domain of my Native American helpers. As Grandmother, the leader of the group, assessed him, she saw immediately what I had seen and determined that she needed some assistance to remove this particularly noxious attachment. She put Gerald's spirit on a horse with a male warrior and all of them rapidly galloped to the base of a mountain close to their compound. There, she forcefully told four of her male warriors to hold and support Gerald to stand upright.

Grandmother approached the base of the mountain and began screaming at an elemental spirit that resides in the mountain. Because it is an elemental spirit, it is amoral (in contrast to compassionate spirits), and its forces must be carefully controlled by a shaman. Soon, the mountain began to tremble and this tall, vibrating, cylindrical Spirit of the Mountain began rumbling and positioning itself right in front of Grandmother. I see this elemental spirit about three stories tall with a cyclonic circulating intensity. It appears more like a very tall column of whirling energy rather than any kind of vortex. It generates tremendous centripetal force and thus is able to draw out harmful entities and intrusions that a person has been harboring in order to transmute them.

Grandmother was screaming at it to begin circulating around Gerald's spirit body but not to touch him. The force generated by the Spirit of the Mountain is like a huge powerful tornado with extreme high-intensity winds. As it circulated around and came to the front of Gerald, Grandmother screamed at it to come closer to him but not to touch him. As this was occurring, I could see the parasitic entity in Gerald's throat chakra powerfully sucked into this circulating cyclone-like elemental force. Grandmother then screamed at it to go back into its mountain home and transmute the entity.

As is often the case in these situations, Gerald's spirit body collapsed. Grandmother directed her warriors to put him on a horse with one of the men. They then galloped rapidly to the river near their compound. She directed two of the warriors to hold onto Gerald and submerge him in the river. The fast-paced current of cold water rushed by and around him, revivifying and restoring him. Afterward, they walked him over to their compound and gave him some power food in the form of dried bison meat.

When we subsequently muscle tested before the end of our session, the parasitic attachment was completely gone and Gerald was now 56 percent embodied. Muscle testing also indicated there was another energetic origin still generating interference on the intention for him to be 100 percent in his body. This next originating event was when he was forty-four years old—the time when he had his major physical collapse mentioned above.

So, we muscle tested to determine if Gerald was carrying residual trauma from this incident. The answer was yes. This residue was determined to be a loss trauma imprint due to the loss of his job and his inability to continue working, as well as his loss of normal function due to his psoriatic arthritis outbreak. There were several elements of traumatic residue including negative emotional charge, an unconscious death wish, soul loss, unresolved repressed anger, and a collective intrusion from his current family. During subsequent discussion, Gerald expressed that his current-day family

CASE STUDY 2

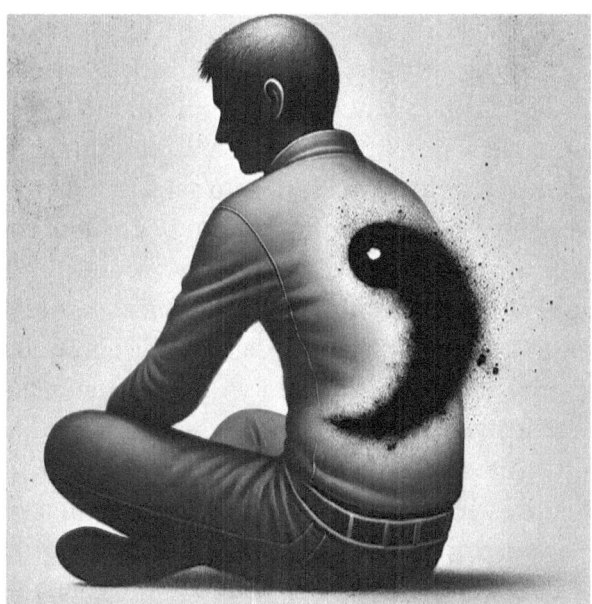

A parasitic attachment

was not sympathetic about his collapse and that he did not feel supported by them. This had been a familial theme that he was all too familiar with because he had suffered through so many of these psoriatic arthritis episodes in the past. When we muscle tested to ask what would be the best intervention to start with (in order to release this energetic intrusion of the subtle negative energy remnants from the trauma), frontal occipital holding tested strong.

As I proceeded, images and awareness began to emerge within me. I experienced and felt into how Gerald felt discounted, devalued and even shunned by his family members. I then perceived my upper-world teacher Odin, whose origins are from the Norse tradition. He came into Gerald's field and reached deep into Gerald's throat, pulling out what appeared as a lump of smoldering coal. I knew immediately that this was his repressed anger from feeling so unsupported when he was most vulnerable. Once Odin pulled out the lump of smoldering coal and threw it into the vastness of the universe to disperse, he then held his staff out and infused power into Gerald. After a short time, Odin withdrew and returned back to his own domain where I frequently visit him. This is when I knew we had completed our task. When I next muscle tested, the intrusion was gone and Gerald was determined to be 95 percent embodied.

I next asked a series of questions through muscle testing, and it was determined that Gerald had to integrate these changes on his own before he could expect to be fully grounded in his body once again. I suggested to him that in our next session, it would be wise to set a new therapeutic intention for him to be in optimal appropriate right relationship with psoriatic arthritis (i.e., establish healthy energetic boundaries with psoriatic arthritis). This would achieve being in harmony with this virus rather than being a victim to it. This is how we ended the session.

When we next met two weeks later, Gerald reported feeling much better overall, but he still had some low-grade anxiety about not ever ridding himself of his propensity to restimulate the persistent psoriatic arthritis. I reiterated his new intention to establish right relationship/energetic boundaries with his disease so that he would no longer remain vulnerable to these recurring attacks of infection. I had been considering this since we met previously, and he agreed that this would be a good way to put language to his therapeutic goal.

Whenever I start muscle testing a client, I always test for sufficient hydration to ensure that the muscle testing will be accurate. I discovered right away that Gerald could not hydrate regardless of how much water he was drinking. It occurred to me to ask if there was subtle negative energy interfering with his ability to hydrate, and in fact that was the case. This required me to step a few feet away as this was in-person. My muscle testing then became non-local or remote, which is what I do when I have Skype or Zoom sessions with people who are out of town. I have corroborated over many years now that my non-local muscle testing is just as accurate as physically testing my client's arms when working in-person.

CASE STUDY 2

As I continued to inquire, it turned out that the subtle negative energy was an energetic intrusion Gerald had been carrying from the very first time he came down with psoriasis when he was fourteen—this was the energetic origin. When I asked for the best approach to address this, my muscle testing indicated the frontal occipital holding intervention.

Standing next to him with my hands gently touching the front and the back of his head, I asked for help and defocused my eyes. Suddenly, I was in shamanic visionary journey mode. Once again, I was taken down to the domain of my Native American helpers where Gerald's spirit body was present and vibrating. I immediately saw the intrusion depicted as something akin to English ivy running down the front of him from where his collar bones come together all the way down to his pubic bone. It was dark, tenacious and deeply embedded in his body.

Grandmother once again emerged and, after a quick assessment, determined that she would need some assistance to release this. As before, she put him on a horse with the other warriors as they galloped toward the base of the nearby mountain. As is her way, Grandmother began screaming to the Spirit of the Mountain to come out and assist her to extract this intrusion. Shortly thereafter, the mountain began to rumble and this powerful, tall vibrating cylinder of ominous moving energy came out. She screamed at it to start moving slowly around Gerald, who was being held firmly by several male warriors. As the Spirit of the Mountain circulated around my client, she once again directed it to hover in front of him in an effort to pull out the intrusion. After what seemed like a substantial amount of time, the intrusion began to peel off from Gerald's collar bone area all the way down to his pubic bone. As it started to rip away from his body, I could see many long waving tendrils that had finally been detached from deep in his body.

Eventually, the intrusion was completely released and absorbed into the swirling mass of this primitive elemental energy. Grandmother then directed the Spirit of the Mountain to go back into the mountain to transmute the intrusion. I saw that there was a deep opening in Gerald's body where the intrusion had been pulled out. Grandmother then directed several of her warriors to travel swiftly to another area in their domain where there are hot springs that have specific medicinal healing properties. They were to bring back bowls of steaming mud from the hot springs (which they did very quickly). She then took handfuls of this wet, steaming gray mud and pasted it into and over the huge gaping vertical open wound. She sensed that this would not be sufficient to complete the healing so she directed several of her warriors to dig a very deep trench. They then laid Gerald's body deep into the earth. I could see dark oily poisons being pulled out of his body by the earth until the extraction was completed. He was then brought back up onto the surface.

Now that all the poisons from the intrusion had been released, I could see that Gerald's spirit body was very pale and needed help to stand up. Grandmother then directed her warriors to take my client on horseback to the river near their compound, and hold him in the river as the powerful current of cold, cleansing water washed over his back as before. He was then turned around to confront the powerful current of water pushing against his front side. After a moment or so, it was determined that he was sufficiently cleansed and he was brought back onto the surface and supported as they walked him over to a small structure. There he was fed power food in the form of dried bison. The journey and the related healing were then completed; I withdrew my attention and the scenario dissipated.

When I next muscle tested Gerald, he was completely hydrated with no need for any additional water—the intrusion was completely released at all levels, and he was finally 100 percent present in his physical body. Additionally, my muscle testing indicated that he now had 100 percent energetic boundaries with psoriatic arthritis. This meant that because all of the significant traumatic residue and subtle negative energy associated with his many experiences with psoriatic arthritis had been released, he was now energetically protected from this disease.

Commentary

Think about Gerald's initial complaint and try to imagine how cognitive behavioral therapy (CBT) might have addressed this. There would have been weeks and weeks of discussion about his early family experiences along with the many internalized beliefs he continued to carry into his current family. In my opinion, changing his thinking about psoriatic arthritis along with how his family marginalized his suffering would likely never have been able to create a healing outcome. He would be even more aware of how painful it was to live with his family of origin and his current family, but the psychotoxic energy he carried would never have been addressed. And, he would have continued to be vulnerable to psoriatic arthritis. As I have described earlier, CBT and Dynamic Energetic Healing™ (DEH) are two completely different psychotherapy models. Each carries different assumptions and uses different strategies. Just because many if not most therapists feel comfortable with talk therapy does not make it more effective. In fact, hashing over old painful trauma often tends to simply reinforce and sustain the suffering.

This case study encompassed three ninety-minute sessions. Gerald's presenting problem of dissociation initiated our inquiry process with the help of behavioral muscle testing, but the underlying issues included a conflicted self-identity generated from a conservative religious upbringing. This mirrored his current family wherein his wife and son were unsupportive of his pain and suffering related to yet another destabilizing bout of psoriatic arthritis.

With the help of muscle testing, I was able to calibrate the degree to which he was dissociated and determine the energetic origins (that identified key points of reference relating to earlier unresolved trauma, along with the subtle negative energy consequences of several of his complaints). The frontal occipital holding intervention was repeatedly selected via muscle testing as the vehicle for me to access several of my trusted helping spirits in compressed-time shamanic journeys. Throughout these three psychotherapy sessions, I was able to help my client release old unprocessed family trauma and identify underlying causes for what generated his chronic dissociation. The most significant shifts occurred when a parasitic attachment was released, along with the intrusion in his throat center and, finally, the penetrating intrusion depicted as deeply embedded English ivy. In subsequent visits with Gerald, his energetic boundaries with psoriatic arthritis remained strong, along with his ongoing experience of staying grounded in his physical body. By staying present with the windy road of Process as I followed the thread, guided by my cultivated sensitivity using muscle testing, my helping spirits facilitated incredible healing outcomes.

As a footnote, *energetic intrusions* are represented to me differently depending on each particular client and the underlying issues that generated them. These issues are usually a consequence of unresolved trauma that perpetuates degrees of chronic dissociation and the various expressions of subtle negative energy. Additionally, *I differentiate between what I call a common earthbound spirit attachment versus a parasitic attachment.* In the case of Gerald, a parasitic attachment was identified as an energetic entity siphoning his life force and thus weakening him cumulatively over time. I have seen them with many clients over the years and they frequently are drawn to people who are overidentified with the victim archetype and have often been scapegoated. Unlike what I have described as earthbound spirits who are typically disoriented, lost and fearful, these particular attachments are the spiritual and energetic analog of an ongoing abusive and persecutory environment or individual(s) that cumulatively shames and exploits the weakness of someone caught up in a cult-like familial environment.

CASE STUDY 2

    These parasitic attachments seem to emerge and are drawn to people who personify the victim archetype in order to perpetuate their suffering. In a way, they are the energetic stand-in for the original abusers. Even when the beaten down individual is able to finally leave their abusive family environment, they sometimes end up with this tortuous parasitic attachment that follows them like some kind of punishing curse. Fortunately, I have many ally figures in nonordinary reality who know exactly what is needed when these aggressive entities are identified. I am always amazed and grateful to be a witness to the remarkable creative and healing strategies demonstrated by my helping spirits. Their intercession is nothing short of miraculous as I hold space for them with my ongoing connection, reinforced regularly through my own personal shamanic journey work. While these case studies may create some cognitive dissonance for you, I assure you that with strong intent, ongoing practice and a persistent commitment to learn these strategies, you too can become *power-filled* and cultivate lifelong relationships with these remarkable compassionate beings.

Case Study 3:
Bowel Dysfunction Relieved from Releasing an Energetic Intrusion

Jonathan is sixty-two years old. He has been an accountant for a regional bank for the last twenty-two years. He was referred to me by his doctor for persistent constipation and intestinal distress. Our initial interview highlighted his frustration with his wife of over thirty-five years. He continues to want a close sexually intimate relationship while his wife seems largely uninterested. Compounding this was his perception that his wife was flirting in a sexual manner with other women when they were out at a gathering with friends. This so shocked him that he didn't know what to say to her, so he said nothing. He acknowledged feeling hurt, angry and resentful for both of these unresolved issues. He described his wife as somewhat critical and controlling, such that he was reluctant to confront her about these feelings he harbored.

As is often the case, once we began muscle testing to identify the energetic origin of these problems, the indicator for subtle negative energy emerged and was identified as an energetic intrusion from an incident that had occurred two years in the past. This original incident was the very first time that he perceived his wife "blatantly" flirting with another woman in a sexual manner. My client was so shocked that he became paralyzed with worry and began to have anxiety that his wife might have latent lesbian tendencies. Adding insult to injury, he remarked that this flirting is something he would love to experience with his wife, but she seemed interested in directing her flirtations toward other women instead of himself.

Frontal occipital holding was the intervention that was called for to address this intrusion. As I defocused my eyes while making gentle contact with his head, I began to see the *intrusion represented as an elastic belt cinched tightly around his solar plexus.* When I asked for help, I saw my upper-world teacher Odin holding his staff out and directing heat and fire at the intrusion around Jonathan's solar plexus. After a short period of time, the tightly cinched elastic belt began to loosen and very quickly completely dissolved. Subsequent muscle testing confirmed that the intrusion was completely released.

At his next appointment two weeks later, Jonathan acknowledged that within a day following our initial appointment he started having normal bowel movements once again. As we continued to discuss his marital relationship, it became evident that he needed to discuss and process these feelings he had harbored for the last two years so that he would no longer carry the anger, hurt and resentment toward his wife that was being internalized, self-directed and somaticized. While this was difficult for him, he came to understand and appreciate in our discussions that there was a direct correlation between suppressing these powerful emotions (instead of discussing them with his wife) and the subsequent tightening in his gut that generated the chronic constipation. I helped him to establish strong energetic boundaries with his wife to enable him to be in a more neutral position to initiate these discussions with her. He said he was prepared to do so and this became evident during our next session.

Jonathan acknowledged that being more forward with her caused him just a little anxiety, since she is a strong and self-possessed person. His task was to notice his reluctance to pursue his own desires with her when she appeared to be resistant to his overtures. As he deepened his understanding of the relational dynamics with his wife, his digestive and elimination issues began to normalize. Much of this short-term therapy was learning to acknowledge his own reticence to occupy the relationship when he was feeling sexual, along with accepting his own choices to step away without carrying resentment. By the last session, he continued to have normal elimination and there were no more energetic intrusions. He did require some minimal reinforcement of his energetic boundaries with his wife, as he decided that he was willing to take greater personal responsibility for his interpersonal choices.

Commentary

On reflection, what was most notable in Jonathan's case was how everything shifted when the intrusion from the original incident had been released. This opened up new insights regarding what was necessary for him to do in order to take care of himself within the context of his marital relationship. He understood from his personal physical experience that should he continue to harbor anger, hurt and resentment instead of sharing his concerns and processing this with his wife, there was a great likelihood that his previous dysfunctional constipation issues would reoccur.

While Jonathan admitted that it felt uncomfortable for him to openly discuss his concerns with his wife, he was committed to initiating the discussion in a way that was not accusatory. I helped him practice new ways to talk about this with her so he felt confident that he could do this without getting angry.

Since I did not hear back from Jonathan, I felt reassured that he met the challenge and redefined his marital relationship. He had become more self-confident occupying the relationship with his wife as he now felt emotionally safer. This was a very good outcome from just four psychotherapy sessions. The extraction and removal of the energetic intrusion was the key to resolving the problem, enabling productive discussions that followed with increasing ongoing awareness. With solid energetic boundaries, Jonathan now had more choices for how to interact with his wife without getting all bound up.

Case Study 4:
How Releasing an Energetic Intrusion Changed a Student's Life

A number of years ago, my son Elias, who was in his twenties at the time, was on a plane returning to New York where he was living and working. Sitting next to him was a man reading a book about ayahuasca. This piqued Elias' interest since he knows about my shamanic abilities and he was curious to know if this man was also interested in shamanic healing. Ayahuasca is a plant-based psychedelic preparation native to the Amazon region. (It is a combination of a shrub and a vine mixed together). When it is prepared in a traditional way and ingested under the oversight of a traditional shaman, it generates fantastical visions and subsequent healings from the spirit of the plants.

Elias engaged this gentleman, Thomas, in conversation and discovered that he was associated with a corporate IT firm and was becoming disenchanted with his job. He had never indulged in an ayahuasca ceremony, but he was becoming curious about different spiritually-based alternative paths. As Elias and Thomas continued their conversation, Elias told him that I am a shamanic practitioner of many years. They exchanged contact information, since the gentleman said he might be interested in contacting me at some point.

About a year later I received a phone call from Thomas. He was seeking help for his high school daughter, Penelope, who was suffering from extreme anxiety. He and his wife had arranged for her to meet with a psychologist specializing in adolescents. Penelope had been meeting with this psychologist for four months prior to this phone call. While she reported that her meetings with the psychologist helped her to better understand her anxiety, they did not mitigate or substantially reduce it.

Apparently, Thomas also thought that his conversation with Elias was a meaningful synchronicity, so he found my website and then purchased and read through my book on Dynamic Energetic Healing™ (DEH). He wanted to know if I would be willing to try to help Penelope. He was trusting his gut on this, and while he didn't understand a lot of what I do, my book and many of the case histories he read persuaded him that I could be helpful to his daughter.

Generally speaking, I do not work with adolescents unless it is a family-related issue that involves one or both parents. However, I made an exception this time because of what I considered to be the fascinating synchronicity when my son was drawn to initiate a conversation with Thomas on the plane. Since the family lived on the East Coast and I am located in Oregon, I suggested Skype sessions providing both Thomas and his wife would be present when I worked with Penelope. He agreed so I sent him my intake forms including my informed consent statement. I requested that Penelope provide me with some background information leading up to her extreme anxiety so I could have some history related to her problems.

Penelope reported in her personal statement that for several months she had been anxious that she was going to die. She felt that somehow it was her destiny and there was nothing she could do to stop it. She also reported having vague fears that someone had poisoned her or was planning to poison her, even though she knew that this thinking was irrational. She reported various somatic symptoms including shooting pains in her chest area, in her head and other parts of her body from time to time. She also felt significant fatigue but wasn't sure whether it was just because of school or her anxiety. She said that during the day she had fears she would pass out and die, and at night she worried that she would die when she fell asleep. Additionally, Penelope feared she would just fade out of existence because her mind would disappear and just stop working. She worried that

CASE STUDY 4

she might have some deadly illness that doctors had overlooked. She was having trouble concentrating, she was feeling hopeless, and she felt helpless to stop the feelings of panic that emerged out of nowhere and engulfed her.

Although she was a high-achieving high school student taking advanced placement courses, the anxiety symptoms Penelope described would not typically be caused by the stress generated by a demanding academic program. At this point, I had to reserve judgment about a prospective diagnosis until I met with her.

I met with Penelope four times. During our first session, remote muscle testing indicated that she was only 51 percent in her body, suggesting significant dissociation. After discussion, we agreed that her starting intention was for her to be 100 percent grounded in her physical body. Through my non-local remote muscle testing, I determined that she was incongruent when she made the statement "It is safe for me to be fully present in my physical body now." In other words, she tested strong on the statement "*It is* not *safe for me to be fully present in my physical body.*" When I asked Penelope if she had any thoughts about this, she said she did not want to be in her body because the feelings of fear, doom and dying were too much for her to bear.

When I began testing for what might be the best approach to address this, it became evident that some kind of subtle negative energy was embedded in this incongruent belief that is called psychoenergetic reversal in energy psychology. Upon further inquiry, it was determined that *this subtle negative energy, an energetic intrusion, was directly connected to the incongruent statement Penelope just made. She felt like she had been cursed!*

When I next asked through muscle testing what the best intervention would be to release this self-devaluing belief, frontal occipital holding was indicated. Mentally, I put a "holographic" image of Penelope in the chair next to me, and placed my hands around where her head would be positioned as if she were physically sitting in the chair. I initiated my invocation and asked for help. As I defocused my eyes, images began coming into my awareness. I saw the energetic intrusion as a large roiling black mass of heavy energy throughout Penelope's solar plexus region. As I felt more deeply into it, I began to feel nauseous. It was seething like a black oily turbulent sea. I then began asking for help and I saw that Penelope's spiritual body was taken down into the lower-world domain of my Native American helpers. The shaman of these Native American compassionate spirits is the wizened old woman who calls herself Grandmother. (This is the same helping spirit who appeared in Case 2 who had called forth the Spirit of the Mountain to assist her in removing an energetic intrusion and parasitic attachment from a different client.)

Grandmother walked around Penelope and saw very clearly what I had seen. Suddenly, she plunged her right hand into Penelope's solar plexus and pulled out what appeared as an aggressive, menacing agitated creature that was a black kinetic mass. Grandmother threw it into a fire that was burning nearby. She then directed one of her assistants (a woman warrior) to quickly go to the river nearby and fill up a wooden bowl with gray river mud. When Grandmother received the bowl of mud in one hand, she scooped out a handful of it with her other hand and smeared it all over Penelope's solar plexus. When she felt she had thoroughly completed the task, she directed two of the warrior women nearby to assist Penelope and walk with her to a nearby open area where she was fed power food in the form of dried bison meat.

After a few more seconds the scene dissolved and I was finished. I asked Penelope if she noticed anything; she said she just felt lighter and her breathing was now more relaxed. While I felt somewhat uncomfortable sharing my perceptions with Penelope, as her parents were on either side of her, I wanted her to know that there was something energetically potent and toxic that had been identified as a causal factor perpetuating her persistent anxiety. Muscle testing indicated that the intrusion was now completely released at all levels of her being.

I then went back to the statement about whether Penelope felt safe to be fully in her body. This time after she repeated it, I tested her and she was congruent on this statement of belief. She no longer reported feeling doomed, and the feeling she had earlier expressed of being cursed had been released when the intrusion was extracted from her solar plexus. To me, this entity represented a cumulative potentized belief reinforced over time that continued to build and intensify as Penelope's anxiety became more pervasive. It represented a series of ongoing fears from unknown sources that consolidated as this underlying, all-encompassing belief that destabilized her. The next muscle test determined that Penelope was now 100 percent grounded in her physical body. This was how we finished up the first of her four sessions.

The following week during her second session, I helped Penelope establish firm energetic boundaries with one of her advanced placement classes and a few annoying classmates. Overall she reported feeling much more calm. She did remark that she had been experiencing transient feelings of anxiety but they would dissipate quickly without any lingering fears. This was very encouraging. She remarked that her sleep was also improving.

By the third session two weeks later, she reported no longer having feelings of doom or despair, her overall energy was better, and the feelings of panic were finally gone.

During our fourth and final session two weeks later, Penelope reported that her anxiety was mostly gone. She still had an occasional thought of doom but said it did not persist and now passed quickly. As we talked, she shared that she would occasionally watch rock and heavy metal music videos. She acknowledged that many of the themes in these videos were dark, and they often left her with an uncomfortable feeling in her gut that translated emotionally as anxiety. As I continued to muscle test, it became clear that she had no energetic boundaries with media in general and heavy metal videos in particular. Her new therapeutic intention was to establish solid energetic boundaries with the media in general, and music videos and heavy metal in particular.

I feel it is important to comment on what I call the *dreaming media*. I have come to realize that while some people are more comfortable with visual media, auditory or multimedia stimulation can have a significant negative impact on sensitive and vulnerable individuals. This is because certain types of music and multimedia tend to bypass our cognitive filters and infuse themselves directly into the limbic brain and powerfully impact our sympathetic nervous system. I am absolutely convinced this is a growing problem with so much multimedia available through YouTube and the plethora of various internet platforms that are always pushing their messages. It is notable that this may have been one of the underlying triggers that initiated Penelope's anxiety. I made sure before we signed off that she had good energetic boundaries with heavy metal music as part of her four-session psychotherapy time with me. I recommended that she limit her exposure to these videos and monitor herself afterward to ensure that the videos were not generating anxiety.

As I next began the muscle testing, the indicator for subtle negative energy emerged, specifically in the form of another energetic intrusion. Upon further inquiry, it was revealed that this intrusion was a direct consequence of the dreaming media. In my DEH training program, I spend an entire day teaching psychotherapists how to identify and address problems related to the dreaming media with their clients. Essentially, this is a newly emergent archetype and it is pervasive cross-culturally throughout the world. Internet interconnectivity is now available nearly everywhere so the media's impact cannot be overstated. I conceptualize the dreaming media to be an enormous collective field of energy made up of billions of individuals that become

Case Study 4

part of this large information float. When people are unable and unwilling to deal with their anger and other powerful lower-chakra, more primitive energies (what Freud referred to as the id), they are essentially splitting off these feeling states because they are unwilling to process them, thus marginalizing them out of their conscious awareness. As a consequence, millions and millions of individuals' primitive split-off energy cumulatively becomes the dreaming media that all different kinds of media platforms unwittingly and unconsciously channel as dark powerful energy that many people are susceptible to.

Whether it is through music videos, television shows, violent movies, angry talk radio, social media or printed matter, this enormous collective field is continually circulating and being channeled and promoted unconsciously by the producers of this content. It has a very powerful negative impact on the billions of people interacting with it. I have the word *dreaming* as part of this description because people are unconsciously splitting off dark and disowned parts of themselves, finding that they are drawn to different media formats as they continue unconsciously to try to reconnect and reunite with that inner disavowed part in order to feel more whole. It is a curious paradox that leads to pervasive problem states.

For Penelope, the frontal occipital holding intervention was called for. As I settled into perceiving what was present within her energy field, themes of death and darkness began to emerge on a feeling level. My inner vision perceived a glowering black snake-like creature in her solar plexus that, once I noticed it, became very agitated and began moving around in an aggressive and evasive manner. Fortunately, my cultivated long-term relationships with compassionate spirits enabled me to call in a powerful helper as I held the space with concentration and awareness of what unfolded in order to extract this psychotoxic energy. This time Panther emerged. It quickly paced around Penelope and then attacked this snake-like intrusion. Panther transmuted its dark and psychotoxic

A Foot in Both Worlds

The dreaming media

energy until Penelope's solar plexus glowed in a golden radiance. Subsequent muscle testing revealed that the intervention released the intrusion completely. I then helped Penelope establish solid energetic boundaries with media in general, and music videos in particular.

The very last process that we did together was establishing solid energetic boundaries with international travel. This therapeutic intention was crafted since Penelope was planning to take a two-week study abroad program in Vienna. We accomplished this handily and she remained 100 percent embodied. I did not hear back from her, so I assumed there was no more need to address her previous problem.

These four sessions took place over six weeks from start to

finish. It was a remarkable transformation from when I first began working with Penelope when she was so anxious and panicky that she had to sleep with her parents in their bed. By the time we were finished, Penelope's persistent anxiety, panic and feelings of doom had dissolved and she was sufficiently self-confident to travel internationally on her own. *The release of two significant energetic intrusions allowed this transformative process to happen in such a relatively short time.*

Commentary

This case is a wonderful demonstration of how shamanic healing is integrated into the traditional psychotherapy context and generates an excellent therapeutic outcome. Before we began working together, Penelope had met with a child and adolescent psychologist for four months. She had also tried psychiatric medications, which did not address the problem in any efficacious manner. Additionally, this healing outcome occurred non-locally over Skype.

To me this is always miraculous and beyond words to adequately describe. How is this possible? From a rational Western psychological model it does not make any sense. The success of my approach is based on my ability to access the compassionate spirits and recruit them for healing. To do that, one must be trained to access nonordinary reality along with the *power* and compassion that these beings bring forth. They inhabit nonordinary reality and are willing to work with us. They create passageways to come through and positively impact our everyday reality in order to effect healing outcomes.

From the many workshops and trainings that I have facilitated over the years on the topic of shamanic healing, I have come to know firsthand that nearly anybody can learn these techniques, providing they have a sincere heart and are open to other dimensions where healing can be accessed. As I tell my clients, I just hold the space for the compassionate spirits to become available. Essentially, I am partnering with these beings of light and love as *they* know what to do to create healing outcomes. It is always a remarkable blessing.

Case Study 5:
Releasing Multiple Layers of an Energetic Intrusion

Olivia came in for therapy to address her anxiety. She had felt it as a knot in her solar plexus for many years. She expressed the desire to be more assertive and feel safe in her interactions with other people. During her sixth session, it was determined that she needed to have a power animal retrieval in order to augment her personal power. The power animal retrieval was successful; her new guardian spirit was a large animal with thick protective skin. Her new guardian spirit was excited to be in her life and help her to stay *power-filled*.

Two weeks later when I next met with Olivia, she reported feeling much more solid within herself. She felt less nervous and more comfortable being around other people. She also reported feeling more grounded, but she was still experiencing tightness in her solar plexus area. After some discussion, we arrived at the following therapeutic intention: "To no longer take on other people's energies, to acquire and maintain protective energetic boundaries with people in general, and to no longer feel guilty for not meeting other people's needs."

After I helped her to restore being fully grounded in her physical body (since she was significantly dissociated), Olivia brought up the difficult and abusive relationship she had endured with her father when she was growing up. We had discussed this briefly a couple of months earlier but a more concretized archetype that her father represented was now emerging. He was controlling, angry and critical. He often ranted that children are selfish, and whenever anything went wrong he angrily blamed Olivia. She also realized that due to her father's anger and control, she did not feel comfortable saying no to requests from most people.

Rather than just focus on her father, I expanded the therapeutic intention to incorporate the archetype he represented and the victim/persecutor dynamic. Her starting therapeutic intention was now modified to establish resilient energetic boundaries with this archetypal figure that her abusive father represented and to step out of the victim/persecutor dynamic.

As I began muscle testing to determine if there was any psychoenergetic reversal on her intention (that is, to discover if she was incongruent), it became evident that she was completely reversed or conflicted related to the intention. During subsequent muscle testing, subtle negative energy was identified. *What emerged was an intrusion that was cumulative over time, relating to her early interactions with her father.*

The first intervention called for was frontal occipital holding. I saw the intrusion as deeply encrusted psychotoxic residue that filled up her solar plexus much like hard, dense coal. I quickly perceived one of my upper-world teachers, Odin, holding out his large staff. For several minutes I saw the energetic *power* being emitted at Olivia from my teacher's staff as the encrusted residue slowly began dissolving. After a few minutes, the *power* from Odin's staff began to withdraw and I knew that the healing was completed. My perception was that nearly all of the encrusted residue was gone.

When I next muscle tested it became clear that the intrusion had been completely released. When I circled back to check on the statements that were initially reversed—reflecting incongruity—they were now all balanced. We were not able to complete the therapeutic intention due to time constraints, so we agreed to continue to work on it in the next session two weeks later.

When we met for her next appointment, Olivia reported feeling much better physically. In particular, she was aware that her solar plexus felt much more spacious, especially in her lower abdomen. It was reassuring that she noticed a positive shift somatically along with an overall feeling of less anxiety.

As I began muscle testing, I discovered that although Olivia was now fully embodied, there was resistance to completing the intention as indicated by more subtle negative energy. *It was identified as another layer of an intrusion that she had absorbed over many years from her father.* This had been deeply veiled and even though she was now fully grounded in her body, the muscle testing process helped me to identify this embedded psychotoxicity. Because I can often tune in to my client's *energy body*, I asked her to begin stimulating several of her energy centers. I directed her to start fanning back and forth in front of them while she reflected on the intention statement. After a moment, I muscle tested to determine the next strategy to use and found that frontal occipital holding was called for.

As I waited with openness, Odin reemerged with his large staff held out in front of him, directing his *power* once again at her solar plexus. This time I saw only a thin layer of encrusted psychotoxic energy within Olivia's solar plexus. I next noticed that my teacher was changing his *power* emanations to a light-reddish ray directed at her solar plexus. As the dark psychotoxic energy that had been lining her solar plexus dissipated, I perceived and understood that Odin was changing Olivia's energetic frequency so that she would essentially be immune from being negatively affected by this angry and controlling negative father archetype and the archetypal dynamic of the victim/persecutor. I realized Odin had just upgraded her energetic frequency signature, since the encrusted residue that had still lingered was now completely gone.

As I have mentioned earlier, during the times I was training with Dr. Michael Harner, he emphasized that while seemingly inexplicable healings were often known to occur when working with the helping spirits, shamanic practitioners should expect to address a particular issue multiple times in order to achieve the desired results. Olivia's experience is a wonderful example of how repeated efforts positively influenced the desired result.

When we debriefed, Olivia reported being aware of a left side/right side balance in her solar plexus area. She then noticed she was spontaneously repeating positive affirmations to herself when thoughts or memories of her father emerged. The muscle testing indicated that the intrusion had been completely released. Additionally, she now had 100 percent energetic boundaries with her father *as well as the archetype he represented.*

Commentary

What was so moving to me was how the same upper-world teacher spontaneously emerged in two consecutive sessions as the healing force to address this angry and controlling negative father archetype. I never program who is to come through when I do frontal occipital holding. This makes it clear to me that the compassionate spirits are truly tuned into us when we ask them for help. In a traditional journey when I rattle or drum, I set the intention to meet a particular helper, but not so in frontal occipital holding—I just ask for help and wait to perceive who shows up. The spirits care deeply and as long as I regularly maintain ongoing relationship with them, they will be there for me when I need them for help and healing. In this case, the same compassionate spirit showed up two weeks later to essentially complete the healing that he had initiated. There was continuity over time with this upper-world helper, and that is inspiring to me. It reinforced my experience that the spirits know when to show up when their special healing powers are required.

Case Study 6:
Healing PTSD in Two Sessions

James is a forty-year-old man who after many years working as a mechanical engineer decided to leave his profession in search of spiritual guidance. He told me that for the longest time he had a growing awareness of his emerging spiritual nature but had no clue how to address it. Unusual things were happening to him that he could not understand. After considering a number of alternatives, he realized that there was nobody close to him who he could turn to for understanding these experiences. Therefore, he decided to try the academic route—he enrolled in a graduate program in religious studies as a way to better understand what many traditions have described as spiritual experiences.

Session One

I met with James several times in 2016, and then he contacted me in 2020 after completing his graduate program. In our first meeting in late 2020, he described not feeling safe in the world. He felt constantly on guard, hypervigilant and dissociated, and had feelings of depersonalization. His affect was flat with no noticeable emotional expressiveness. He said, "I fundamentally believe I'm not worth being taken care of. I do not feel safe. I do not feel supported by humans, Earth, or the cosmos. Sensations of embodiment are powerful and scary. I feel abandoned with a lack of meaning and purpose. I am scared, sad and alone." He was going through the archetypal dark night of the soul.

Using my Dynamic Energetic Healing™ (DEH) protocol, I initially asked him via behavioral kinesiological muscle testing to what percentage he was fully occupying his physical body. The feedback was an alarming 5 percent. This is almost comatose, suggesting James was having great difficulty staying mentally focused and concentrating. That's when I began to appreciate his overtly depressive state.

We decided to establish the therapeutic goal for James to restore full embodiment. As we progressed, it became clear that an inner part of him was voicing resistance to proceed. Through dialogue it was determined that this was old repressed anger that this inner part harbored. Once we had identified it, James became fearful that it would consume and overwhelm him. As I continued to ask more questions via muscle testing, it soon became apparent that *he had been contaminated with an energetic intrusion* from an encounter with a particular individual some months earlier. This encounter left him feeling betrayed.

James became in touch with his growing anger and resentment related to this particular individual. Ultimately, he had to leave the relationship as it no longer felt safe to him.

When I asked via muscle testing what the best approach would be to attempt to release this anger and resentment, the frontal occipital holding intervention came up positive. Even though we were conducting sessions via Skype, I was able to do this intervention non-locally with the same efficacy as in an in-person session. As I settled into the frontal occipital holding while James reflected on his fears of being overwhelmed by old anger, images and impressions began to come into my awareness. The first thing I saw was roiling anger in his solar plexus. This represented the intrusion. When I next asked for help, we were taken to one of my upper-world teachers, who assessed the situation and saw what I had seen in James' solar plexus.

Suddenly, the scenario shifted and we were all by a riverbank of a tributary of a large river in an Amazonian jungle. My teacher called forth a massive anaconda that emerged from the banks of the river and began slithering up and around James' body, squeezing progressively harder and harder. Very soon I witnessed a large quantity of oily black psychotoxic material—it looked like viscous tar—being squeezed out of his solar plexus area. It plopped onto the riverbank and the earth absorbed it until it was no longer visible. During the frontal occipital holding, which lasted about three minutes, James was agitated. He had to move his body back and forth with intense heavy breathing until it all began to gradually subside. When he was calm enough to muscle test, it was determined that he was completely back in his body and the intrusion had been released. We were both in awe.

Session Two

When I met with James several days later, he remained fully embodied and felt more present than he had been in a very long time. But now he was feeling his bodily sensations, which included anxiety and hypervigilance. We discussed this, and the bottom line was his desire to feel safe in his body now that he was able to stay connected to it. After some discussion, I let him know that the experience he was describing was classic post-traumatic stress disorder (PTSD). After further discussion, it was decided to establish the intention *to heal his PTSD*. I decided to frame it this way as it was a more comprehensive approach that simply addressing anxiety or depression independently. The dissociation, depersonalization and hypervigilance are all different interconnected aspects of the larger diagnostic category of PTSD.

We started the muscle testing to determine if there were any psychoenergetic reversals to address. (As explained in my first book, *Dynamic Energetic Healing*™, these reveal internal conflicts surrounding the intention or therapeutic goal). He tested weak on the statement "It is safe for me to completely heal my PTSD." I next asked through muscle testing what would be the best approach to treat this reversal; frontal occipital holding tested strong.

As I held my hands in position and asked for help, I perceived an upper-world teacher I have worked with for many years. It was Odin holding his staff out in front of him. The *power* radiating from his staff was being directed at James in very powerful waves. The next thing I saw was James' energy field with a large black wedge cemented in his solar plexus. The *power* radiations were being focused on this black wedge, which soon started becoming a pale color and eventually dissolved completely. I next noticed James' energy field greatly expanded; apparently it had been contracted previously due to the black wedge.

During this procedure, James became very agitated, moving back and forth, twisting and turning, making moaning sounds and making remarks that he wasn't sure he could handle whatever was happening to him. When I was finished and sat down, he was in quite a state. His face was red and distorted and he continued to make strange noises including burping and vocalizations of fear that he wasn't sure he was going to be able to survive this. He said he was sweating profusely and was scared by this out-of-control experience. He wasn't out of the woods yet.

I directed James to do some emotional freedom techniques (EFT) tapping as a rapid way to balance his vital energy by stimulating all of the major acupuncture meridians. I then guided him to ground, describing a specific visualization followed by having him fold his hands over his heart center accompanied by long deep breathing. He told me that he had a strong feeling of something pressing down on his chest, and that he had been aware of this feeling for years. As I continued to direct him to tune into his heart center and continue his long deep breathing, he next told me his heart was starting to feel full. I directed him to feel and visualize his heart expanding throughout his body and then beyond his body to fill the entire room. When James was stable enough to collect himself somewhat, he told me, "Before my heart felt vacuous. Now it feels dense and full—a new experience and perception."

Following up with muscle testing, he now tested strong on the statement "It is now safe for me to heal my PTSD." When James was calm enough to debrief, he told me he felt a little anger along with feeling like crying and screaming. "That part was separated," he said. "Now it is integrating." He felt it was a reunion of a younger part of him that was now able to join all of his other inner parts. The pressure in his chest was quickly dissipating, and he had completely stopped his physical writhing. He told me that it felt like "Little James finally came home. He's back." This was evidence that he also experienced a spontaneous soul retrieval of a part of him that was regularly dissociated. As a footnote, James did have a personal history of significant trauma when growing up with his family.

James told me his voice sounded full and unfamiliar. He felt like he was going to cry tears of joy with feelings of profound gratitude. By this time, we had spent ninety minutes together and he was feeling stable enough emotionally and physically to end our session.

We met again the following week. None of the PTSD symptoms remained. James told me he felt profoundly different with no hypervigilance or anxiety. He again remained fully embodied. When I muscle tested about his previous experience and the therapeutic goal we had worked on, it was determined that his PTSD was indeed healed. We spent the rest of the session reviewing what had transpired in the first two sessions, and we discussed what direction he might take moving forward in his life.

Commentary

To say the least, apparent recovery from long-term PTSD in so short a time is very unusual. Yet all of James' presenting symptoms had abated. When we first met, he was able to articulate clearly his thinking and feeling states. By the end of his second ninety-minute session, he was able to calmly relate and describe the contrast between how he had been feeling before and how he experienced himself now. It was really quite extraordinary.

I should note that as a seasoned psychotherapist, I can never anticipate just how long it may take for someone with a PTSD diagnosis to resolve. Some people never fully recover from what has been long-term PTSD. James was unusual in that he was very focused on seeking to understand how spiritual interventions could foster healing and recovery. He had been studying many spiritual traditions and had implemented a meditation practice to augment his studies.

While James initially acknowledged that feeling anxious and hypervigilant had become his normal state of being, he was also pushing himself to find ways not just to understand but to heal his ongoing anxiety. My muscle testing results were corroborated by his self-report that after his sessions with me he no longer had the constant anxiety. This improvement was palpable. It was also reassuring that he was able to stay solidly connected to his physical body and no longer chronically dissociated.

Through the intercession of the compassionate spirits, a remarkable transformation had occurred. It was now James' task to integrate these changes so he could get on with the rest of his life. All of what he experienced is in striking contrast to traditional cognitive behavioral therapy, with its emphasis on talking about one's symptoms and thoughts. I feel blessed to be able to call on these beings of great compassion and *power*.

Case Study 7:
Energetic Intrusion and Soul Stealing

Sarah is twenty-three years old. She had gone out for the second time with a guy she had recently met. She reported that her first date with him was fun; they had dinner and a drink. They talked and walked afterward and she decided to meet him a second time for a simple dinner and then a comedy show at an upscale nightclub. After their dinner, they went back to her car and she recalled stumbling on the way, finding it hard to coordinate her movements. She told me that she was hardly able to walk.

The next thing she remembered was waking up in her car feeling drugged out. It was hard for her to physically function and her only concrete memory was feeling pressure and the weight of someone on top of her. She somehow managed to drive home, even as she continued to feel woozy and unsteady. When she finally got to her apartment, she collapsed on her bed and slept for hours. She said she was in some surreal state of unconsciousness the entire time. She began to suspect that her date had slipped a drug into her drink at dinner.

When she woke up the next morning, trying to piece it all together, she began to suspect that she had been raped, but due to her mental confusion she could not be certain. Even though she was still suffering from the effects of being drugged, she managed to drive herself to the hospital to get tests and to make sure she wasn't poisoned. She was hoping tests at the hospital would confirm her suspicions. She reported the incident to the police and they put out a warrant for the man's arrest in order to acquire a sample of his DNA for testing.

Sarah came in to see me four months later. She had been asking around for a therapist and a friend who had met with me previously and experienced a positive therapeutic outcome encouraged her to see me. Sarah told me that she felt uncomfortable talking about the event but was willing to try my energy-based approach since her friend found it extremely helpful.

Sarah told me that since the incident took place, she was experiencing uncharacteristic awkwardness talking to people and was having difficulty looking at people when interacting with them. She was also having panic attacks, something she had never experienced before. Additionally, she was feeling dissociated with a noticeable lack of her normal mental acuity.

We began the session using muscle testing and it was determined that she was only 41 percent embodied. As I continued to ask questions through the muscle testing process, the indicator of subtle negative energy emerged. Very quickly it became clear to me that she was being affected by *a psychotoxic intrusion*. After using some energy psychology strategies to get her overall energy system more balanced, frontal occipital holding was indicated as the best strategy to address the intrusion. My compressed-time shamanic journey follows.

As I gently placed my hands on the front and back of Sarah's head, I defocused my eyes and asked for help from my allies. The intrusion was represented to me as a dark gray, metallic-clad apron bolted onto her pelvic area covering her second chakra. It was restricting her normal flow of life-force energy. In other words, this energy center was significantly contracted. When I asked for help, I saw that her spiritual body was taken into the lower-world realm of my Native American helpers with Grandmother, the tribe's preeminent shaman, facilitating the healing.

Grandmother assessed the metallic apron with great concentration and determined the best way to release this intrusion was through the agency of the Spirit of the Mountain. She put Sarah on a horse accompanied by a large number of women warriors and they all rode up to a large mountain. They dismounted and two warriors held Sarah's arms out to the sides while two other

CASE STUDY 7

warrior women kneeled down and held tightly onto her feet. Immediately, Grandmother started screaming to the Spirit of the Mountain that resided within. This is a powerful and wild elemental spirit that Grandmother has some power and control over, but she must scream at it with all her power to direct it. Elementals can be used and directed by powerful compassionate spirits such as Grandmother but they are primitive and must be cautiously directed.

This elemental spirit is large and tall (As I mentioned earlier, I perceive it as a towering column of swirling, rotating and vibrating energy, three stories tall and whirling around like a tornado). She screamed at it to come close to Sarah but not to touch her. As it rotated around her closely, its centripetal energy tore off the apron and the spirit absorbed the apron into itself. Grandmother screamed at it to go back into the mountain to transmute the psychotoxic energy. When it was gone, enormous amounts of black oily sludge began pouring out of the contaminated area of Sarah where the metallic apron had been. Once it was completely depleted, Sarah collapsed into a heap.

The women warriors placed her onto a horse and slowly rode back to their compound. They took her to their women's tent and were gentle and nurturing with her as she slowly came around. They fed her dried bison *power food* and stayed with her until she was feeling herself once again. Then the scene dissolved and I removed my hands. Sarah reported feeling very emotional during the frontal occipital holding experience but it was fleeting and afterward she came back into emotional balance quickly. My muscle testing indicated that the intrusion had been completely released and she was back to being fully grounded in her body after months of being dissociated. She immediately reported feeling mentally clearer and more present than she had felt in the months since the event.

My next muscle testing question asked if she was harboring any blocked memories of the event. While it tested positive, it also indicated she was harboring more subtle negative energy to process. Through muscle testing questioning, it was determined to be an intentionally externally generated "curse" that we needed to know the content of. Somebody had "cursed" Sarah with some type of negative attribution. After some dialoguing supported by muscle testing questioning, the negative energy directed at her from the rapist was determined to be "*You are just an object to be used.*"

We discussed this briefly, and as Sarah reflected on this statement, I directed her to stimulate her central meridian by tapping on it for about ninety seconds. I asked her about her experience and she said she felt the tapping had been effective. My muscle testing corroborated this as it indicated that the predatory sentiment she had internalized was now completely released. Going back to my original question, it was determined via muscle testing that she had indeed blocked memories of the event. However, it was best to not re-elicit these memories from her subconscious, so we left it alone. This is an example of how beneficial muscle testing can be—Sarah's inner knowing directed us to go no further on this issue at the time. Some therapists tend to believe that it is always important to elicit repressed trauma. But in this case, *her deeper self* was protecting her from having to re-experience the event and retraumatize herself.

We had an additional fifteen minutes left of this seventy-five-minute session. After discussion, I explained that it would be very helpful for Sarah to establish solid energetic boundaries with the perpetrator so she would stay empowered and remain grounded whenever she might think about him. When I began asking questions through my muscle testing on how to proceed, the indicator for subtle negative energy once again emerged. As I continued to inquire if there was any additional information we needed to elicit from the energetic origin of the event (i.e., the rape itself), it became clear that it was time to identify what the subtle negative energy was that still persisted from the rape.

As I inquired via muscle testing, what emerged was *soul*

stealing and the connected soul loss. I explained to Sarah what this meant and how people who are controlling and dominating in relationships often take and absorb components of the other person's (the victim's) vital essence as a way to maintain dominance and weaken them. This often happens when the victim is codependent and thus complicit by tacitly agreeing to offer themselves up by submitting to their partner.

Sarah's event did not fulfill the criteria for soul stealing/soul loss as explained above since it was a single incident within a very new and fleeting exploitive relational context (again, this was just the second time they went out together). But Sarah *was* suffering from soul loss and unable to stay fully present in her power. She was not complicit because it was not an ongoing relationship and he had not appeared to her as dominating. Neither was she acting in a codependent manner. Nevertheless, he exploited her and, energetically speaking, he stole some of her vital essence by disregarding her need to be treated respectfully and treating her as an object. Thus, Sarah's various symptoms had continued to amplify over time. Frontal occipital holding was indicated with the following compressed-time shamanic journey.

At first, I saw the perpetrator's spirit carrying a bag of what I immediately knew to be several stolen soul parts, Sarah's among them. When I asked for help, my spirit Horse emerged and instantly ripped open the bag. Horse then reclaimed/absorbed Sarah's stolen essence while the other stolen soul parts were now free as well, hopefully to find their way back to their respective individuals. I next observed Horse merging with Sarah in my office as it returned her stolen vital essence into her second, third and fourth energy centers. This soul retrieval/rescue was a complete success. When I next inquired via muscle testing, it was determined that there was no more traumatic residue from the event. Interestingly, all of Sarah's trauma had ended up as subtle negative energy along with the expected dissociation. In other words, because Sarah was drugged and unconscious, her trauma became repressed at the unconscious level and impacted her by leaving various remnants of subtle negative energy in her *energy body*. If her date had tied her up or physically hit her, her trauma would have been more acute. We did not need to spend any more time processing the event or discussing it. When I next muscle tested, she was indeed completely occupying her physical body once again.

Before we concluded the session, I muscle tested Sarah to ensure she had excellent energetic boundaries with her perpetrator and her unfolding future to ensure she would not have any ongoing anxiety. Her boundaries were solid and intact, so we ended the seventy-five-minute session there.

Sarah scheduled a follow-up appointment to meet with me four weeks later. She reported good sleep and the curious transient symptom (following her first session) of sore shoulders for two days. She felt physically lighter and emotionally strong. She remarked with a smile that she was feeling like herself before the rape occurred. She was also aware that she was staying present in her body most of the time. However, there were occasions when she sensed that she had dissociated, since she found it hard to stay focused. Yet she added she was no longer preoccupied with the event whenever it crossed her mind. When I asked Sarah how she was sleeping, she reported that she had had a couple of nightmares of people trying to lure her away but she did not allow them to do so. This was a positive indicator that while she was continuing to process the events, the work she had done with me had fortified her sufficiently so that she was no longer overidentified with the victim archetype.

We next began the muscle testing process. To ensure that she remained fully embodied, she only needed to stimulate her seventh energy center while reflecting on her relationship to her physical body. I next had her verbalize two statements to test for congruency about staying fully self-empowered. The two statements tested strong: "I am not safe in my body" and "I cannot be safe in my body." This is indicative of what in energy psychology is referred to as being psychoenergetically reversed. It reflects being internally conflicted, often at the unconscious level. This was understandable as lingering doubt and fear after being sexually assaulted. I directed her to internally reflect on these statements and any feelings that were associated with them. Then through my ability to perceive her chakra centers, I directed her to fan in front of her throat center and then her solar plexus center. After one minute, I perceived that they both came back into balance so I directed her to stop. The subsequent muscle testing indicated that any lingering fears about these two statements had dissolved. When she repeated the same two statements, they both tested weak. When she stated them in the affirmative, (i.e., "I am now safe in my physical body" and "I can remain safe in my physical body"), Sarah was now congruent about being safe in her physical body as the muscle tested confirmed this. She exhaled deeply after this muscle testing reassurance.

There was just a little bit more to do to complete this seventy-five-minute session. We set three therapeutic intentions: 1) Establish and maintain energetic boundaries with her memory of the event; 2) Establish and maintain energetic boundaries with having sex; 3) Establish and maintain energetic boundaries with sleep. Implementing various energy psychology strategies, she was easily able to restore her right relationship with all three therapeutic goals.

Sarah is a self-reliant and self-confident young woman. This event really shook her up and threw her into understandable acute post-traumatic stress. The symptoms she experienced are understandable given that she was sexually assaulted. Sarah did not need to return for any subsequent appointments as she was able to let go of the trauma through this unique Dynamic Energetic Healing™ (DEH) approach. The deepest traumatic residue she was carrying was resolved through the agency of shamanic healing.

Commentary

Since I am very skilled in this work, I teach other psychotherapists how to incorporate both the energy psychology component (including the muscle testing) as well as the shamanic healing

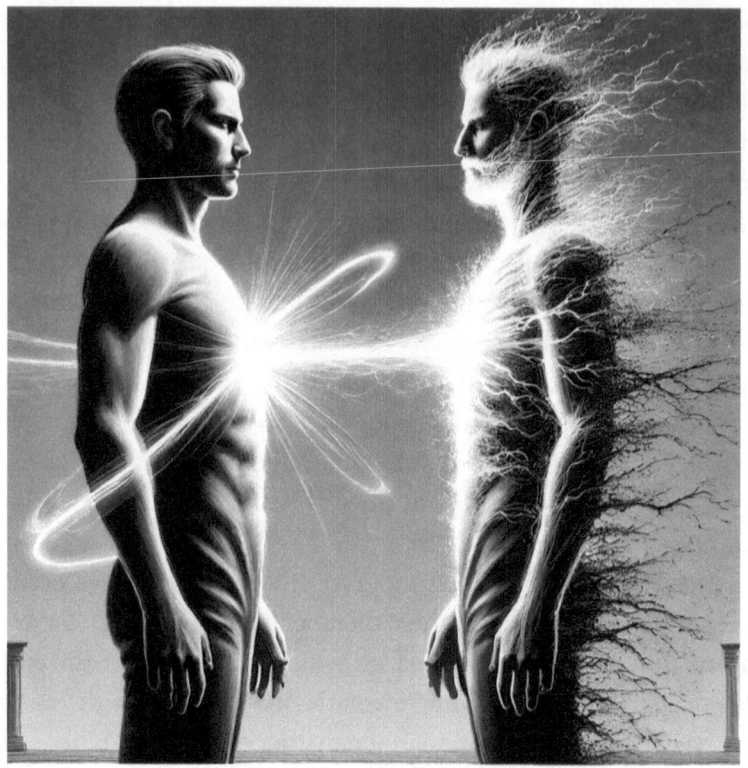
Soul stealing

aspect. These descriptions of what goes on in these psychotherapy sessions may raise eyebrows, because Western psychotherapy has approached treating mental and emotional disorders in a cognitive and psychopharmacological/scientific evidence-based approach. I have presented an overview of this Western approach in Part 1 of this book. While many clients receive benefit from Western approaches to psychotherapy, clearly there are other effective approaches—such as DEH—that are profound and healing. This does not presume an either/or proposition. I am simply asking you to open your mind to consider other largely unfamiliar approaches to mental and emotional healing within the psychotherapy setting.

Case Study 8:
Covid Collective Field Discharged via Dismemberment

Toni contracted her second bout of Covid-19 over the holiday season in December of 2022. When I met with her in March 2023, she said she had recovered from the acute phase fairly quickly, but now, more than two months later, she was still experiencing persistent fatigue and a cough. She told me that nearly everyone she knew was getting sick with the virus.

I had originally met with Toni in late 2021; she consulted me about her first bout of Covid-19. At that time, she had compromised energetic boundaries with the Covid-19 energetic collective field and had a Covid-19 collective energetic intrusion. The same was true this time. However, this time the collective intrusion came on the heels of her recent Covid infection. She was still feeling a little ragged around the edges but she was mostly over her symptoms.

Frontal occipital holding was indicated through muscle testing as the first intervention. We were meeting via Zoom, so I placed my hands where Toni's head would be as I visualized her body sitting in the chair next to me. I asked for help and waited for the visions to begin. It was my Hawaiian teacher who emerged; he is the one who always appears for addressing Covid-19 collective contamination by recruiting the natural elements. This time, as in the past, he began by doing the sacred hula dance and generating a powerful storm. The storm clouds began emitting bright streaks of lightning as the rain became torrential. I saw Toni sitting on a lava rock platform overlooking the Pacific Ocean. I then perceived the collective intrusion as a dark, Velcro-like blanket wrapped around her body several times. It was thick and vibrating, and it appeared as dark particles pervading her body to her very core. As the storm with the wind, rain, thunder and lightning intensified, he directed and focused his hula dancing movements directly at Toni, targeting the collective intrusion.

As the storm continued to intensify, I noticed that the vibrating collective intrusion was penetrating Toni's physical body and had now begun circulating inside her body. I had never seen this so pervasive within an individual before. This was likely the case because Toni had just recovered from her Covid infection and was still feeling weak and vulnerable. As the storm built up, her body suddenly exploded apart, reflecting what is known as a *dismemberment* for complete system-wide purification and cleansing. Sometimes this happens spontaneously, as was the case here. Other times, shamanic practitioners deliberately ask their helping spirits to initiate this as a way to create a new spiritual body devoid of persistent energetic toxicity.

Shortly afterward, the storm began to recede and Toni's new spiritual body emerged as golden, glowing and expansive. The fierce winds died down and the sun came out as the larger collective field of Covid-19 was blown far away from her, reaching toward the horizon. My teacher stopped dancing and approached her, telling her that her healing was completed. He looked her over and smiled. He was carrying a banana, tore it in half and gave her one half to eat as *power food*. He ate the other half. Shortly thereafter, the vision faded and I removed my hands.

After relating the experience to Toni, she told me she felt a little spacy but much lighter than when we started. Subsequent muscle testing indicated that the Covid-19 collective intrusion had been completely released, and Toni's energetic boundaries with both the Covid-19 virus and the collective field of Covid-19 were now restored.

Commentary

I find it intriguing that it is always the same compassionate spirt who emerges in my awareness when addressing this collective intrusion related to the Covid-19 virus (i.e., my Hawaiian teacher).

CASE STUDY 8

Global collective energetic intrusion

It has been my experience over many decades of shamanic journey work that each of my helping spirits specializes in particular issues brought in by clients. One of my power animals specializes in finding and retrieving split-off soul parts in order to enable a soul retrieval. Another power animal specializes in releasing individual energetic intrusions and then transmuting the dark, heavy energy. Every one of my helping spirits exists in their own particular domain, providing very specific healing approaches. This is the case whether the helping spirit is represented in the form of an animal or an anthropomorphic being. For example, I have been working with an upper-world Mayan teacher for over twenty years who takes me into a rainforest. This teacher has introduced me to numerous plant spirits, each of whom shares with me a unique representation and transmission of *power* for healing and rejuvenation.

All of these journeys just unfold, since I have learned to let go of my preconceived ideas and trust the journey process to lead me to where I need to go next. This process is all about allowing and trusting that the compassionate spirits know what is best for me—and my clients—when recruited for healing purposes. This is an ability that I have honed over many years but it is available to anyone with an open heart, and a willingness to open up to a sacred and accessible nonordinary reality.

A Foot in Both Worlds

Dismemberment via the elements

Case Study 9:
Collective Energetic Intrusions

In 2021, Mary Ann described herself as significantly dissociated and suffering from collective anxiety due to the Covid-19 pandemic.

When I muscle tested her, it was determined that Mary Ann was indeed dissociated (only 15 percent embodied), and she reported subjectively that she felt like she was dying. We set the intention for her to be fully embodied once again. As I muscle tested to determine if there was any specific interference on this intention, the indicator for subtle negative energy emerged. As I inquired further, it became evident that she was being affected by the media and all of the frightening information about the pandemic that she was ingesting on a daily basis. I identified this disturbance as the Covid-19 virus albeit as a global collective field of split-off primal emotional energy that had essentially metastasized into a collective energetic intrusion being funneled through the media.

Frontal occipital holding was selected through muscle testing as the best intervention to address this. As I defocused my eyes and asked for help, I could see this *collective intrusion* moving around her like a swirling field of energy stuck like Velcro to her energy field. I then saw my Hawaiian Kahuna teacher on the edge of a lava rock outcropping overlooking the ocean. He began dancing the hula as he faced the ocean, soliciting the spirits of the elements to dissolve this collective intrusion. The wind then picked up and I saw lightning as rain started to pour down onto Mary Ann's energy field where this collective intrusion was still swirling around her. I could see and feel the intensity of this storm that was being generated by my Hawaiian teacher.

Shortly thereafter, I could see that there were openings and slits being made in this Velcro-like swirling vortex of dark energy around Mary Ann's body. Soon, this swirling mass of dark psychotoxic energy began to dissipate and disperse. I could see the storm pushing the collective Covid-19 psychotoxicity further and further away to the very edge of the horizon.

This was the sixth time in the preceding four weeks that this Covid-19 collective intrusion had attached itself to one of my clients causing significant dissociation and anxiety. In every case, this swirling mass of dark psychotoxic energy was pushed far away to the edge of the horizon, suggesting it could return and negatively impact these clients unless they took significant measures to protect themselves from it.

As I made further muscle testing inquiries, it became very apparent that this collective intrusion had been completely released. Subsequent muscle testing indicated Mary Ann was restored to being fully present in her physical body, and she was in right relationship with her body as well.

After releasing a Covid-19 collective intrusion, I always follow up by asking about the sources of media information that the client has been ingesting. This is because certain media platforms generate more anxiety than others for each individual. For example, television is generally highly anxiety-inducing because it is a multimedia format. This is in contrast to reading a newspaper or listening to the radio. Multimedia television captures our attention and stimulates our nervous system in a way that reading the newspaper does not. Thus, I always ask my client how they are getting their news and information. Similar to Case 4, this case study also involves the penetrating influence of the dreaming media archetype.

For Mary Ann, information was being funneled into her awareness through watching the TV news, getting a daily email from the Oregon Health Authority about the rising numbers of Covid-19 documented cases and deaths, Facebook, and MSN.com. When I muscle tested her asking which of these sources of news and information were triggering her, it was the TV news and Facebook. Muscle testing further indicated that to avoid re-experiencing this collective intrusion along with the accompanying anxiety, she needed to eliminate all TV news as well as stop using Facebook. While we can wonder why these particular news sources overstimulated her sympathetic nervous system versus the others, it has become apparent to me that different people are more sensitive to different media inputs. Muscle testing is an excellent way to identify these distinctions.

As we discussed the ramifications of all of this, it began to make sense to Mary Ann that by allowing herself to become oversaturated with frightening news every day about this highly contagious microbe that was infecting and killing millions of people worldwide, she could acknowledge how this all fit together. Near the end of the session, when I muscle tested her for energetic boundaries with both the media and the Covid-19 virus, she tested strong and reported that her thinking mind and memory had suddenly returned, now that she was once again fully present in her physical body.

Commentary

We are energetic beings. Most people don't think about this on a regular basis, but we are always being affected by other people's energies and, in particular, larger collective fields of energy. I describe this particular phenomenon as the *dreaming media.*

Carl Gustav Jung developed the concept of universal archetypes—large collective fields that everyone throughout history and the present day recognize (such as soldier, martyr, hermit). I suggest that the dreaming media is a new archetype that circulates everywhere throughout the world. As more people *unconsciously* participate in the dreaming media, they are potentizing this media-related collective field every time they choose not to process their fear (or anger, or other strong persistent emotion). Thus, instead of integrating these feeling states within themselves they are disavowing them. These feeling states then become part of the larger and growing collective field that is strengthened each time someone splits off the part of themselves they are not dealing with on an unconscious level. These split-off parts then circulate in the larger collective fields. If nothing else, this case study should heighten your awareness about your sensitivity to other people's fields of energy.

As a form of subtle negative energy, *energetic intrusions* come in two flavors. Usually, they are a result of interactions with just one individual with whom a person has lost (or never had) sufficient energetic boundaries. However, when a person has been negatively influenced or affected by two or more people simultaneously, a *collective intrusion* may result.

Note: See Case 10 for my two personal examples dealing with collective intrusions.

Case Study 10: Author's Personal Examples of Collective Intrusions

Example One: Chronic Muscular Tightness

When the pandemic started in North America in early March of 2020, everyone in our city went into lockdown. It was very eerie driving to my office as there were hardly any cars out—it felt like driving at 6:30 a.m. on a Sunday. There wasn't much known about the coronavirus initially and contagion was spreading rapidly. People were reluctant to go into stores to buy groceries so curbside pickup quickly became popular. It was all very frightening and strange.

In the third week of April, I began to notice that one of my left gluteal muscles became very tight. No matter how much I walked or massaged it, the continual tightness persisted. It was so tight that it began to pull my pelvis out of normal stable alignment, so I initiated chiropractic treatment. It did not help. I then got a referral to a massage therapist and after three massages nothing changed. This gluteal tightness had never happened to me before. After three months of chiropractic treatment nothing changed. I was flummoxed. Then it finally occurred to me to consider that an intrusion might be the cause.

Once the light of awareness began to shine brightly, I started to journey shamanically in my effort to find a solution. In my first journey, I ended up in the realm of my Hawaiian teacher. I explained to him my chronic symptom and he began to do his spirit-derived hula dancing. This recruited the *power* of the elements. A fierce storm emerged with thunder, lightning and torrential rain that bore down on me. As this continued, I saw that my body had been contaminated by the enormous collective field of worldwide fear generated by the coronavirus. I was but a minute part of this worldwide fear and it manifested as several layers of Velcro-like soot wrapped around my body. The power of the elements directed at me by my teacher dissolved the layers of contamination that were part of this worldwide collective intrusion.

As is often typical of energetic intrusions, I was manifesting a physical symptom, though I cannot say why it manifested in this particular way. After about fifteen to twenty minutes of being purified by the elements in nonordinary reality, the storm receded and was pushed out to sea to the edge of the horizon. The sun came out and my teacher told me that the healing had been done. I was aware that the Velcro-like soot around my body had dissolved completely. My teacher came over to me as I thanked him, and we sat together for a few minutes overlooking the calm Pacific Ocean. He gave me some coconut meat to eat as *power food* and the journey ended.

Within the next two days, the rope-like gluteal tension completely dissipated. It has never returned. I was once again grateful and amazed that my shamanic healing connections with my helping spirits assisted me to come back into balance. It was in this way that I discovered that it was not just the Covid-19 virus that was affecting people but the larger collective Covid-19 global field of fear, uncertainty and anguish.

Over the next two years, I treated many clients to help them establish energetic boundaries with this Covid-19 collective field of fear. Many clients were able to come back into balance quickly, and it was then much easier for them to establish and maintain reliable energetic boundaries with the Covid-19 virus itself. When one has energetic boundaries, one is in optimal appropriate relationship.

Example Two: Exacerbation of Achilles Tendonitis

Some years ago, my wife and I were returning from London. I had completed teaching a four-day Dynamic Energetic Healing™

Case Study 10

(DEH) training and subsequently enjoyed being in London as a tourist. On our way back to Oregon, we first needed to change planes in Vancouver, Canada. This was where we needed to go through passport control. It so happened that two other international jets had also just landed and within minutes, hundreds of passengers were being funneled into the passport control area. There were probably forty kiosks where we could insert our passports with picture ID technology before heading toward the immigration agents who would stamp our passports so we could continue on our trip.

As is common with international travel, we had needed to be at Gatwick airport outside of London three hours prior to our flight, so we had to start our taxi ride to the airport very early in the morning. The flight was about eleven hours, so with our early morning start we were quite tired by the time we got to Vancouver. People were exhausted, stressed and anxious (as were we). We began to get anxious that we wouldn't get to our connecting flight to Oregon in time due to the long lines. Once we got through passport control, we literally had to run to our gate and got there just as they were preparing to finish the boarding process. We made it but were very stressed.

To back up for a moment, before our trip to London, I had developed Achilles tendonitis in my right foot from overuse on some weight machines at my local gym. For the week prior to our departure, I was plunging my foot into a bucket of ice water every night and taking Advil to reduce the inflammation. I was quite concerned about how I would manage getting around in London since one walks on the cobblestone streets in order to get to the underground subway. After the first three days in London, I was relieved to discover that the inflammation in my foot had receded and I was able to walk normally throughout the rest of our trip without any discomfort. The swelling was gone and did not return for the duration of our trip.

The day after settling in back home, the inflammation in my foot returned. It was bright red and puffy and had become inflamed once again. I could not understand why it suddenly returned after walking on it for over two weeks on uneven surfaces in London. Reluctantly, I started taking Advil and plunging my foot into the bucket of ice water. After three days, the inflammation had not abated. I began to speculate about possible causes and started using muscle testing in an effort to determine an underlying cause.

Shortly into initiating the muscle testing, the indicator for subtle negative energy emerged. As I continued to inquire, it became evident that the source of this pain and inflammation was a collective intrusion. I was able to narrow it down to the collective stress and anxiety generated by the hundreds of people I was with who were going through passport control in Vancouver. Because I was exhausted, worn down and anxious about making our next flight, my normally robust energy field was compromised and more porous than it would otherwise be. I was part of this collective field of stress and anxiety. Consequently, I had absorbed the collective stress, which turned out to be a psycho-toxic collective intrusion. This negative energy nested in the most vulnerable physical area of my body, namely my foot. This was the source of the inflammation that everyday conventional approaches were unable to resolve. I was glad to have discovered the underlying origin of this and, once confirmed, I journeyed to one of my helping spirits to release this collective intrusion. Thirty-six hours later, all of the swelling and pain dissolved and never returned.

Commentary

We are all energetic beings sensitive to the impacts of other people and other environments. These two personal anecdotes illustrate the importance of remaining *power-filled*, which requires daily self-care strategies along with ongoing responsible energetic hygiene practices. In my DEH trainings, I teach the protocol that I have referred to as the *dreaming media* that

Case Study 10

addresses the collective fields of different forms of information that we regularly expose ourselves to daily. This is what I describe above in Case 9. When we are overloaded, we become susceptible to the larger collective fields of negative energy circulating throughout the media. These massive collective fields of shared psychotoxic energy also inform and affect individuals as collective intrusions, since much of the media we now take in is *multimedia* that affects us in multiple perceptual channels. These channels include our visual channel (internal and outer visual), our auditory channel (internal and outer auditory), as well as proprioceptive and parapsychological.

The continuing diet of frightening and bad news that is often amplified through social media postings presented in a multimedia format is simply overwhelming to many people's sympathetic nervous system. This does not always result in traumatization, but when bad and frightening news is repeatedly highlighted, we are prone to media overwhelm. This overwhelm can and does end up as contamination reflected as subtle negative energy, often identified as collective intrusions. Repeated bad news cumulatively erodes our overall well-being, generating various degrees of fear, overwhelm and ennui. It is wise to check one's energetic boundaries with the many media sources we tend to rely on regularly, so we can consciously determine when it is prudent to take short vacations from all the bad news.

We are inundated by information, and thus we need to pay attention to our thoughts and feelings (i.e., reactions) about what we are hearing, seeing and reading about so we can maintain proper balance in our lives. Consider the various categories of bad news circulating in the world: the ongoing impacts of global climate change, daily mass shootings, pandemic-related contagion (at the time), threats of tactical nuclear weapons, ongoing wars, political divisions and on it goes. These larger global concerns may compound our own daily challenges related to our health concerns, work and family responsibilities. Perhaps it is time to step back for a moment and reevaluate how you are choosing to live your day-to-day life and emphasize making self-care a priority. There are many reasons to take some personal time and truly reevaluate how we choose to interact with the world and these larger collective fields. It is imperative that we do so now.

Case Study 11:
Confronting Ancestral Spirits That Contribute to Physical Illness

Stuart came in for his second appointment, asking for help with some autoimmune issues he was struggling with. This session ended up being a new experience for Stuart.

He was comfortable with my Dynamic Energetic Healing™ (DEH) approach since we had previously done some muscle testing along with energy psychology approaches. When I began muscle testing for the best strategy to start with, shamanic journey emerged. Stuart expressed the therapeutic intention to mitigate the chronic pain and discomfort that was wreaking havoc to his body, which was associated with his progressively worsening illness. He was hoping for a complete cure for the painful physical condition that he had been struggling with for the previous seven years. He said he was always hoping for a miracle.

Stuart's wife agreed to write out the journey as I narrated my journey experience. As I put on my eye mask and began my shamanic journey to the drumming music from my portable speaker, I was quickly taken into the lower world realm of my Native American allies with the help of Horse. After riding through a green valley, the landscape changed as we galloped onto the plains. Shortly, I saw the many tents in the distance where the compound of my allies is located. I met with my tribal council as I entered a large tent. After honoring the spirit of tobacco by passing the pipe around the interior to the three tribal members, it was my turn to draw on the pipe and then return it to its place on hooks attached to the interior of the tent.

The shaman of the tribe, named Grandmother, summoned Stuart's spiritual body standing upright in the center of our small group. She walked around him, looking intently at him and through him. I saw (through her) a dark ball of gaseous, vibrating, charcoal-colored psychotoxicity located in his upper solar plexus. This represented an energetic intrusion. She immediately determined that this was caused by Stuart's ancestral spirits. I asked Grandmother if it would be appropriate and helpful to bring forth any of his ancestors. She thought for a moment and said it would.

She began rattling around Stuart to bring forth his ancestral spirits. Soon a *Stargate*-like luminous shimmering portal appeared, and immediately one of his ancestral spirits came through wearing black clothes. Grandmother began talking to this spirit in a strong voice. She told him he needed to stop this unauthorized behavior as it was poisoning Stuart. He responded that Stuart is part of their clan and thus he and the others could continue to send energy into Stuart to ensure that he stayed with and would return to his clan upon his death (Stuart's ancestral lineage is Irish).

This representative of Stuart's clannish ancestral spirits was possessive and intrusive. Grandmother understood this right away and began lambasting him, telling him that they must stop this right now. This ancestral spirit's negative and possessive attention directed onto Stuart had been poisoning Stuart. Grandmother went on to say that Stuart has his own path that is his to pursue. These clannish ancestral spirits were interfering in Stuart's life, and also poisoning him. She told him this must stop NOW.

This ancestral spirit began looking down onto the ground and was clearly uncomfortable. After Grandmother continued to lambast him, he finally relented and consented to withdraw his and the others' focused possessive energy onto Stuart. Grandmother then dismissed him and he went back through the energy portal that then condensed to a pinpoint of light and disappeared.

Grandmother then had Stuart lie down and I noticed that the toxic energy of the dark ball was now a light beige. Grandmother kneeled down beside him with a small hollow bone and extracted and sucked out the remains of the gaseous toxicity, spitting it onto the ground. I then noticed that the poisonous dark energy that had been circulating throughout his body was much lighter now and had much less volume than was there initially. She then decided that Stuart and the other warriors needed to go to the mud-spattering hot springs nearby at the base of the foothills.

Once they arrived, one warrior smeared hot mud all over Stuart's body and then had him lie on his back so the hot sun could dry out the mud and pull out any residual poisons. I noticed that Stuart looked very weak. After a time, it was decided that they needed to take Stuart to the river for cleansing and purification. Stuart was put onto a horse with another warrior and they all rode back to the river by their compound. Two warriors dragged the very weak Stuart into the river, which had a powerful current. Stuart slowly revived and became increasingly alert. Then they helped him out and Stuart slowly came into his full presence. Now, Stuart was easily walking on his own to the men's hut, where one of the warriors covered him with a thick blanket. Then another warrior gave him some dried bison meat for ingesting *power*. Soon thereafter, Horse and I rode back and the journey ended.

When we began discussing and reviewing the journey, Stuart's wife mentioned that Stuart's relatives never accepted her or other in-laws, as they were very clannish. I had not known this before. This was an interesting reinforcement of what Grandmother had identified in the journey. I found this quite fascinating.

Stuart subsequently reported that he was sleeping much better after this journey, and only had to get up once during the night to visit the toilet. He also told me that he had much better overall energy and felt encouraged that we had discovered an important component of his longstanding illness. This healing experience significantly mitigated many of his chronic symptoms. We discussed making subsequent appointments to continue to ameliorate his illness.

Commentary

In my experience over many years of shamanic journeying, ancestral spirits tend to be protective and supportive. As part of our intergenerational lineage, they are referred to as "ethnocentric" spirits, and they typically only want the best for us. While this representative of his ancestors believed that he and his clan were acting in this way in order to help Stuart, the information gleaned through the intercession of Grandmother was quite to the contrary. The energetic intrusion represented not just cumulative psychotoxic energy but what had been an ongoing intrusion into his current physical life experience that was contributing to a longstanding chronic illness. I would never have considered this a factor related to his physical health and well-being. This is but another remarkable example of the wondrous *power* (including wisdom and information) proffered by compassionate spirits when they are called upon for assistance.

CASE STUDY 12:
AN ANCESTRAL SPIRIT COMES IN LOVE

Stacy found herself in the hospital for two days due to an unusual medical issue with her left eye. She described it as a small circle just to the side of her pupil. It was determined this was not at all related to her use of contact lenses. The attending doctor theorized that she might have been affected by some type of chemical exposure that burned her eye. She had to wear her glasses for two to three weeks while it healed. She was in the hospital with a patch on her eye for a couple of days before being released.

We had an appointment already scheduled and it had been a couple of weeks since Stacy had been out of the hospital. She felt fine and her eye was healing. When we began our session, it was determined that she was only 17 percent embodied. Stacy acknowledged that she had been feeling dissociated, alternating between coming back into her body and then dissociating again. To be fully present and grounded in her physical body became her starting therapeutic intention.

As I started muscle testing it became evident to me that subtle negative energy was likely responsible for her dissociation. This was identified as some kind of spirit attachment. When I brought this out, Stacy asked if it was an ancestral spirit. Indeed, it turned out to be just that. She thought to ask this because when she was growing up, her paternal grandfather lived with them and he was a very loving man. He was devoted to her, almost like a surrogate loving father she never felt she had. She said *he had a damaged left eye from an accident and this was why she thought to ask if it was him.*

It was determined that the frontal occipital holding intervention would be the best strategy to proceed with. After doing my invocation, I perceived that it was indeed her ancestral spirit grandfather who had actually merged with her in an effort to support her and protect her during her recent pregnancy. It is unusual for an "attached" spirit to be actually merged with someone—they are usually either in a person's energy field or hovering loosely around and above the person. I had to explain to him that he could not stay merged with her or she would experience possession illness, the eye problem being one aspect of this. He said he just wanted to help and protect her, so he merged with her. (We did not know exactly when he first merged with her, but it was earlier in her pregnancy. As he continued to stay merged, she began absorbing some of the damage from his eye.) He went on to say that he would be praying for her and her baby. After a brief dialogue, he understood that he needed to disengage from her and he immediately left.

When the frontal occipital holding was completed, we shared our respective perceptions. Stacy perceived that her grandfather had merged with her with love at some point earlier in her pregnancy. During the frontal occipital holding, he showed her some very dark energy that was part of her paternal ancestral lineage and that while it was still there in her lineage, she would no longer be affected by it. She then felt the healing spirit of Jesus come into her and felt his love, light and peace.

When we next muscle tested, she was completely embodied and there was no longer any indication of an intrusive spirit in her energy field or physical body. Stacy felt very good about it and came to realize that her eye problem would heal more rapidly now. She was grateful for the message embedded in her eye symptom and grateful she was able to sort all of this out by working with me in a collaborative manner.

Commentary

Ancestral spirits are part of our spiritual legacy and can be intentionally accessed and worked with for beneficial reasons.

CASE STUDY 12

A compassionate ancestral spirit

As these spirits spend more time in nonordinary reality, they become more compassionate with increasing desires to help if called upon.

In this case, Stacy's grandfather's spirit intervened unilaterally without being solicited—he believed that he could support her during her pregnancy. Stacy is a very sensitive individual and suspected that something was up since she was dissociating and then coming back into her body. She knew that there was nothing going on in her life that was threatening or disturbing; her pregnancy was uneventful and she was excited about having a baby. While her grandfather's spirit was coming from a place of compassion, he was naive about how his merged presence would eventually cause her problems. In this case, it was particularly on the physical level because his merged presence affected her eye as well as her groundedness. Stacy was reacting energetically by dissociating, opening up the possibility for other potential problems to occur.

I have mentioned earlier that when a shamanic practitioner chooses to merge with one of their compassionate spirits for facilitating healing, it is for a relatively short time with the practitioner being the one to decide when to disengage. We must assert and claim our spiritual sovereignty and remember that it is never helpful to stay merged with one's helping spirit or any other spirit or problems will ensue. An experienced shamanic practitioner often merges with their helping spirits for different healing outcomes but realizes this is done with control and awareness for achieving a specific healing result. We can cultivate loving relationships with our ancestral spirits, but as with any other compassionate spirit, these guidelines must be well understood and respected.

Case Study 13:
Spontaneous Healing through Shamanic Merging

Several years ago, I was working with a client named Jane, who I saw once a month for nearly a year. During the session described here, Jane explained that she had an awareness of a wall around her. She was aware of this particularly when in social situations, and the wall kept her from deeply connecting to others. She described the overriding concern as "a subtle trust issue." As a child, Jane was sexually abused over several years by her uncle. Possibly, this wall was related to the abuse.

As I started muscle testing her to ensure that she was congruent to heal and that she was fully present in her physical body, it quickly became evident that she was only 65 percent embodied with one internal objection: "I'll be too vulnerable to others if I'm fully present in my body." Her therapeutic intention then became to restore full embodiment by targeting the specific objection. Her muscle testing indicated fanning in front of her solar plexus as the first intervention, followed by dialoguing with me to release this objection. During our discussion, I asked her what had been the most painful thing she experienced growing up. She said being abandoned by her father. She then became very emotional, so I directed her to tap through a sequence of emotional freedom techniques (EFT; read about this in my book *Dynamic Energetic Healing*™). Jane became even more emotional doing this, and when I inquired she said, "It's all about not being accepted—it's my fault!"

As she continued to cry, I asked Jane to rate her subjective units of distress on the scale of zero to ten. She said she was at about nine and a half. She was becoming increasingly distraught, so I directed her to rub the points under her collar bones while repeating the following statement three times out loud: "I totally and completely love and accept myself even though it's my fault." This was followed by another sequence of tapping on the EFT acupressure points accompanied by lots of tears. As she began to calm down, I asked her to pause and reflect on any new awareness that had become apparent to her.

What Jane heard was an inner voice: "You can't do it right—you're not good enough." She commented that this voice hides a lot and moves in and out of her awareness. I began using the neurolinguistic programming (NLP) representational systems model to help her further define this inner voice. I asked her about the tone of the voice, how loud it was, how soft it was, and so on. She said the voice was just critical and the tone was not angry but it was very cruel, repeating "Of course you can't do anything right." The voice was neither male nor female. It was loud and then soft, moving in and out of her awareness, hiding and then returning.

I asked her to begin a dialogue with this inner voice and to ask it to come out of the shadows. I began thinking of different ways to externalize it, such as the gestalt empty chair or voice dialogue techniques. All of my suggestions attempting to help her personify it or give it some shape or form had not been successful up to this point.

Suddenly, I had a strong *second attention* awareness that I needed to grab my rattle, so I started rattling around her. As I did, my helping spirit Grandmother merged with me and directed the rattling as I moved into a shamanic dreamtime trance. In my shamanic visionary state, I began to see a dark malleable form that I perceived as an energetic intrusion emerging from Jane's first chakra at the base of her spine. I then saw Eagle come into the scene and escort this intrusion away as I continued to rattle. At a certain point Grandmother disengaged from me and I stopped the rattling. Jane later told me that during this time *she* went into the dreamtime space and saw an eagle take away a menacing rat and snake. The *power* of Grandmother that infused the interpersonal space was so strong that Jane spontaneously opened herself up to nonordinary reality (NOR). Essentially, she perceived the dynamics of the healing process in real time concurrently with my own merged experience.

Next a dragon appeared that Jane perceived was *not* benevolent. It was a black, scaly dragon with a pointed tail and red eyes that came right in front of her and stared at her in a threatening manner. She called for help for lack of anything else that she could think of. What next appeared to Jane was another dragon that was green and to her felt incredibly close and loving. It "wrapped herself around me and snuggled up to me." She felt safe and protected as it subsequently chased the threatening black dragon away. Jane had an impression that the Green Dragon had been with her since she was a child, and upon muscle testing this was confirmed. It was truly a guardian spirit that had helped Jane survive many difficult circumstances throughout her early life.

When Jane had collected herself and the rattling was over, she commented, "It's more important to get to the root of what attracted the bad dragon and other beings who would come into me in the past." She elaborated on this by saying that as a child, she often had the perception, especially when going to sleep at night, that entities or negative spirits were coming into her. One could theorize that this might have had something to do with early sexual abuse. However, there is no way to know for certain whether this represented physical intrusion by the abusing uncle or heightened sensitivity into the realm of NOR.

When we were done, Jane said she felt *very* good and felt she was glowing internally, having confirmed her reconnection to this "new" power animal (the Green Dragon). I proceeded to muscle test her, inquiring whether the root cause was resolved; the answer was yes. Additionally, Jane was now 100 percent present in her physical body and thus no longer dissociated.

It is interesting that NLP and energy psychology "cutting edge" techniques were unable to alleviate Jane's extreme emotional distress as she dropped into the black hole of some old residual trauma that was reflected by a painfully judgmental and critical inner voice. Part of my Dynamic Energetic Healing™ orientation is the cultivation of *second attention awareness*. This awareness provided greater perceptual acuity to subtle energies in the interpersonal therapeutic field, allowing for openness and ease of moving back and forth between ordinary reality and NOR. It was precisely this second attention awareness that provided me with the "impression" to grab my rattle as an intervention, thereby allowing for the intercession of one of my helping spirits to initiate and facilitate the transformation that unfolded within Jane.

Jane left the session completely restored and feeling positive regarding what had occurred during her session. There was no lingering negative affect, only appreciation and awe for what had happened. I mentioned to her that the next session should include inquiring if she needed to install new beliefs relating to self-esteem, along with ensuring that her energetic boundaries with the abstract inner critic figure (in this case the disembodied inner voice) were secure and solid. In the shamanic paradigm, negative thought forms that penetrate a person's normal healthy boundaries or biofield can be characterized as intrusions and can create a host of problems, including physical and mental illness. As the session concluded, I harbored the strong belief that Jane would continue to have secure and solid energetic boundaries with the inner critic figure, since the intrusions that she perceived as a menacing rat, snake, and malevolent black dragon were all released.

Commentary

It would be all too easy at this point to get into debating exactly what happened, but that debate would only be from each individual's perceptual and theoretical bias. Some of these therapeutic biases might include a traditional, Western

CASE STUDY 13

Freudian-based psychoanalytic orientation, a Jungian depth psychology orientation, an energy psychology approach or a core shamanic healing orientation. Rather than get mired in academic theoretical discussions, I chose to respect my client's subjective experience before, during and after her abreaction. I also chose to acknowledge and accept my own subjective experience, resulting from many years of training in a variety of models that propose constructive altered states of consciousness as the underlying foundation for transformative change in the psychotherapy context.

Jane had taken one of my beginning shamanic journey classes, but with inconsistent results. Since she had previously acknowledged an interest in learning about core shamanic practices, she was already in a greater state of openness and receptivity to the reality of power animals as guardian spirits and NOR in general. Not too long after that session, Jane emailed me expressing interest in continuing to learn shamanic journey work. It was understandable to me that because of her early life experiences (of being "invaded" by what she described as entities or negative spirits), Jane's initial shamanic journeying workshop experiences were blocked. Now that these fears or blocks had been removed, she suddenly became available to shamanic journeying and was eager to learn.

When individuals experience overwhelming life experiences such as repeated abuse, it is not uncommon for them to be more open to the realm of NOR. However, without the proper training, negative and frightening experiences can occur spontaneously without the context to understand what is happening and what to do about them. Many more people than you would suspect experience these extraordinary perceptions during times of overwhelming trauma. Yet, because core shamanic practices are little known within the general population, these experiences are marginalized and, when revealed to others, are often regarded as a sign of mental illness and delusional thinking. Thus, it is normative for people who experience these perceptions to suppress them and suffer silently. It was Jane's good fortune that I was able to follow the thread of Process in order to support her for a good therapeutic outcome.

This case study also illustrates how the *power* and compassion of one of my compassionate spirits merged with me as I became identified with it. I sensed the nudge of my helping spirit's desire to merge so her *power* could more directly impact my client in our everyday reality. Through me, her presence became embodied—she was directing the rattling to infuse *power* into my client in very specific ways. It is a special experience for me to surrender to my helping spirit as I, too, benefit from the absorption of her *power* moving through me. These mergings occur when my helping spirits feel it is important to be more present. I always defer to them. Sometimes, I call on one of my helpers in order to deliberately merge, but it is usually something that happens in the moment without much premeditation. This merging happens as a result of cultivating relationships with compassionate spirits over time. It is one aspect of the shamanic practitioner's skill set and it is always a blessing when it occurs.

Case Study 14:
Soul Stealing and Soul Retrieval

Leslie came to me with a therapeutic intention to be free to speak her truth without the fear of retribution. One of her associated fears was that someone would get hurt by her telling the truth.

I started the session by addressing her fears using emotional freedom techniques (EFT; see my first book, *Dynamic Energetic Healing*™) tapping. This strategy involves repeatedly tapping on the end points of each of the major acupuncture meridians while attuning to the particular problem state. As each meridian is associated with one or more specific emotional states, the tapping (also referred to as needleless acupuncture) unblocks the stuck emotional energy related to the specific problem state. After two sequences of tapping, her fear and bodily tension related to this intention were reduced by 50 percent according to her subjective self-report (or subjective units of distress, which went from an eight to a four).

Leslie then explained that her father had always been tense after visiting his own father, who was critical and judgmental. I wondered if perhaps there was an ancestral link that was an intergenerational pattern from her paternal grandfather to her father and then to her. As we began to muscle test it was determined that subtle negative energy was interfering with her intention. Muscle testing determined that the issue is what in shamanic healing is referred to as *soul stealing*.

My muscle testing indicated that the best intervention was frontal occipital holding. After gently placing my hands around her head and reciting my silent invocation, I saw Horse traveling down a tunnel-like corridor into Leslie's past, where I saw her father holding her five-year-old soul part just like a parent holds their new baby. Her father was holding her to protect her, but as a consequence he unwittingly absorbed or "stole" part of her vital essence. I then understood that this prevented her from developing her own power to be authentic and courageous, since she was no longer whole. Once this was understood, Horse returned with the appropriated soul part and brought it into Leslie's throat (her fifth energy center).

I should note that before I asked for interventions, I had *the second attention awareness* to muscle test each of Leslie's chakras and, not surprisingly, her fifth center was weak. When this center is balanced, we are typically free to represent ourselves to the world in full integrity and authenticity. Once the soul retrieval was completed, muscle testing indicated that the soul stealing had been resolved. The soul retrieval had been successful and when retested, her throat center was balanced. As I placed my hand in front of her throat and muscle tested it, I saw it become a large golden sun radiating outward several feet.

Perhaps Leslie's father was trying to protect her from *his* father's judgment and maybe even his own. While we cannot know motive for why the soul stealing occurred, it is more common that we realize. This can also happen in adult relationships when one individual is codependent and the other person is all too willing to take the other's vital energy for his or her own sense of power and control. Some people can become energetic vampires, literally taking other people's energy for their own selfish ends.

Leslie has been working hard for some time to be honest with her partner, but she still has some occasional resistance to being completely honest with her true feelings. This *soul retrieval* will no doubt shift her relationship with her partner.

Commentary

When individuals acquire and reintegrate lost parts of themselves, their vital energy gets a tremendous boost as they return to greater wholeness. Additionally, the inner part that dissociated or left returns with the information about the underlying trauma that had previously been consciously inaccessible. This is because when a traumatized inner part splits off, it carries the information about the trauma with it, so that information cannot be accessed through cognitive discussion. This is often one of the limitations of talk therapy—the memory of important aspects of the event is no longer consciously available. Soul retrievals create a more empowered individual simply because that person is now more present to themself.

Soul retrievals generate one of the most profound healing outcomes that the shamanic practitioner can provide. It is often said that the helping spirits know what needs to happen in order for healing to transpire. It is up to us to learn how to cultivate relationships with these remarkable beings of great compassion and *power*. By sharing these clinical examples, I am simply describing what is possible when we embrace this shamanic healing paradigm and partner with our helping spirits.

Case Study 15:
Clearing a House of Residual Psychotoxic Energy

When a middle-aged couple, William and Charlotte, moved into the home they had recently purchased, they began to perceive some "lingering negativity" which they believed was from the previous occupants. They wanted to know if the house was actually haunted or contaminated in some way.

They really liked the house, but they were suspicious about the Realtor® and the previous occupants. The sellers essentially rented back the house for sixty days after the transaction was completed to better prepare for their own move out, and my clients told me that the sellers were very nasty to them. William and Charlotte remarked that the sellers left miscellaneous debris in and around the house when it all should have been removed. They also felt that the Realtor® who handled the transaction was unprofessional, and bordering on rude at times.

After William and Charlotte finally moved in, they noticed unusual events going on in the house. They described weird streaks on their new table that they had not noticed previously; they exchanged it for a table that was unmarked. There were scratches on other pieces of furniture, and stains that were not previously noticed on some of the carpet. There were bites all over William's legs, some of which dissipated and then recurred ten days later. But when they hired a bedbug analyst to go through the house, that person declared it clear of bedbugs. Charlotte experienced unexplained bruising and scratches, along with one scary dream that was nightmarish and upsetting.

Their therapeutic intention was to ensure that their house was energetically clean. They had worked with me in the past and were harboring suspicions that the overall feeling and energy in the house was perhaps toxic in some way. As I began

CASE STUDY 15

muscle testing Charlotte for psychoenergetic reversal on the intention, the indicator for subtle negative energy immediately emerged. After further inquiry, it was identified as a *collective energetic intrusion* from the previous occupants. Both Charlotte and William were being adversely influenced by this psychotoxic energy. They were not surprised.

Through the energy checking process, frontal occipital holding was selected for Charlotte, who was representing both of them, to address the collective intrusion left by the previous owners. Our sessions were being conducted in my office, but I saw the collective intrusion as a large gray film that filled their entire house, similar to dense fog. When I asked for help to clear this collective intrusion, a number of my helping spirits appeared to extract this residual psychotoxic energy. This included one of my upper-world teachers and Panther, fire sprites, and the Spirit of the Wind. They worked both individually and collaboratively until the space appeared to me to be crystal clear. Muscle testing of Charlotte confirmed my perceptions that the collective intrusion was released completely.

As we continued to energy check, more subtle negative energy became apparent. Upon further inquiry, an earthbound spirit occupying the house was identified. As I went into the frontal occipital holding position, I perceived this being (who some people might call a poltergeist because it appeared to be mischievous) but I was unable to identify its reason for being in the house. It was in some way representing and expressing the nasty, negative qualities of the people who sold the house to Charlotte and William. Perhaps it was the spiritual analog of the human energy of the sellers that was most untoward. When I asked for help, I immediately saw another one of my powerful upper-world helping spirits come into the field of the house and with one arm grasp this being and ascend with him into the upper world.

Once the collective intrusion and the mischievous earthbound spirit were released, my clients reported that the strange phenomena that they had been experiencing no longer bothered them. Muscle testing revealed that William and Charlotte now had excellent energetic boundaries with their new house as well as the former occupants. There was nothing more that needed to be done—their new home was now energetically clean.

Commentary

As I wrote about in my first book, *Dynamic Energetic Healing*™, it is not uncommon for people to leave residue of their energy behind when they leave a place, such as a hotel room. This residue affects and sometimes contaminates a space that someone else might subsequently occupy. During many of my DEH trainings over the nine years I was teaching in Oregon, some participants flew in from out of town and stayed in hotels. It seemed that there was always at least one person in the group who had picked up some kind of earthbound spirit attachment or energetic intrusion that was left behind by previous occupants in their hotel room. This occurred despite the vacuuming and tidying that is done by the hotel's maid service before new occupants arrive.

Many years ago, I became aware of this phenomenon while staying in a large hotel in Denver. Among other events, I uncharacteristically became very angry at the front desk clerk when we were told our reservation had never been confirmed. (It had been.) When we went to a late dinner in the hotel restaurant, the waiter disappeared after taking our order. My sister-in-law then became very angry when we were eventually told that the cook had simply left his late shift, so no food was being prepared. It became very clear to me that the hotel was being affected by strange negative energy that was circulating throughout the entire complex. Later that week, when I was in Estes Park, Colorado, I became contaminated again, this time from the motel room we were staying in. (You can read more about my experience in my book *Dynamic Energetic Healing*™.)

I hazard to guess that most people do not know why they may feel so poorly upon leaving a motel or hotel room since they are not as sensitive to energetic phenomena as I have become. Nevertheless, the energetic intersection of our everyday reality and nonordinary reality often occurs in ways that impact us. These energetic remnants can be perceived by anybody who chooses to train in becoming more sensitive to subtle energy. With commitment, persistence and determination, you too can become aware of subtle energy in different environments. In the long run, this can be most helpful for staying healthy and *power-filled*.

Case Study 16:
Spirit Attachment and Releasement

Joan is a forty-year-old client who called me in a crisis. Her mother (seventy-five years old) had just had major surgery and Joan and her stepfather (eighty-seven years old) were the only ones present to support her after her surgery. Joan spent ten hours at the hospital during the day of her mother's surgery. Her mother was released the next day and for the next two days, Joan assisted her mother and her stepfather at her mother's home.

Joan told me that when she left the hospital, she felt fine. But upon returning home after spending two days with her mother, she felt weighted down, dizzy, disoriented and very emotional. She also told me she had been doing things very uncharacteristic of her. These included painting her fingernails dark purple and driving to the local mall after her family went to bed so she could shop. (It was the holiday season, so the mall was open all night.) In fact, she bought a lot of expensive electronic equipment that she had not intended to before she left the house. She was also uncharacteristically staying up until about 3:30 a.m., reading, watching TV and cleaning her house. Additionally, she sheepishly reported that she and her husband had wild sex and did things that they had never done before at her initiative.

I considered the possibility that she had some form of caregiver burnout and her behaviors were compensatory as a way to deal with the stress of attending to her ailing mother.

Joan set the intention to feel normal again since she sensed her behaviors were out of character for her. As I initiated muscle testing, I perceived that she was not fully embodied; in fact, she was only 26 percent embodied. Her first therapeutic goal was to restore full embodiment so she could be fully present. However, there was one objection from an unconscious inner part. It was concerned about

CASE STUDY 16

Joan having too much responsibility if she was fully present.

Frontal occipital holding was the intervention that was selected by muscle testing. About halfway through it, while her eyes were still closed, Joan suggested that I open the window. I continued to stay focused and maintained my concentration. As I was still in a visionary state, I briefly told her that when we were finished with the frontal occipital holding, I would open the window for her.

Usually, I have visions of helping spirits and of elements of subtle negative energy that I see being released from my client. In this case, however, it was Joan who had the vision. She told me that she perceived some kind of spirit attached to her, and as I continued with the frontal occipital holding, she also saw it being released. When I had completed the frontal occipital holding, she suggested that I open the window—she said she knew that she had picked up an errant earthbound spirit and she wanted to make sure that it could escape out the window. The next muscle test indicated that she was now 100 percent embodied and the objection that had been identified had been completely resolved.

What Joan described and experienced is what shamans call *possession illness*. She believed that she had picked up an earthbound spirit as she got worn down physically and emotionally at the end of her stay in the hospital. This earthbound spirit had attached to her during her hospital stay, and it was influencing her to act out in these ways that were very uncharacteristic of her. These uncharacteristic behaviors were satisfying its own desires through Joan. Joan had worked with me in the past, so she was aware of the possibility of being affected by an earthbound spirit; that's why she had set up the appointment.

I next muscle tested to find out if Joan had any energetic boundaries with these nonordinary reality phenomena. She did not. It was easy to establish these energetic boundaries through a series of quick interventions in order to provide a sense of safety and protection to Joan. I explained how important it is to maintain a sense of personal power and self-confidence in order to maintain one's sense of well-being. This is especially important when one is around people who are very vulnerable, such as those in hospitals, where there is a lot of fear and anguish in the general environment.

When we were done, Joan felt completely better, her affect returned to normal and she felt confident about moving forward with her life, including supporting her mother during her convalescence.

Commentary

While it is unusual for a client to be the one to perceive the presence of an earthbound spirit, many individuals who are particularly empathic (or who suffered repeated trauma during their formative years) pick up on subtle energy phenomena more frequently than most people realize. This is a prime example of why empaths need to be particularly careful to ensure that they have excellent energetic boundaries in all contexts.

When aspects of one's life become out of tilt, it is time to check in with one's therapist and find out if there has been an incident that created the imbalance. What Joan experienced was not just normal stress—she experienced behaviors that were unusual and out of character for her. Fortunately, she had the self-awareness to suspect that there was more going on beyond normal caregiving stress.

Conclusion
Shamanic Practices and the Living Earth

The earth does not belong to man, man belongs to the earth.
All things are connected like the blood that unites us all.
Man did not weave the web of life, he is merely a strand in it.
Whatever he does to the web, he does to himself.
 — Chief Seattle's *Letter to All*

Shamanism has been described in many ways, but most who have studied and practice it agree that it is a way of being in the world that honors and respects all aspects of the living Earth. To a large extent, one's deep connection to the living Earth can be considered a remedy to feeling alone and isolated. Earth's beauty is intoxicating, should one choose to pay attention. A dilemma remains that we humans, as a collective race, are becoming more and more estranged from the natural world with its omnipresent beauty and diversity. As shamanism is a nature-based orientation to life, all plants, animals and even the various elements are respected and honored as unique expressions of the mysterious intelligent life force that animates all things. At its center is the acknowledgment of an ecologically based Earth *wherein all things and all beings are interrelated and interconnected*. I remind you of how James Lovelock redefined our relationship to our planet:

> James Lovelock will always be associated with one big idea: Gaia. *The Oxford English Dictionary* defines this as "the global ecosystem, understood to function in the

manner of a vast self-regulating organism, in the context of which all living things collectively define and maintain the conditions conducive for life on earth". It cites the independent scientist as the first to use the term (ancient Greek for Earth) in this way, in 1972.[143]

The experience of connection to all things is at the very core of shamanic healing approaches. Thus, these approaches are an antidote to peoples' growing experience of alienation and isolation, especially now that so many are sequestered in their home office in front of a computer monitor, often without real human contact. The ramifications of this seclusion are profound. When species become extinct because of modern industrial incursions and encroachment into wildlife and forest habitats, there are reverberations throughout the entire living Earth's ecosystem. Our growing distance from the natural world alone is reason enough to incorporate shamanic practices into the psychotherapy context as so many clients suffer from feeling disconnected, not just from other humans but from the sacred living Earth as well.

We are social beings. Hidden away in our home offices in front of a computer monitor is reason enough for many to feel depressed and disconsolate. I fear this new paradigm is becoming the norm. With increasing climate change, our addiction to a capitalistic fossil-fuel-based industrial economy, and a relatively comfortable way of being with all of the amenities we so desire (and think we need), we in the West are rapidly approaching another new paradigm shift that presages a great deal of turmoil, suffering and uncertainty. Industrialized cultures continue to exploit Earth for its natural resources. As James Hillman has commented,

> The coming ecological disaster we worry about has already occurred, and goes on occurring. It takes place in the accounts of ourselves that separate ourselves from the world.[144]

Have you ever thought about where the basic components of all of the vehicles on the road all over the world come from? They come from mineral deposits being mined from Earth's crust—iron ore that is transformed into steel, lithium for our rechargeable batteries, silica and quartz for our glass, and oil and petroleum products used for gasoline and the synthesis of plastics that are now endemic throughout our oceans and food. William Commanda, who was an Algonquin elder, spiritual leader, and promoter of environmental stewardship, presciently commented that Western industrialization would have a devastating impact on native peoples and on the living Earth itself.

> Traditional people of Indian nations have interpreted the two roads that face the light-skinned race as the road to technology and the road to spirituality. We feel that the road to technology… has led modern society to a damaged and seared earth. Could it be that the road to technology represents a rush to destruction, and that the road to spirituality represents the slower path that the traditional native people have traveled and are now seeking again? The earth is not scorched on this trail. The grass is still growing there.[145]

Eating heart-healthy fish and nearly all foods now means ingesting microplastics. And it is getting worse. Much of this arises from the persistent belief that we have dominion over nature and thus the right to pursue our endless voracious appetite for beef, dairy products and a shiny new car, all of which are using up the natural resources from our living Earth as our population continues to grow. How different this is from the consciousness of indigenous peoples as expressed by The Great Law of the Iroquois:

> In our every deliberation, we must consider the impact of our decisions on the next seven generations.[146]

Conclusion

The lives of indigenous peoples and shamanic cultures have always depended on the accessible natural resources of Earth and thus value it in ways most of us do not. I am not naive about how much arable land will continue to be needed to feed the growing human population, even as great swaths of fertile farmland are drying up because of global warming creating persistent droughts. But contaminating our soils with herbicides and pesticides in order to meet these growing population needs is a Faustian bargain. More and more people are developing cancer and other diseases, likely in part from the daily ingestion of toxic chemicals. I recently read an article about dark chocolate in *Consumer Reports*.

Through rigorous laboratory analysis, most of the chocolate bars and cocoa we now enjoy are contaminated with substantial amounts of lead and cadmium. Dark chocolate, famously touted for its health-related antioxidant benefits, has become one more glaring example of how nearly everything we consume is becoming a health risk.[147] As I enjoy dark chocolate in various forms, I am now deeply saddened because of what this represents about how Earth is becoming poisoned. And we must not forget all of the factories burning fossil fuels worldwide that are reducing our numbers collectively at an alarming rate due to air pollution. It is grievously happening now throughout our planet Earth. The very air we breathe is slowly killing us. In 2022, *The New York Times* had this to say:

> How unhealthy is unhealthy air? A whole spectrum of impacts can fall under that term. But while pollution means something very different in Dallas than it does in Delhi, globally, the impacts are remarkably grim. Perhaps 10 million people worldwide die each year from the acute and cumulative effects of air pollution, and as many as eight million of those deaths are linked to the particulate matter produced from the burning of fossil fuels. That is one death in five.

Some estimates run lower; nearly all of them run into the millions. This is a global toll, each year, to match the pandemic death totals for each of the past two; it is death, each year, at the scale of the Holocaust. And with fossil fuels continuing to burn, the totals add up: Ten million premature deaths every 12 months is 100 million a decade. It is 400 million in my lifetime.[148]

While blind indifference to the tradeoffs of maintaining a comfortable life style abounds, global warming and climate change are marching inexorably toward a tipping point that will spare no one. It is time to make the effort to educate ourselves about the values and practices of traditional indigenous shamanic beliefs. Those who reach out for this updated psychotherapy approach will be the beneficiaries, as will the therapists who are willing to broaden their considerations for how people heal and recover from protracted trauma. There can no longer be a disconnect between one's inner psyche and the natural environment we all depend on. Increasing climate catastrophes will surely create more climate-related trauma on a global level, requiring more than cognitive behavioral therapy (CBT) to address eco-anxiety. Buhner provides this quote from Fukuoka:

> Alienated from nature, human existence becomes a void, the wellspring of life and spiritual growth gone utterly dry. Man grows ever more ill and weary in the midst of his curious civilization that is but a struggle over a tiny bit of time and space.[149]

Learning to become more aware and understanding of the need to change personal habits will become more and more necessary, not just to help us to survive now but to ensure that our progeny do not end up in a dystopian future living in underground sanctuaries as troglodytes. Shamanic approaches to mental and emotional healing by definition address these escalating concerns, as the ecological needs of Earth *must* be taken into account.

Conclusion

It has always been through indigenous peoples' relationship to the living Earth that the shaman's skill set emerged. More shamanic practitioners with growing sensitivity to our natural world and the changing climate are needed as the planet's glaciers and ice sheets melt and ocean temperatures continue to rise. This growing concern has been labeled existential—it is keeping many awake at night, anxious about how our children and grandchildren will cope as these frightening realities grow more real every day.

More psychotherapists sensitive to these growing Earth-related concerns will provide therapeutic solace. For those trained in shamanic healing techniques, the ability to access shamanic states of consciousness specifically will address and support clients about how to feel more deeply connected to the threatened natural world. This will be one way to help console those with growing eco-anxiety, and to help teach respect and reverence for our living Earth. Our collective sense of entitlement to exploit Earth in an effort to preserve our comfortable way of life is becoming threatened. Shamanic engagement and sensitivity to the living Earth is needed now more than ever before.

Indigenous peoples' worldviews are based on a nature-based animistic relationship to life and the world. Their experience is of being connected to all things in and around the natural world. This includes the living Earth itself, Gaia, encompassing animals, plants, mountains and rivers, weather patterns, and energy-based subtle energies that we in the West might call supernatural or parapsychological. To reiterate, shamans make a distinction between what the West refers to as ordinary everyday reality (mostly based on a left brain, dominion-over-nature orientation to life) and a dimension of consciousness that can be accessed and interacted with that is "nonordinary." This nonordinary reality (NOR) is populated by sentient compassionate spirits. As plant and animal species are disappearing at an alarming rate and the rainforests in the Amazon are being bulldozed, indigenous peoples are increasingly being forced out of their native lands to assimilate to Western cultural values.

The harsh reality that this reflects is the systematic marginalization and even cultural genocide of indigenous peoples throughout the world, in order to make way for Western industrial colonization and the spread of Western values. One might muse to what degree we are complicit and what changes each of us can make in order to begin a collective shift toward becoming more sensitive to preserving the living Earth that nourishes us in so many ways. When will we humans wake up to this ecological threat? We must all do our part to raise awareness of how we live on this beautiful planet without creating more planetary pain.

Shamanic practitioners who work in NOR quickly become initiated into the oneness of all things on this living Earth. When psychotherapists who are shamanic practitioners realize they can directly interact with the spirits of the elements, the flora, and the fauna, and impart replenishment and *power* to their clients from these connections with the living Earth, this knowledge and healing creates reverberations throughout all aspects of the Gaian collective field. An ancient Navajo warns us in a poetic way about this.

> If you kill off the prairie dogs there will be no one to cry for rain.[150]

NOTES

1. Raines, G. N. (1953). Comment: the new nomenclature. *American Journal of Psychiatry*, 109, 548–549, https://www.ncbi.nlm.nih.gov/pmc/articles/
2. List of Psychotherapies. (2025, May 29). In *Wikipedia*. https://en.wikipedia.org/wiki/List_of_psychotherapies
3. Association for Comprehensive Energy Psychology. (2025). *Home*. https://www.energypsych.org/
4. Brockman, Howard. (2006). *Dynamic energetic healing: Integrating core shamanic practices with energy psychology applications and processwork principles*. Columbia Press.
5. Brockman, *Dynamic Energetic Healing*, 259–264.
6. The Foundation for Shamanic Studies. (2025). *Home*. www.shamanism.org
7. Webster. (2010). Neurasthenia. In *Webster's new world college dictionary*. (4th ed.).
8. Maloney, P. (2013). *The therapy industry: The irresistible rise of the talking cure, and why it doesn't work*. Pluto Press, 11.
9. Jung, C. G. (1961). *Memories, dreams, reflections*. Richard and Clara Winston (Trans.) Vintage, 167.
10. Jung, *Memories, dreams, reflections*, 138
11. Shamdasani, S. (2015). 'S.W.' and C.G. Jung: Mediumship, psychiatry and serial exemplarity. *History of Psychiatry*, 26(3), 288–302, doi: 10.1177/0957154X14562745
12. Carl Gustav Jung. (2025, March 2). In *Wikipedia*. https://en.wikipedia.org/wiki/Carl_Jung
13. Jung, *Memories, dreams, reflections*, 167, 169.
14. Jung, *Memories, dreams, reflections*, 176.
15. Jung, *Memories, dreams, reflections*, 183.
16. Bowlby, J. (1988). *A secure base: Parent-child attachment and healthy human development*. Routledge, 4, 11–12.
17. The Nobel Prize (2025). *Ivan Pavlov: Biographical*. https://www.nobelprize.org/prizes/medicine/1904/pavlov/biographical/
18. The Nobel Prize. *Ivan Pavlov: Biographical*.
19. The Nobel Prize. *Ivan Pavlov: Biographical*.
20. Rilling, M. (2000). How the challenge of explaining learning influenced the origins and development of John B. Watson's behaviorism. *American Journal of Psychology*, 113(2), 275–301.
21. GoodTherapy. (2015). *John Watson (1878–1958)*. https://www.goodtherapy.org/famous-psychologists/john-watson.html
22. Watson, J. B., & Rayner, R. (1920). Conditioned emotional reactions (The Little Albert study). *Journal of Experimental Psychology*, 3(1), 1–14.
23. Burgess, A. (2012) *A clockwork orange*. W. W. Norton & Company. (Original work published 1943)

[24] Bartholomew, A. (2013). *Behaviorism's impact on advertising: Then and now* [Master's thesis]. Available at DigitalCommons@University of Nebraska-Lincoln. https://digitalcommons.unl.edu/cgi/viewcontent.cgi?article=1042&context=journalismdiss

[25] Mcleod, S. (2024, February 2). Operant conditioning: What it is, how it works, and examples. *Simply Psychology.* www.simplypsychology.org/operant-conditioning.html; and Skinner, B. F. (1953). *Science and human behavior.* The Free Press.

[26] Skinner, *Science and human behavior*, 186–187.

[27] Skinner, B. F. (2005). *Walden two.* Hackett Publishing, 246. (Original work published 1948)

[28] Skinner, *Walden two,* 95.

[29] Skinner, B. F. (2002). *Beyond Freedom and Dignity.* Hackett Publishing, 155. (Original work published 1971)

[30] Beck Institute. (2025). *Dr. Aaron T. Beck.* https://beckinstitute.org/about/dr-aaron-t-beck/

[31] Rogers, C. R. (1951). *Client-centered therapy.* Houghton Mifflin Company.

[32] Maslow, A. (2013). *A theory of human motivation.* Martino Fine Books. (Original work published 1943)

[33] Kirsch, I. (2011). *The emperor's new drugs: Exploding the antidepressant myth.* Basic Books, 121.

[34] Brownawell, A., & Kelley, K. (2011, October). Psychotherapy is effective and here's why. *American Psychological Association.* http://www.apa.org/monitor/2011/10/psychotherapy.aspx

[35] American Psychological Association. (2009). *How psychotherapy works.* https://www.apa.org/news/press/releases/2009/12/wampold

[36] Stubbe, D. E. (2018, October 19). The therapeutic alliance: The fundamental element of psychotherapy. *FOCUS the Journal of Lifelong Learning in Psychiatry, 16*(4), doi: 10.1176/appi.focus.20180022

[37] Rogers, C. (2012). *On becoming a person: A therapist's view of psychotherapy.* Houghton Mifflin Harcourt.

[38] El-Hai, J. (2001, February 4). *The lobotomist.* The Washington Post. https://www.washingtonpost.com/archive/lifestyle/magazine/2001/02/04/the-lobotomist/630196c4-0f70-4427-832a-ce04959a6dc8/

[39] Lewis, T. (2021, October 13). *Lobotomy: Definition*, procedure and history. Live Science. https://www.livescience.com/42199-lobotomy-definition.html

[40] Lewis. *Lobotomy: Definition.*

[41] Day, E. (2008, January 13). *He was bad, so they put an ice pick in his brain....* The Guardian. https://www.theguardian.com/science/2008/jan/13/neuroscience.medicalscience

[42] El-Hai, *The lobotomist.*

[43] Day, *He was bad.*

Notes

[44] Matthias, M. (2025, June 24). *How Many People Actually Got Lobotomized?*. Encyclopedia Britannica. https://www.britannica.com/story/how-many-people-actually-got-lobotomized

[45] Read, C. F. (1940). Consequences of Metrazol shock therapy. *American Journal of Psychiatry, 97*(3), 667–676. doi: 10.1176/ajp.97.3.667

[46] Read, Consequences of Metrazol. Online abstract.

[47] Schimelpfening, N. (2024, May 28). *Common antidepressant medications: What you should know about SSRIs and other common antidepressants*. Very Well Mind. https://www.verywellmind.com/most-common-antidepressants-1066939

[48] Reardon, S. (2016, April 6). *Mysterious antidepressant target reveals its shape*. Nature. https://www.nature.com/articles/nature.2016.19711

[49] Kramer, P. D. (1993). *Listening to Prozac: A psychiatrist explores antidepressant drugs and the remaking of the self*. Penguin, 18.

[50] Miller, S. G. (2016, December 13). *1 in 6 Americans takes a psychiatric drug*. Scientific American. https://www.scientificamerican.com/article/1-in-6-americans-takes-a-psychiatric-drug/

[51] Carey, B., & Gebeloff, R. (2018, April 7). *Many people taking antidepressants discover they cannot quit*. The New York Times. https://www.nytimes.com/2018/04/07/health/antidepressants-withdrawal-prozac-cymbalta.html

[52] Fluoxetine. (2025, January 28). In *Wikipedia*. https://en.wikipedia.org/wiki/Fluoxetine

[53] Wu, Y., Tao, M., Cao, H., Ye, M., Wang, K., & Zhu, C. (2023, November 7). Changing trends in the global burden of mental disorders from 1990 to 2019 and predicted levels in 25 years. *Epidemiology and Psychiatric Science, 32*(e63). https://pmc.ncbi.nlm.nih.gov/articles/PMC10689059/

[54] Nikkel, R., & Whitaker, R. (2018, October 22). *Flooding the world with psychiatric drugs could boost the burden of mental disorders*. STAT. https://www.statnews.com/2018/10/22/flooding-world-psychiatric-drugs-boost-burden-mental-disorders/

[55] Jorm, A. F., Patten, S. B., Brugha, T. S., & Mojtabai, R. (2017). Has increased provision of treatment reduced the prevalence of common mental disorders? Review of the evidence from four countries. *World Psychiatry, 16*(1), 90–99. doi: 10.1002/wps.20388

[56] Glenmullen, J. (2000). *Prozac backlash*. Simon & Schuster, 14.

[57] Kramer, *Listening to Prozac*, xvi.

[58] Whitbourne, S. K. (2015, July 21). *Psychotherapy vs. Medications: The Verdict Is In*. Psychology Today. https://www.psychologytoday.com/us/blog/fulfillment-any-age/201507/psychotherapy-vs-medications-the-verdict-is-in

[59] Nikkel and Whitaker, *Flooding the world*.

[60] Nikkel and Whitaker, *Flooding the world*.

[61] Brownstein, J. (2011, December 22). *Prozac works better when given with talk therapy*. Live Science. http://www.livescience.com/17625-prozac-works-talk-therapy.html

[62] Brownstein, *Prozac works better*.

63. Grose, J. (2023, December 20). *We know how to put people on Ozempic. Do we know how to get them off it?* The New York Times. https://www.nytimes.com/2023/12/20/opinion/ozempic-oprah.html
64. Glenmullen, *Prozac backlash*, 8.
65. Ghorayshi, A. (2023, November 9). *What to know about the sexual side effects of antidepressants*. The New York Times. https://www.nytimes.com/2023/11/09/health/antidepressants-ssri-sex-side-effects.html
66. Ghorayshi, *What to know*.
67. Nikkel & Whitaker, *Flooding the world*.
68. Nikkel & Whitaker, *Flooding the world*.
69. Grose, *We know how*.
70. Grose, *We know how*.
71. Grose, *We know how*.
72. Grose, *We know how*.
73. Breggin, P. R. (n.d.). *Antidepressants: Far more harm than good*. Breggin.com. http://breggin.com/antidepressant-drugs-resource-center/
74. Cosci, F., & Chouinard, G. (2020). Acute and persistent withdrawal syndromes following discontinuation of psychotropic medications. *Psychotherapy and Psychosomatics, 89*, 283–306. https://www.karger.com/article/PDF/506868
75. Goedeke, A. (2021, October 14). *How many Americans are taking antidepressants because severe withdrawal symptoms are preventing them from stopping?* Newswires. https://www.einnews.com/pr_news/553802797/how-many-americans-are-taking-antidepressants-because-severe-withdrawal-symptoms-are-preventing-them-from-stopping
76. Davies, J., & Read, J. (2019). A systematic review into the incidence, severity and duration of antidepressant withdrawal effects: Are guidelines evidence-based? *Addictive Behaviors, 97*, 111–121. www.sciencedirect.com/science/article/pii/s0306460318308347?via%3Dihub.
77. Goedeke, *How many Americans*.
78. Stockmann, T., Odegbaro, D., Timimi, S., & Moncrieff, J. (2018). SSRI and SNRI withdrawal symptoms reported on an internet forum. *The International journal of risk & safety in medicine, 29*(3-4), 175–180. https://pubmed.ncbi.nlm.nih.gov/29758951/
79. Penn Today. (2002, May 23). *Study finds cognitive therapy at least as effective as drugs in long-term treatment of severe depression*. https://penntoday.upenn.edu/news/study-finds-cognitive-therapy-least-effective-drugs-long-term-treatment-severe-depression#
80. Barry, E. (2022, February 22). *The 'nation's psychiatrist' takes stock, with frustration*. The New York Times. https://www.nytimes.com/2022/02/22/us/thomas-insel-book.html?searchResultPosition=31
81. Barry, *The nation's psychiatrist*.
82. CBS News. (2024, December 27). *Homelessness surged 18% to a new record in 2024 amid a lack of affordable housing across the U.S.* https://www.cbsnews.com/news/homelessness-record-level-2024-up-18-percent-housing-costs-migrants/

NOTES

[83] Quoted by Academy of Ideas: Free Minds for a Free Society. (2018). *Aldous Huxley and Brave New World: The dark side of pleasure* [video]. https://academyofideas.com/2018/06/aldous-huxley-brave-new-world-dark-side-of-pleasure/

[84] Whitaker, R. (2015). *Anatomy of an epidemic: Magic bullets, psychiatric drugs, and the astonishing rise of mental illness in America*. Broadway Books, 8–9.

[85] My Online Therapy. (n.d.). *How much does it cost to see a psychologist in the UK?* https://myonlinetherapy.com/cost-to-see-a-psychologist/

[86] Pajer, N. (2019, September 9). *This is what therapy is like around the world*. The Huff Post. https://www.huffpost.com/entry/what-therapy-is-like-around-the-world_l_5d2f2930e4b02fd71dddab1c

[87] Pajer, *This is what therapy is like*.

[88] Pajer, *This is what therapy is like*.

[89] Pajer, *This is what therapy is like*.

[90] Greenbaum, Z. (2019, May). The expat life. *Monitor on Psychology, 50*(5). https://www.apa.org/monitor/2019/05/cover-expat-life.

[91] Pajer, *This is what therapy is like*.

[92] Pajer, *This is what therapy is like*.

[93] Greenbaum, The expat life.

[94] Orlinsky, D., Rønnestad, M. H., Ambühl, H., Willutzki, U., Botersman, J.-F., Cierpka, M., John Davis & Davis, M. (1999). Psychotherapists' assessments of their development at different career levels. *Psychotherapy: Theory, Research, Practice, Training, 36* (3), 203–215. doi:10.1037/h0087772

[95] Koc, V., & Kafa, G. (2019). Cross-cultural research on psychotherapy: The need for change. *Journal of Cross-Cultural Psychology, 50* (1), 100–115. doi: 10.1177/0022022118806577

[96] Yalvac, H. D., Kotan, Z., & Unal, S. (2015). Help seeking behavior and related factors in schizophrenia patients: A comparative study of two populations from eastern and western Turkey. *Düşünen Adam: Journal of Psychiatry and Neurological Sciences, 28* (2), 154–161. doi:10.5350/DAJPN2015280208

[97] Avasthi, A. (2011). Indianizing psychiatry—Is there a case enough? *Indian Journal of Psychiatry, 53*, 111–120. doi:10.4103/0019-5545.82534

[98] Uzoka, A. F. (1983). Active versus passive therapist role in didactic psychotherapy with Nigerian clients. *Social Psychiatry, 18* (1), 1–6. doi: 10.1007/BF00583381

[99] Beattie, M. (1986). *Codependent no more: how to stop controlling others and start caring for yourself*. Hazelden.

[100] Kumaraswamy, N. (2007). Psychotherapy in Brunei Darussalam. *Journal of Clinical Psychology: In Session, 63*, 735–744. doi:10.1002/jclp.20388

[101] Smith, T. B., Rodriguez, M. D., & Bernal, G. (2011). Culture. *Journal of Clinical Psychology: In Session, 67*, 166–175. doi:10.1002/jclp.20757

[102] Buhner, S. H. (2002). *The lost language of plants*. Chelsea Green Publishing, 35.

[103] University of Sheffield. (2025). *Epistemology*. https://www.sheffield.ac.uk/philosophy/research/themes/epistemology

[104] Buhner, *The lost language of plants*, 38.

[105] Narby, J., & Huxley, F. (2001). *Shamans through time: 500 years on the path to knowledge.* Tarcher, 258.

[106] Gardner, J. (1991). *The art of fiction: Notes on craft for young writers.* Vintage, 30–31. (Internal quote is from Buhner, *The lost language of plants*, 70).

[107] Gardner, *The art of fiction* (quoting Buhner), 71.

[108] The Why Not 100. (2014, January 27). *92 commentaries on imagination.* http://thewhynot100.blogspot.com/2014/01/92-commentaries-on-imagination.html

[109] Naparstek, B. (2004). *Invisible heroes: Survivors of trauma and how they heal.* Bantam Dell, 150.

[110] Naparstek, *Invisible heroes*, 149.

[111] McKenna, T. (n.d.). *Shamanism.* https://psychedelicsalon.com/transcripts/TMcK-Shamanism1.html

[112] Harner, M. (1980). *The way of the shaman: A guide to power and healing.* Bantam.

[113] Narby & Huxley. *Shamans through time*, 7.

[114] Campbell, J. (1949). *The hero with a thousand faces.* Princeton University Press, 21.

[115] Pollen, M. (2018). *How to change your mind: What the new science of psychedelics teaches us about consciousness, dying, addiction, depression, and transcendence.* Penguin Putnam, 406. Kindle Edition.

[116] Campbell, J. *The Hero*, 30.

[117] Eliade, M. (1972). *Shamanism: Archaic techniques of ecstasy.* Princeton University Press. (Original French work published 1951)

[118] Harner, M. (2013). *Cave and cosmos: Shamanic encounters with another reality.* North Atlantic, 40–41.

[119] Harner, *Cave and Cosmos*, 42.

[120] Harner, *Cave and Cosmos*, 43.

[121] Harner, *Cave and Cosmos*, 44.

[122] Cowan, T. (1993). *Fire in the head: Shamanism and the Celtic spirit.* HarperSanFrancisco, 30–31.

[123] Wilshire, B. (2000). *The primal roots of American philosophy: Pragmatism, phenomenology, and Native American thought.* Pennsylvania State University, 33.

[124] Mindell, A. (1993). *The shaman's body: A new shamanism for transforming health, relationships, and the community.* HarperSanFrancisco, 84.

[125] Mindell, *The shaman's body*, 85.

[126] Diamond, J. (1979). *Your body doesn't lie.* Warner Books, 33.

[127] Diamond, *Your body doesn't lie*, 27.

[128] Diamond, *Your body doesn't lie*, 33–34.

[129] Goodman, L. (2017, October 4). *Shamanic messages from the future: An interview with Hank Wesselman.* Medium. https://moonmagazineeditor.medium.com/shamanic-messages-from-the-future-an-interview-with-hank-wesselman-4429e3cadbd1

NOTES

[130] Harner, M. (2013). *Cave and cosmos: Shamanic encounters with another reality*. North Atlantic, 77.

[131] Wilshire, B. (2000). *The primal roots of American philosophy: Pragmatism, phenomenology, and Native American thought*. Pennsylvania State University, 21.

[132] Harner, *Cave and cosmos*, 77.

[133] Jahnke, R. (2002). *The healing promise of Qi: Creating extraordinary wellness through Qigong and Tai Chi*. Contemporary Books, 10–11.

[134] Jahnke, *Healing promise of Qi*, 12–13.

[135] The Foundation for Shamanic Studies. (2025). *Workshops and Training Programs*. www.shamanism.org

[136] Narby, J. & Huxley, F. (2001). *Shamans through time*. Tarcher, 257–258.

[137] Wilshire, B. (2000). *The primal roots of American philosophy: Pragmatism, phenomenology, and Native American thought*. Pennsylvania State University, 227.

[138] Wilshire, *Primal roots*, 257.

[139] Wilshire, *Primal roots*, 257.

[140] Naparstek, B. (2004). *Invisible heroes: Survivors of trauma and how they heal*. Bantam Dell, 77.

[141] Harner, M. (2013). *Cave and cosmos: Shamanic encounters with another reality*. North Atlantic Books, 48.

[142] Naparstek, B. (2004). *Invisible heroes: Survivors of trauma and how they heal*. Bantam Dell, 159.

[143] Radford, T. (2019, June 29). *James Lovelock at 100: The Gaia saga continues*. Nature. https://www.nature.com/articles/d41586-019-01969-y

[144] Quoted in Buhner, S. H. (2002). *The lost language of plants*. Chelsea Green, 52.

[145] William Commanda. (n.d.). In *AZQuotes*. Retrieved February 15, 2025. AZquotes.com. https://www.azquotes/quote/590877

[146] Farmer, S. D. (2009). *Earth magic: Ancient shamanic wisdom for healing yourself, others, and the planet*. Hay House. Preface.

[147] *Consumer Reports*. (2023, February), 34–41.

[148] Wallace-Wells, D. (2022, July 8). *Air pollution kills 10 million people a year. Why do we accept that as Normal?* The New York Times. https://www.nytimes.com/2022/07/08/opinion/environment/air-pollution-deaths-climate-change.html

[149] Fukuoka, M. Quoted in Buhner, *The lost language of plants*, 41.

[150] Buhner, *The lost language of plants*, 61.

SUGGESTIONS FOR FURTHER READING

American Psychiatric Association. (2022). *Diagnostic and statistical manual of mental disorders, DSM-5-TR.* (5th ed.).

Aron, E. N. (1996). *The highly sensitive person: How to thrive when the world overwhelms you.* Birch Lane Press.

Association of Comprehensive Energy Psychology. (2001). Three in one concepts. *Participant's Manual of the Third International Conference in Energy Psychology.*

Beijing College of Traditional Chinese Medicine. (1980). *Essentials of Chinese acupuncture.* Foreign Languages Press.

Bjork, D. W. (1997). *B. F. Skinner: A Life.* American Psychological Association.

Blake, D. D. (1993). Treatment outcome research on post-traumatic stress disorder. *NCP Clinical Newsletter, 3*(2), 14–17.

Bohm, D. (1980). *Wholeness and the implicate order.* Routledge and Kegan Paul.

Bradshaw, J. (2005). *Healing the shame that binds you.* Health Communications.

Bry, A., & Bair, M. (1978). *Visualization: Directing the movies of your mind.* Barnes and Noble Books.

Callahan, R., & Trubo, R. (2002). *Tapping the healer within: Using thought field therapy to instantly conquer your fears, anxieties, and emotional distress.* McGraw-Hill.

Campbell, J. (1992). *This Business of the Gods: In Conversation with Fraser Boa.* Windrose.

Suggestions for Further Reading

Castaneda, C. (1987). *The power of silence*. Simon & Schuster.

———. (1998). *The active side of infinity*. HarperCollins.

Childre, D., & Martin, H. (1999). *The HeartMath solution*. HarperSanFrancisco.

Cowan, T. (1993). *Fire in the head: Shamanism and the Celtic spirit*. HarperSanFrancisco.

Cowley, G. (1990, March 26). The promise of Prozac. *Newsweek*.

Craig, G., & Fowlie, A. (1995). *Emotional Freedom Techniques™: The manual*. Self-published.

Deloria Jr., V. (2006). *The world we used to live in: Remembering the powers of the medicine men*. Fulcrum.

Denning, M., & Phillips, O. (1980). *Practical guide to creative visualization: Manifest your desires*. Llewellyn.

Diamond, J. (1979). *Your body doesn't lie*. Warner Books.

Dispenza, J. (2007). *Evolve your brain: The science of changing your mind*. Health Communications.

Dossey, L. (1996). *Prayer is good medicine: How to reap the healing benefits of prayer*. HarperSanFrancisco.

———. (1999). *Reinventing medicine: Beyond mind-body to a new era of healing*. HarperSanFrancisco.

Durlacher, J. V. (1994). *Freedom from fear forever*. Van Ness.

Eden, D. (1998). *Energy medicine*. Jeremy P. Tarcher/Putnam.

Einstein, A. (1955). *The meaning of relativity*. Princeton University Press.

Eisenberg, L. (1996). Commentary: What should doctors do in the face of negative evidence? *Journal of Nervous and Mental Disease, 184*(2), 103–105.

Farmer, S. D. (2009). *Earth magic: Ancient shamanic wisdom for healing yourself, others, and the planet.* Hay House.

Feinstein, D. (1994). *Energy psychology interactive: An integrated book and CD program for learning the fundamentals of energy psychology.* Innersource.

———. (2008). Energy psychology: A review of the preliminary evidence. *Psychotherapy: Theory, Research, Practice, Training, 45*(2), 199–213.

Figley, C. R. (Ed.). (1995). *Compassion fatigue: Coping with secondary traumatic stress disorder in those who treat the traumatized.* Brunner-Routledge.

Fisher, R. L., & Fisher. S. (1996). Antidepressants for children: Is scientific support necessary? *Journal of Nervous and Mental Disease, 184*(2), 99–102.

Freud, A. (1992). *Ego & the mechanisms of defense.* Routledge. (Original work published 1936).

Freud, A. (1955). *Civilization and its discontents.* Norton. (Original work published 1929)

Gallo, F. P. (1999). *Energy psychology: Explorations at the interface of energy, cognition, behavior, and health.* CRC Press.

———. (Ed.). (2002). *Energy psychology in psychotherapy: A comprehensive sourcebook.* W. W. Norton.

Gallo, F. P., & Vincenzi, H. (2000). *Energy tapping.* New Harbinger.

Suggestions for Further Reading

Gawain, S. (1978). *Creative visualization: Use the power of your imagination to create what you want in your life.* Nataraj.

Gaynor, M. (2002). *The healing power of sound: Recovery from life-threatening illness using sound, voice, and music.* Shambhala.

Ghorayshi, A. (2023, November 9). What to know about the sexual side effects of Antidepressants. *The New York Times.*

Gladwell, M. (2005). *Blink: The power of thinking without thinking.* Penguin Books.

Grof, S., & Grof, C. (Eds.). (1989). *Spiritual emergency: When personal transformation becomes a crisis.* Jeremy P. Tarcher.

Harner, M. (1982). *The way of the shaman.* Bantam Books.

Hass, R. A. (2009). *EFT: Emotional freedom techniques for the highly sensitive temperament.* Energy Psychology.

Hillman, J. (1996). *The soul's code: In search of character and calling.* Random House.

Huxley, A. (2002). *Island.* Harper & Row. (Original work published 1962)

Ingerman, S. (1991). *Soul retrieval: Mending the fragmented self.* HarperSanFrancisco.

Kaplan, H. I., & Sadock, B. J. (1988). *Synopsis of psychiatry: Behavioral sciences, clinic psychiatry.* Williams & Wilkins.

Kardec, A. (2008). (A. Blackwell, Trans.). *The spirits' book.* Conselho Espirita Internacional (International Spiritist Council).

Katherine, A. (2000). *Where to draw the line: How to set healthy boundaries every day.* Simon & Schuster.

Kharitidi, O. (1996). *Entering the circle: Ancient secrets of Siberian wisdom discovered by a Russian psychiatrist.* HarperSanFrancisco.

Kirsch, I. (2010). *The emperor's new drugs: Exploding the antidepressant myth.* Basic Books.

Laney, M. O. (2002). *The introvert advantage: How to thrive in an extrovert world.* Workman.

Liu, Master H., & Perry, P. (1997). *The healing art of Qi Gong.* Warner Books.

McCraty, R. (2001). *Science of the heart: An overview of research conducted by the Institute of HeartMath.* HeartMath Research Center.

McTaggart, L. (2002). *The field: The quest for the secret force of the universe.* HarperCollins.

Mindell, A. (1985). *Working with the dreaming body.* Routledge and Kegan Paul.

———. (1990). *Working on yourself alone: Inner dreambody work.* Penguin Books.

———. (1993). *The shaman's body: A new shamanism for transforming health, relationships, and the community.* HarperCollins.

———. (2000). *Dreaming while awake: Techniques for 24-hour lucid dreaming.* Hampton Roads.

———. (2000). *Quantum mind: The edge between physics and psychology.* Lao Tse Press.

Modi, S. (1997). *Remarkable healings: A psychiatrist discovers unsuspected roots of mental and physical illness.* Hampton Roads.

Nenquimo, N. & Anderson, M. (2024). *We will be jaguars: A memoir of my people.* Harry N. Abrams.

Newberg, A., & Waldman, M. R. (2009). *How God changes your brain: Breakthrough findings from a leading neuroscientist.* Ballantine Books.

Orloff, J. (2004). *Positive energy: 10 extraordinary prescriptions for transforming fatigue, stress and fear into vibrance, strength and love.* Three Rivers.

Pellegrino, E. D. (1996). Clinical judgment, scientific data, and ethics: Antidepressant therapy in adolescents and children. *Journal of Nervous and Mental Disease, 184*(2), 106–108.

Perkins, J. (1997). *Shape shifting: Techniques for global and personal transformation.* Destiny Books.

Prabhavananda, Swami, & Isherwood, C. (Trans.) (1953). *How to know God: The yoga aphorisms of Patanjali.* New American Library.

Radin, D. I., Rebman, J. M., & Cross, M. P. (1996). Anomalous organization of random events by group consciousness: Two exploratory experiments. *Journal of Scientific Exploration, 10*(1), 143–168.

Rilling, M. (2000). How the challenge of explaining learning influenced the origins and development of John B. Watson's behaviorism. *American Journal of Psychology, 113*(2), 275–301.

Rinpoche, S. (1994). *The Tibetan book of living and dying.* HarperSanFrancisco.

Robertson, I. (2002). *Opening the mind's eye: How images and language teach us how to see.* St. Martin's Press.

Ruiz, Don M. (1997). *The four agreements.* Amber-Allen.

Rysdyk, E. C. (2013). *Spirit walking: A course in shamanic power.* Weiser Books.

Schaef, A. W. (1986). *Co-dependence: Misunderstood—mistreated.* Harper & Row.

Schwartz, G. E. R., & Russek, L. G. S. (1999). *The living energy universe.* Hampton Roads.

Shapiro, F. (1995). *Eye movement desensitization and reprocessing.* Guilford Press.

Skovholt, T. M. (2001). *The resilient practitioner: Burnout prevention and self-care strategies for counselors, therapists, teachers, and health professionals.* Allyn & Bacon.

Spangler, D. (2001). *Blessing: The art and the practice.* Riverhead Books.

Stevenson, I. (1974). *Twenty cases suggestive of reincarnation.* University Press of Virginia.

———. (1997). *Where reincarnation and biology intersect.* Praeger.

van der Kolk, B. A. (Ed.). (1984). *Post-traumatic stress disorder: Psychological and biological sequelae.* American Psychiatric Press.

———. (1987). *Psychological trauma.* American Psychiatric Press.

van der Kolk, B. A., McFarlane, A. C., & Weisaeth, L. (Eds.). (1996). *Traumatic stress: The effects of overwhelming experience on mind, body, and society.* Guilford Press.

Villoldo, A. (2000). *Shaman, healer, sage.* Harmony Books.

Watson, J. B., & Rayner, R. (1920). Conditioned emotional reactions (The Little Albert study). *Journal of Experimental Psychology, 3*(1), 1.

Watzlawick, P. (1978). *The language of change: Elements of therapeutic communication.* Basic Books.

Weiss, B. L. (1992). *Through time into healing.* Simon & Schuster.

Wesselman, H. (1995). *Spiritwalker: Messages from the future.* Bantam.

———. (2003). *The journey to the sacred garden: A guide to traveling in the spiritual realms.* Hay House.

INDEX

Note: References that begin with C refer to Case Study numbers, not page numbers.

active imagination, 16
acupuncture meridian system, 47, 52, 177. *See also* tapping
Africa, 99
ancestral spirits, C11, C12
anima, 13
animism, 146, 152, 202
animus, 13
anxiety, 145, C4–C6
archetypes, 11, 14, C5
avoidance, 6
Beck, Aaron, 32
behavioral kinesiology, 130–31
behaviorism, 23–30
Bergstrom, Betsy, 161–62
bowel dysfunction, C3
Bowlby, John, 19–21, 24, 181
Brazil, 93
Castaneda, Carlos, 123–24
CBT. *See* cognitive behavioral therapy
chakras, 52, 177
    first, C13
    fifth, C2, C14
    second, C7
chi, 147–49. *See also* subtle energy
China, 93–94
chronic pain, C11
client-centered therapy. *See* person-centered therapy
Clockwork Orange, A, 26
codependency, 99
cognitive behavioral therapy (CBT), 31–34, 42, 64, 66, 135, 169
collective intrusion, C8

compassionate spirits, 113, 116
conditioning, behavioral, 23–28
consensus reality, 123–24
core shamanic practices, 114
Covid-19, C8–C10
Cowan, Tom, 120
cross-cultural considerations, 97–101
defense mechanisms, 3–7
denial, 4
depression, 70–71, 76, 145, 186, 297, C1
    lobotomy and, 56, 59
    medication and, 40, 42, 62, 66
    psychoanalysis and, 32
    psychotherapy and, 42
Diamond, John, 130–31
dismemberment, 258
displacement, 7–8
dissociation, 5–6, 167, 201
    energetic intrusion and, 178
Dolphin (power animal), 165
dreaming, 108–10, 121–22
    lucid, 115
dreaming media, 234–35, C9, 268–70
drumming, 118–19, 158, 164
DSM III, 66
Eagle (power animal), 143, 165, C1, C13
earthbound spirits, 135, 143, 189–95
emotional freedom technique (EFT), C6, C13. *See also* tapping
ego, 3, 12
Ellis, Albert, 31–32
energetic boundaries, 172, 181–84, 205
    cases, C3–C5, C7, C16
    earthbound spirits and, 194
energetic intrusion, 133, 134, 159, 182, 186–87

INDEX

cases, C2–C7, C11
collective, 205, C9, C10, C15
energy body, 131, 132, 175, 176
  earthbound spirits and, 190
energy checking, 131, 132, 205. *See also* muscle testing
energy-based therapy, 47, 50, 52, 127, 135
eye movement desensitization and reprocessing (EMDR), 48, 65
fanning, 177, 203, 205, 241, C13
Fiamberti, Amarro, 55–56
fire walking, 120–21
France, 92
Freeman, Walter J., 54
Freud, Sigmund, 3–10, 14, 19
Friedman, Richard, 71–72
frontal occipital holding, 127, 128, 132, 133, 178, 203
genetics, 86–87
Glenmullen, Joseph, 70–71, 75
Gould, Linda, 206–7
Grandmother, C2, C4, C7, C11, C13
Great Mystery, 128
Great Spirit, 127
Green Dragon (power animal), C13
grief, C1
guided imagery, 110–12
Harner, Michael, 202
  Foundation for Shamanic Studies, 152
  on power animals, 139–40, 142
  on physical healing, 160
  research, 114, 117–18
Horse (power animal), 143, 172
  cases, C7, C11, C14
hydration, 130, C2
id, 3, 235
India, 94–95
indigenous knowledge, 106–7, 113
indigenous worldview, 298–99, 301

individuation, 11–12
inner critic, C13
Insel, Thomas, 86
Jahnke, Roger, 148
James, William, 140
Jung, Carl Gustav, 11–17, 263
Kahuna, C9
Kramer, Peter, 67, 71
Kundalini yoga, 147, 149
libido, 14–15
Little Albert Experiment, 25
lobotomy, 53–62
Lovelock, James, 296–97
marital issues, C3
Maslow, Abraham, 30, 36
mental disorders, incidence of, 69–70
merging
  with compassionate spirit, 155–56, 163, 164, C12
  with power animal, 165
Mexico, 93
middle-world realm, 161, 170
Mindell, Arnold, 16–17
Moniz, Egas, 54–55
Mouse (power animal), 137–39
muscle testing, 133, 176, 179, 199–201, 203. *See also* energy checking
  remote, 129–30
Myers-Briggs Type Indicator (MBTI), 13–14
natural world, connection to, 296–300
negative energy, 130, 132, 200
neurolinguistic programming (NLP), C13
nonordinary reality (NOR), 111, 119, 128, 133, 134, 136, 143
  accessing from a distance, 158
  soul loss and, 170
Odin, 161, 162–64, C2, C3, C5, C6
out-of-body experiences, 168

Panther (power animal), 143, 158, 159, 165, C4, C15
parasitic attachment, C2
Pavlov, Ivan, 23–24, 27
persona, Jung's concept of, 12
personal power, loss of 135
person-centered therapy, 35–38
pet, death of, C1
possession illness, C16
post-traumatic stress disorder. *See* PTSD
power. See also subtle energy
  accumulating, 150
  archetypal experiences and, 119
  in compassionate spirits, 115
  derived from power animals, 139, 142
  effect on nervous system, 112
  effecting healing, 133
  energetic boundaries and, 185–86
  experienced by shamanic practitioner, 132, 152
  gaining from NOR, 113, 115, 149
  of Spirit, 123
power animals, 137–43, 149, 259
  soul retrieval and, 170–72
power food, C2, C4, C7, C8, C11
power-infused sites, 146
prana, *See power*, subtle energy
processwork, 17, 46–47, 51
projection, 4, 6–7
psoriatic arthritis, C2
psychoanalysis, 8, 9–10, 35
psychoenergetic reversal, C4, C5, C7
psychopharmacology, 63–90
psychopomp work, 193, C1
psychotoxic intrusion, 135, 143, C7
psychotropic drugs, 40, 42
  sexual side effects of, 75–76
  withdrawal from, 78–82

prevalence of, 68–69, 74, 80
  vs. CBT, 85
PTSD, 6, 33, 39, 145, C6
  dissociation and, 168–70
  energetic origin of, 179
  guided imagery and, 111
  lobotomy and, 57
  traumatic residue and, 176
Qigong, 147–48, 149
Read, Charles F., 60
regression, 4
relationships, development of healthy, 44–45
residual psychotoxic energy, C15
Rogers, Carl, 30, 35–36, 43–44, 45
schizophrenia, 73
second attention awareness, C13
sexual abuse, C13
sexual assault, C7
shadow, Jung's concept of, 12–13
shaman vs. shamanic practitioner, 114
shamanic journey, emotional response to, 206–7
shamanism, 115
  sacred imagination and, 112–13
shapeshifting, 156–57
Shark (power animal), 165
Skinner, B. F., 27–30
SNRIs, 66, 81
solar plexis, C3–C6, C11, C13
soul loss/soul stealing, 135, 170, 173–74, C7, C14
soul retrieval, 143, C14
spirit attachment, C16
Spirit of the Mountain, C2, C7
Spirit of the Wind, C15
SSRIs, 66–67, 69, 71, 75–76, 81
subtle energy, 52, 124, 146–47. *See also* chi
superego, 3
talk therapy, 135

    energetic imprints and, 179–80
    limitations of, 64, 65, 287
tapping, 47, 63–64, C7, C14. *See also*
    emotional freedom technique
therapeutic alliance, 37, 39–52,
    83–84
therapeutic relationship, defense
    mechanisms and, 46
transference, 182–83
trauma, 65, 206
traumatic residue, 176
unconscious, the 3–8, 122
        collective, 11, 12, 14, 15–16
        personal 12, 14
United Kingdom, 91–92
upper world, 170
visualization, 246. *See also* guided
    imagery
Walsh, Roger, 153–54
Watson, John B., 24–25
Watt, James, 55
weight loss drugs, 77–78